"Jackson W. explores the interplay of metaphor and atonement—thus this book is about the core of salvation in the New Testament. Atonement is complex, but this is a reliable and well-written guide through the variety of biblical images. Its contextualization offers the key to understand the core of the mission of Jesus Christ. A must-read for all who want to know what the Christian gospel means in diverse cultures!"

Christian A. Eberhart, professor of religious studies at the University of Houston and author of *The Sacrifice of Jesus: Understanding Atonement Biblically*

"What would it look like if we allowed the apostle Paul's statement that 'Christ died for our sins' to be truly explained 'according to the Scriptures' (1 Cor 15:3)? In this provocative book, Jackson W. carefully peels back layers of church tradition, systematic theology, and folk Christianity to reexamine what Scripture actually says about the death of Christ. The result is a whole-Bible approach to sin and atonement that mounts a stimulating challenge to scholars and laypeople alike. Whether or not you agree with his conclusions, you will undoubtedly come away with a deeper appreciation for the richness of what Christ's death accomplished!"

Jerry Hwang, academic dean and associate professor of Old Testament at Singapore Bible College

"Given the importance of atonement and the breadth of imagery used in Scripture to describe it, any work on atonement is sure to invite criticism. As Jackson W. himself notes, this book will not avoid that fate. Still, it remains a rewarding read because of the light it sheds on some of the often underappreciated biblical imagery used to describe what Christ accomplished for sin-stained image bearers. Read, wrestle, discern, critique, and worship your way through this book. Even the critic will be grateful for the reminder of the gospel's multifaceted salvation presented in *The Cross in Context*."

Matthew Bennett, assistant professor of missions and theology at Cedarville University

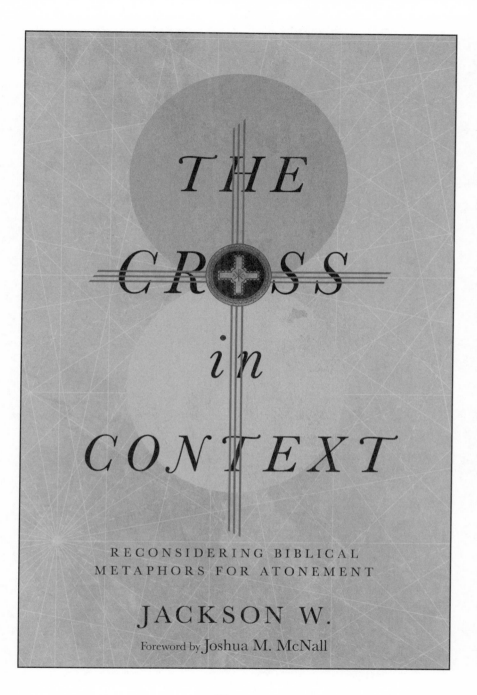

THE CROSS in CONTEXT

RECONSIDERING BIBLICAL METAPHORS FOR ATONEMENT

JACKSON W.

Foreword by Joshua M. McNall

ivp
Academic
An imprint of InterVarsity Press
Downers Grove, Illinois

InterVarsity Press
P.O. Box 1400 | Downers Grove, IL 60515-1426
ivpress.com | email@ivpress.com

InterVarsity Press® is the publishing division of InterVarsity Christian Fellowship/USA®. For more information, visit intervarsity.org.

Scripture quotations, unless otherwise noted, are from the New Revised Standard Version Bible, copyright © 1989 National Council of the Churches of Christ in the United States of America. Used by permission. All rights reserved worldwide.

While any stories in this book are true, some names and identifying information may have been changed to protect the privacy of individuals.

The publisher cannot verify the accuracy or functionality of website URLs used in this book beyond the date of publication.

Cover design and image composite: David Fassett
Interior design: Jeanna Wiggins

ISBN 978-1-5140-0028-1 (print) | ISBN 978-1-5140-0029-8 (digital)

Printed in the United States of America ♾

InterVarsity Press is committed to ecological stewardship and to the conservation of natural resources in all our operations. This book was printed using sustainably sourced paper.

Library of Congress Cataloging-in-Publication Data
A catalog record for this book is available from the Library of Congress.

26 25 24 23 22 | 6 5 4 3 2 1

THIS BOOK IS DEDICATED

TO A DEAR FRIEND AND BROTHER IN CHRIST.

To John L.,

O what debt Christ has paid

And cleansed without guile

On Him the weight was laid

That we be reconciled

CONTENTS

FOREWORD

Joshua M. McNall

"SAY *SHIBBOLETH!*" UNFORTUNATELY, that menacing line from the Hebrew Scriptures comes to mind when some Christians debate the doctrine of atonement. The story, from Judges 12, describes a fractious moment in which one tribe sought to identify and condemn outsiders—not merely by the words they used, but by their favored pronunciation. In recent decades, atonement shibboleths center around particular versions of penal substitution, whether Christ truly died for all, and the place of violence in the drama of redemption. All these discussions are important. And none of them are easy. Yet in some cases, readers get the sense that the many-splendored work of Jesus is being both reduced and weaponized by the attempt to equate it with a particular local accent.

Thankfully, this is not one of those atonement books.

Jackson W. rightly notes the need to recontextualize the cross if we are going to move forward in our gospel proclamation. That means taking a step back from our modern fights over particular models or theories of atonement to understand afresh how *Scripture* speaks of themes like sacrifice, purification, and sin-bearing. The purpose of that step back, however, is not that we would leave behind forever the worlds of Athanasius, Anselm, or Aquinas. To do so would be to endorse a kind of naive biblicism that is itself a regional "twang" that badly mispronounces *sola scriptura*.

W.'s claim is that it is only when we have wrestled with the biblical context more thoroughly that we can *return* to later questions with a fresh and more nuanced perspective. (See especially chapter ten and the book's appendixes.) No amount of "both-anding" or faultfinding with regard to particular atonement models can substitute for this foundational work of biblical contextualization. And that's just one reason I'm glad you're holding this book.

Admittedly, as a systematic theologian, I am not equipped to sit in final judgment on every single fine-grained discussion within the labyrinth of biblical material—or within W.'s work. Because the Scriptures are complex and we are fallen, there will be points at which we disagree; so be it. Nonetheless, I am convinced that we need each other to better understand Christ's work: Bible scholars and theologians, historians and philosophers, pastors and missionaries, little children and senior citizens. Only when we listen carefully to these contextualized insights and perspectives will we be able to proclaim the good news in language that is both faithful and compelling.

ACKNOWLEDGMENTS

A BOOK LIKE THIS requires years of reflection, conversation, and encouragement. Many of the people who have assisted me in this journey live in restricted access countries, and so I cannot list their full names.

First, I am grateful to John, a longtime colleague, supervisor, and brother who suggested many years ago that I develop a course on the atonement. That opportunity gave me the space to work out most of the core ideas found in this book. His willingness to engage in conversation and debate sharpened my thinking on the topic.

Several others deserve mention for their contribution. When I moved to Mission ONE, William Strickland constantly encouraged my progress and protected my time so that I could organize my notes into a manuscript. My students in China were faithful dialogue partners who helped me to identify unanswered questions and clarify my communication. My colaborers at Mission ONE have cheered me on and supported my family as we transitioned to the States, the precise time I was writing my first manuscript. Of course, this book wouldn't be possible without the enthusiastic backing of my wife, who always spurs me on to take new risks for Christ.

Finally, every book worth its salt has someone willing to put fresh eyes on early drafts. Anna Gissing served as my editor from book proposal to final manuscript submission. Her comments improved the quality of writing immeasurably. Thank you also to those friends who were willing to provide feedback on select chapters, especially Tim Gombis, Matthew Bennett, Ched Spellman, Jackie Parks, Will Brooks, Scott Callaham, Ryan Arneson, and John Crawford.

INTRODUCTION

I HAVE GRIEVED THROUGHOUT the writing of this book. I will lose friends. This book will make some people wary of me. Ironically, this is what the doctrine of atonement has done to people. The very thing that should bring church unity instead undermines it.

Jesus' death is central to Christianity. You'd think we could agree about why he died. In fact, few things divide the church as does the atonement of Christ, whose death brings about the reconciliation of all creation. While his sacrifice reconciles us to God, it seems to split the church into factions. This observation is as ironic as it is tragic.

I have found that many people, including Christian scholars, harbor doubts about this or that point of doctrine, but they know speaking up will cause a kerfuffle. The risk to their reputations or careers is too much. So, they choose to "stay in their lane" and away from controversy. Within some Christian sub-cultures, one can hardly challenge popular authors and conventional thinking. To do so means you will be branded a "liberal" or even "heretic." If you listen to some talk about people with opposing viewpoints, the problem you'll see is not mere division but disgust.

Without question, every reader will find something to disagree with in this book. By the time it's published, even I might disagree with something it says. No writer or book is entirely right or wrong. This work is no exception.

Knowing that you'll never get everything correct is paralyzing for some people; instead, it should be freedom giving. We can accept ambiguity, embrace nuance, and learn from others. As teachers, we must guard against heresy. But we should equally fear a lack of genuine humility.

THREE GOALS OF THIS BOOK

This book has three interconnected purposes. First, it attempts to guard church unity. It is commonplace to compare the doctrine of atonement to a multi-faceted diamond. Christ's atoning work abounds in significance. Its richness is incalculable. Nevertheless, Christians all too often feel compelled to emphasize one aspect of the atonement over another. In doing so, one picks a "theological team." Debates about the "most central" or "most fundamental" theory of atonement have long divided Christians.

While some authors attempt to mediate such debates, their explanations might perpetuate the problem. Theologians assume the validity of conventional, systematic theories of atonement. They do not always interact sufficiently with or incorporate the wealth of insight provided by biblical scholars. Such systematic treatises focus more on philosophical assumptions than on the inherent logic of the biblical narrative and its metaphors. Although many authors acknowledge the partial truth of various historical theories, their treatments still lead readers to prioritize one theory over another. Some debates refuse to die. Pilate killed Jesus, but we theologians sacrifice the atonement.

A second purpose is theological. In light of these disputes, this book seeks to add clarity and cohesion amid the clutter of theories. It shows how biblical writers harmonize the various atonement metaphors that span the canon. As a result, readers will not pit one set of biblical texts against another. This broader perspective of Christ's atonement is both humbling and hope giving. It can calm the cackle and clatter that stifles genuine dialogue among Christians. It helps to reconcile theological camps and enables us to interpret the Bible more faithfully.

Third, this book assists readers in contextualizing the Bible's teaching concerning the atonement. It equips the church to explain the gospel of salvation in ways that are meaningful in diverse cultural contexts. Furthermore, this volume lays the groundwork for practitioners to better comprehend how the atonement affects various aspects of life.

An important result follows from this study. It highlights several ways in which honor and shame shape biblical passages that speak of atonement. These observations provide a more robust view of Christ's work through the cross and opens fresh applications for the church.

DO WE REJECT OR RECONCILE THEORIES?

The atonement is the crux of Christianity. Despite this fact, or perhaps even because of it, the atonement remains an enduring source of contention among theologians. For centuries, writers have offered theories to explain the significance of Christ's death. Scholars take sides in the debate whenever they defend their preferred view of Christ's atonement. Systematic theologians catalog an array of biblical texts to highlight the superior logic of *their* theological perspective.

Several recent books take a more accommodating approach.[1] They take pains to demonstrate how competing theories can coexist. Accordingly, authors insist that popular theories, like penal substitution and Christus Victor, are complementary, not mutually exclusive. Yet even in such cases, readers may invariably conclude that one theory is more "fundamental" or "central" to the doctrine. As a result, theologians create a hierarchy of atonement theories founded on the logic of countless hidden assumptions.

Much of the literature that exists concerning the atonement is inaccessible to nonspecialists. Most readers do not have sufficient time or background to grasp the nuanced arguments found in the journals of biblical studies. What's more, one finds discontinuity between the way many Old Testament scholars describe atonement in the Pentateuch, for example, and the treatments provided by systematic theologians, who synthesize texts from disparate contexts to construct an atonement theology.

Many welcome the movement away from either-or debates about the atonement; however, both-and solutions are inadequate unless we can explain *how* the Bible integrates the various aspects of Christ's atonement. A fresh approach is needed.

In this book, I propose a way to reconcile popular theories of atonement that sometimes seem to conflict or at least have tension. To do so, we'll consider the influence of context on our understanding of the atonement. The biblical narrative uses several metaphors that help us find the intersection of the biblical text with contemporary contexts. The biblical narrative has an inherent logic that gets lost amid endless theory-laden debates.

AN OVERVIEW

The following chapters fall into three major parts. Section one consists of five chapters. The first chapter explains why all atonement theories are

---

[1]For example, Scot McKnight, *A Community Called Atonement* (Nashville: Abingdon, 2007); Jeremy Treat, *The Crucified King: Atonement and Kingdom in Biblical and Systematic Theology* (Grand Rapids, MI: Zondervan, 2014); Ben Pugh, *Atonement Theories: A Way Through the Maze* (Eugene, OR: Cascade, 2014); Joshua McNall, *The Mosaic of Atonement: An Integrated Approach to Christ's Work* (Grand Rapids, MI: Zondervan, 2019); Oliver Crisp, *Approaching the Atonement: The Reconciling Work of Christ* (Downers Grove, IL: IVP Academic, 2020).

contextualized. We are often ignorant of the role that context plays in shaping our theories of atonement. Our cultural context narrows the focus and scope of our theological questions. Because of our historical situation, we might ask too much of our theories. These observations create the need and opportunity for writing this book.

Chapter two provides critical background needed to make sense of Israel's rituals. Ancient Israelites viewed the world quite differently than we do. They even categorized space, time, people, and objects around them in ways we would think peculiar. Lacking this framework, our theology of atonement collapses under the stress of oversimplification. It becomes reductionistic. We sacrifice a biblical understanding of atonement when we substitute our assumptions in place of those held by ancient Israel.

Chapter three opens with an overview of the major types of offerings and their significance. It highlights important aspects associated with sacrifice that are underappreciated in discussions concerning atonement. Chapter four asks several fundamental questions: What does "atonement" mean in the Bible? At a basic level, what does atonement accomplish? Chapter five first explores how the biblical writers use honor-shame language to discuss various related concepts such as holiness, sacrifice, and sanctification. Specific attention is given to Old Testament passages. Second, we'll consider how these observations inform a biblical understanding of the sacrificial system.

Section two demonstrates how biblical writers consistently use several key metaphors when speaking of atonement. Accordingly, chapter six explains why purification is a primary metaphor that describes atonement. Atoning sacrifices cleanse impurity. We will give attention to passages such as Leviticus 17 and Hebrews 8–10. In chapter seven, readers examine the metaphor of "bearing sin." Intriguingly, this imagery routinely conveys opposite theological ideas. We will especially focus on the Day of Atonement (Leviticus 16). Chapter eight considers the Bible's use of economic language to explain atonement. Atonement is often depicted as payment or compensation for debt. Offering sacrifices or gifts to God is one way that worshipers provide recompense. What are the implications for a biblical doctrine of atonement? We will study the Passover, a fundamental paradigm used by New Testament writers to explain Christ's death on the cross. Next, chapter nine raises objections and questions concerning several weighty passages, such as Psalm 22, Isaiah 53, Romans 8,

2 Corinthians 5, and Galatians 3. Some readers will be tempted to skip immediately to this chapter. I recommend against that plan for the simple reason that my comments there will make little sense apart from the preceding chapters.

Finally, section three highlights various implications and applications. Chapter ten ties together the insights from this study. It shows the relationship between the interpretation in this book and popular theories of atonement. In the process, I respond to common questions that arise from the view of atonement proposed in this book. Chapter eleven offers a meaty conclusion. It surveys various applications that stem from the previous chapters. It raises theological and practical questions that deserve further discussion. For example, how does Christ bear our shame? How might the ideas in this book affect contextualization in crosscultural missions? Also, how does a biblical view of atonement expand our understanding concerning the need for reconciliation between people?

MY FEAR OF TREE ROOTS

When I was around seven years old, my uncle and I took a walk through the forest. We came across a large fallen tree. A huge crater remained where the roots had formerly been. A puddle of rain filled the hole. I had no idea how deep the cavity sunk into the ground. So, I asked my uncle, "What's down there?" His reply was straightfaced and simple, "Hell." I was petrified. For many years later, I veered from such holes, *just in case* he was right. I hate being suckered.

As humans, we are desperate for certainty and clarity. It provides a sense of security. Sadly, this natural desire can lead us to forfeit other values, like humility and richness. What do I mean? In seeking certainty, we hedge our bets against humility, even though we all know that everyone is fallible with limited perspectives. Wanting clarity, we sometimes demur at the Bible's richness with the label "complex." Scripture is deemed complicated. Our brains' longing for certainty and clarity sets us up to be duped.

We even become blind to reality. Consider this: at one level, the picture I paint in this book is a simple one. The Bible uses a few common metaphors. Ironically, various atonement theories actually complicate our view of atonement. Verses and images are taken from context and reordered according to our limited wisdom. In trying to make the doctrine simpler than it is, we end up twisting the Bible to fit our desires and assumptions. This is a type of theological syncretism whereby one compromises the gospel by settling for ideas that are merely true.[2]

CONTEXTUALIZATION AND THE CROSS

Why is this book called *The Cross in Context*? Words and ideas have meaning based on their context. This is why contextualization is so important. I define contextualization as "the process wherein people interpret, communicate, and apply the Bible within a particular cultural context."[3] Contextualization begins with interpretation. It cannot be otherwise. Most chapters consider how the biblical authors contextualize the concept of atonement. However, I don't want us to stop there.

Sprinkled throughout the book are ideas and suggestions to help readers communicate and apply their insights about the atonement. Healthy contextualization should be both biblically faithful and culturally meaningful. Contextualization cannot be done well in the abstract. It requires a concrete, historical context. Accordingly, no book can hope to tell every reader how to contextualize the atonement for their specific setting.

How then might I offer real-world suggestions given the limited size of this work? I'll demonstrate the practical significance of contextualization in at least three ways: First, we will use the observations made in this book to evaluate certain attempts to contextualize the cross of Christ. Second, I'll propose constructive ideas for communicating the atonement in contextually meaningful ways. Third, readers will see a few implications for applying the atonement within our daily lives. Such application is found most clearly in the book's last chapter.

Finally, I offer a brief word to scholars. This book does not intend to give a history of how interpreters explain the atonement and related concepts. Therefore, some specialists will be disappointed that I do not explicitly interact with certain renowned authors. To allay such concerns, I can only state that I've

---

[2]"Theological syncretism" prioritizes certain texts over others due to tradition. The interpreter's priorities, questions, and assumptions are read into the Bible. In contrast to *cultural* syncretism, which forces unbiblical notions into Scripture, *theological* syncretism limits the biblical message, silencing parts of the Bible as a result of one's theological subculture.

[3]Jackson Wu, *One Gospel for All Nations: A Practical Approach to Biblical Contextualization* (Pasadena, CA: William Carey Library, 2015), 8.

engaged such scholars in my research but, due to the larger goals of this book, I'm forced to limit my interaction with them here. In some cases, other writers seem to participate in a quite different conversation than the one I put forth in this book. Consequently, some specialists might be less than satisfied with certain parts of my arguments; however, I trust readers will assess my proposals with generosity.

A Constellation of Theories

Humans are pattern-making machines. This is why we see a "man in the moon." Our brains construct the image of a face from a cluster of lunar craters. When reading the Bible and doing theology, this instinctive skill set goes into high gear. Our many theories of atonement are comparable to various constellations. The Big Dipper belongs to the constellation Ursa Major (the "Great Bear"). Others, like Perseus, Hercules, and Aries, fueled the minds of ancient peoples, who envisioned cosmic powers in conflict in the sky.

Stars and planets are real. Patterns help us organize those astronomical bodies within our minds. The more we humans contemplate those interstellar patterns, the more we open our imaginations to a thousand other speculations and stories. Our theories can become larger than life. Meanwhile, we forget the stars and planets.

This book brings our attention back to basics. My objective is not to present a definitive or final interpretation, which is not possible in such a limited space. I suggest reasons why certain evangelical views should not be assumed as obvious nor taken as default positions. But ultimately, my goal is constructive. This work is an attempt to reconcile those who love Jesus, "the root and the descendant of David, the bright morning star" (Revelation 22:16).

SECTION ONE

THE ATONEMENT

in BIBLICAL and

CULTURAL CONTEXT

1

RECONCILING ATONEMENT THEORIES

Very simple was my explanation,
and plausible enough—as most wrong theories are!

H. G. WELLS, *THE TIME MACHINE*

CHINESE PARENTS ARE CONSUMED WITH WORRY about their children's grades. By the time a child is two years old, parents have planned that child's path to successfully passing the *gaokao*, the test that students take in their final year of high school. It is the single most significant factor determining whether students attend college. In a country with well over a billion people, competition is fierce. A Chinese idiom explains these parents' anxiety. They are afraid their children, lacking the most rigorous education, will "lose at the starting line."

This expression aptly captures much of the debate that surrounds the doctrine of atonement. Countless books and articles start in the wrong place. They begin with certain atonement theories in mind. They look either to evaluate or reconcile those theories as they are typically presented. To the degree a person tries to harmonize different views, one effectively assumes the truth of those theories. We too quickly debate already-developed systems of doctrine. The problem, however, is that we then "lose at the starting line."

Theories are necessary and useful. They simplify vast amounts of information. At the same time, theories often make ideas feel overly complex. They can obscure reality as much as clarify it. This is certainly true with respect to theories of atonement.

I don't imply that traditional atonement theories are wrong and should be cast aside. Rather, it is possible to overemphasize certain parts of a theory and neglect other aspects. The virtues of a theory can blind us to its weaknesses. Taken as whole systems, atonement theories can seem irreconcilable. From the start, we limit the potential ways one might understand the Bible. We have three or four choices to pick from. In our minds, we tend to choose one outright. Or, at the very least, we rank them in some sort of order.

We are often ignorant of the role that context plays in shaping our theories of atonement. Our cultural context narrows the focus and scope of our theological questions. Because of our historical situation, we might ask too much of our theories. We expect them to provide answers not given in the biblical text. In defense of a long-held theory, we are prone to overemphasize certain parts of the Bible at the expense of others. We have a hard time separating Scripture from speculation.

WHAT ARE THE INGREDIENTS?

The law of Moses placed numerous dietary restrictions on ancient Israelites. Shrimp, pork, and various birds were forbidden. By and large, the early church did not follow these regulations. Christians today enjoy a more expansive menu.

When it comes to doctrine, however, we find an ironic reversal, especially with respect to atonement. Not only are many Christians content with a small menu of "atonement dishes," they argue over which dish is most important or inspired by God. Historically, theologians offer a select group of atonement theories from which to choose. By contrast, the Bible never presents such systematic formulations. Biblical writers instead act as master chefs who offer a succulent buffet of truth even while using only a few basic ingredients.

Envisage a society with only a few meal choices: fried chicken, pasta, scrambled eggs, chicken and dumplings. In this imaginary culture, factions arise that claim the superiority of one dish over another. Debates rage about the relative virtue of eggs over fried chicken. By analogy, these dishes are like the popular atonement theories we've inherited from history. They nourish us. We are thankful for them. But restricting ourselves to these few options looks increasingly unnecessary, even harmful, the more we look at the situation.

Someone familiar with cooking will notice an oversight on the part of our imagined society. Each food item above can be made with just a few ingredients. There is no reason that people must restrict themselves to those specific dishes. With only flour, chicken, eggs, milk, and potatoes, we have an array of culinary options. For example, one could also make chicken soup, waffles, breakfast skillets, potato soup, grilled chicken, and a basic omelet.

In this analogy, the ingredients represent a small set of biblical metaphors that can be rearranged to form numerous doctrinal theories. Nevertheless, we tend to start with a limited set of atonement theories and *overlook the more fundamental elements that are common to each theory*. When discussing the Bible's teaching on atonement, we "lose at the starting line." The Bible provides a collection of theological ingredients, but we often don't start here. Instead, we settle for a narrow set of doctrinal dishes. Although nourishing, they do not represent the biblical medley available to us.

To put it another way, we need something like a "Taco Bell approach" to the doctrine of atonement. This popular, Tex-Mex inspired, fast-food restaurant urges people to "think outside the bun" and serves an impressive variety of dishes. The vast menu has tacos, nachos, burritos, and quesadillas, yet also includes original creations like the Naked Chicken Chalupa. Why do I say "impressive"? When you look at its menu, Taco Bell uses a relatively small set of ingredients and, still, it always boasts an assortment of options for customers. With respect to doctrine, we need to think outside the box of convenient cat-egories. By delving deep into the Bible, we find a handful of motifs that combine to form a richer, more robust theology of atonement.

Our context largely influences how we combine biblical themes and texts. Church tradition, personal experiences, education, and culture shape our ques-tions and assumptions. They affect what we see *and* what we don't. In church history, particular theories of atonement arose to explain Christ's death in fresh ways. Such formulations are helpful, but they are not our starting point. *Merely comparing atonement theories is a recipe for failure*. We need to look back at both history and the Bible in order to savor the fullness of Christ's atoning work.

The Atonement in Historical Contexts

In appendix A, I provide a brief survey of several major atonement theories, highlighting their historical background and emphases. Each theory attempts to contextualize the Bible's teaching on atonement. Still, we are left with a question: To what extent do these common theories of atonement reflect biblical logic?

Theology is not equivalent to biblical truth. Hopefully, these two have much overlap. However, we cannot assume that our theology—our understanding of Scripture—wholly captures the Bible's teaching.

We all have limited perspectives. We live in particular cultures and historical periods. No one studies the Bible in a vacuum. Our cultural, historical, and personal contexts influence how we interpret the Bible. In this sense, all theology is contextualized.

"Context" is not just culture; it also includes history. Different historical ages are different contexts. How does context influence our theology? Specifically, how do our assumptions and history shape the way we understand the atonement?

Different historical periods and subcultures have varying perspectives on Christ's death. Sometimes these views complement one another. At other times, they contradict. In every case, people's historical context influences how they explain atonement.

As I write this, the world wrestles with Covid-19. Before the pandemic, if my daughter developed a small cough and fever, we'd have given her some medication, kept an eye on her, and thought little about it. But in the context of the Covid-19 virus, we now fixate on her symptoms with new seriousness. The only thing that's changed is the context.

Of course, every generation has a limited vantage point. We all have blind spots. This is as true for theology as it is with medicine. Just a hundred years ago, doctors recommended drinking radium to cure arthritis and impotence. We need people from other generations to give us an alternative perspective. They challenge our modern assumptions and priorities. By studying history, we dialogue with historical thinkers. Historical views of atonement inevitably affect our interpretations. Even seemingly novel perspectives resemble older views in some way.

What Versus How

When theologians speak of Christ's atonement, we can't assume they are answering the same questions. Atonement theories generally fall into two categories: The first kind of theory explains *what* atonement achieves. The second type explains *how* Christ achieves atonement. I will list several popular theories according to their kind.

The following primarily emphasize *what* atonement achieves:

- recapitulation theory
- Christus Victor

The following primarily emphasize *how* Christ effects atonement:

- ransom theory
- satisfaction theory
- penal substitution

It's more difficult to categorize moral influence theory, though I think it probably fits in the second group better.

Even the questions we ask and emphasize will shape our doctrine of atonement. This single factor sets our theology on one of various possible trajectories. Our questions and assumptions naturally lead us to use different texts and stress different metaphors. As we'll see in the coming sections, our culture and ministry contexts further influence how we explain this doctrine.

Reading the Atonement in Context

Theology involves synthesis. Theology combines our analysis of various passages to make conclusions. As a result, readers' questions and assumptions influence our understanding of doctrines more than we might think. Our backgrounds and basic view of the world shape which doctrines we prioritize. They make us think certain texts are clear while others seem unclear. The questions of our age lead us to give too much (or too little) weight to certain passages. We might even try to force the Bible to answer our questions. We could say that theological doctrines are the conclusions we reach when we interpret the Bible using various cultural and historical lenses.

As an example, we'll use the doctrine of atonement to illustrate culture's impact on theology. The fact that culture influences theology does not at all imply that all theology is mistaken. Rather, it simply means we purposely need to diversify our perspective. We must consistently look for blind spots and critically assess common conclusions.

Adonis Vidu demonstrates the point well. He explores the influence of context on the doctrine of atonement. He says, "The history of atonement thinking could be read as an ongoing conversation with the history of thinking about justice and the law."[1] During the patristic age, Vidu explains, "the interests of the gods in relation to justice are not first and foremost the preservation of the law. Laws are very much secondary to a justice understood primarily as order."[2] Many people assumed "laws apply between humans, but they are not binding on God."[3]

With time, views on law and justice evolved. By the medieval period, "in both law and theology, justice comes to be approximated as law. Law is now regarded as defining the framework for human and divine relationships."[4] Furthermore, law is an expression of God's own being. Sin demands satisfaction or punishment that is proportionate to the crime.

The Reformers sharpen the distinction between natural law and temporal, social laws. The former could not be discerned through fallen reason. The latter imperfectly reflects the revealed will of God. This perspective led to differing ways of relating law and Christ's atoning work. For Luther, the law is merely a guide that condemns and so "curbs" crime.[5] Christ's death overcomes the penalty levied against us by the law. For Calvin, the law becomes central to the mechanism of salvation itself. He not only accepts the punishment meted out by law; Christ perfectly obeys its commands. Accordingly, Vidu says, "Rather than construing law as the enemy that must be defeated, it is rather the means by which the ultimate victory is won."[6]

This short overview cannot do justice to Vidu's study. Still, it suggests just one way that context subtly shifts the way we form doctrine. To be sure, even when views on the atonement differ, they do not necessarily contradict Scripture or each other. Our culture influences and shapes our theology. One's environment and experiences act like lenses.

---

[1] Adonis Vidu, *Atonement, Law, and Justice: The Cross in Historical and Cultural Contexts* (Grand Rapids, MI: Baker Academic, 2014), xiv.
[2] Vidu, *Atonement, Law, and Justice*, xvi.
[3] Vidu, *Atonement, Law, and Justice*, 46.
[4] Vidu, *Atonement, Law, and Justice*, xvi.
[5] Vidu, *Atonement, Law, and Justice*, 100.
[6] Vidu, *Atonement, Law, and Justice*, 120.

How Theologians Contextualize the Atonement

In what follows, we will glance back at the landscape above. Planted in each atonement theory is an agenda or purpose. Each view wants to contextualize Christ's work for its age. In other words, they want to make clear how the atonement affects their audience's life. To be sure, they also connect with many of the same needs seen around the world today.

Recapitulation theory stands in contrast to ancient Gnosticism. In antiquity, this philosophy increasingly influenced how people saw the world. Gnostics divided flesh from spirit. The former belonged to the material world, which was thought to be corrupt. Thus, they asserted that the flesh of our physical bodies is corrupt.

Early proponents of recapitulation theory counter that assumption. They affirm the inherent goodness of God's creation. Recapitulation theory challenges gnostic thinking. We should not expect God ultimately to cast aside our bodies with the physical world. In fact, the atonement aims to restore the world to its original state. The present sinful world is not its natural state.

Ransom theory utilizes "debt" language, which is pervasive in Scripture. The Bible routinely uses debt specifically to talk about atonement. In the ancient world, debt led to slavery. Slavery as a consequence of debt was a daily reality. Naturally, the average person could easily understand the import of this theory.

Christus Victor emphasizes kingship and victory. These concepts are universal throughout history and the world. Territories and kingdoms have suffered from tyranny. People long for a deliverer. Fittingly, the gospel inherently has kingdom connotations. Christ's life, death, and resurrection manifest his royal victory.

The gospel magnifies Christ's power. For this reason, Christus Victor addresses concerns found in so-called fear-power cultures. These cultures stress demons, evil spirits, ancestors, and spirits. They exist throughout the world, especially among tribal peoples in Sub-Saharan Africa and south Asia. The ancient and medieval worlds also were very sensitive to the influence of spirits. People needed to know that Christ overcomes all the world's spirits.

Anselm's satisfaction theory was influenced by the feudalism of his age. According to that system, the tenant had a duty to honor the landowner. Upholding justice entailed maintaining social harmony and order. Humans are God's tenants who owe God honor.

However, our disobedience disrupts the natural order. It dishonors God. Harmony (i.e., justice) entails restoration. How does this happen? The tenants must make compensation. God's demand for honor requires satisfaction. If we don't give God recompense, he will restore his honor himself. Without some satisfying compensation, harmony would require that God destroy humanity. Anselm's honor-shame perspective provides him with assumptions about harmony, justice, and honor. In this way, his culture influences his theory.

From this point, we begin to observe a historical transition. Previous atonement theories mainly concern the grand biblical story. They speak about God's design for the world and especially how God conquers enemies. Early theories have a more cosmic scope. The closer we get to penal substitution, theories become increasingly individualistic. They explain how Christ atones for an individual's sins.

Penal substitutionary atonement (PSA) and satisfaction theory share a common historical background. Both emerge from a medieval worldview. The Reformers insist that God requires satisfaction; yet they adjust the conditions for satisfaction. Rather than God's honor, it is God's law that needs satisfaction. According to this view, God is less a landowner than a judge. Calvin and Luther both had legal backgrounds. Not surprisingly, they naturally appeal to judicial imagery when explaining the atonement.

Anselm's view of justice concerns harmony and honor whereas PSA is based on retributive justice. This view of justice claims that God must punish every single sin without exception. Sinful people cannot compensate for their sin. Only punishment satisfies justice. Without this view of justice, the argument for PSA is substantially weakened.

What about moral influence theory? As liberalism increasingly spread throughout Christianity, people began to underscore religion's practical elements above its abstract parts. Theology became even more compartmentalized and individualized. In this way, moral influence theory is more subjective than prior perspectives. It emphasizes moral transformation. It seeks to spur concrete life change. Advocates want the atonement to have practical importance. While this goal is laudable, it forsakes objective aspects of the atonement. This theory tends to be popular with people who doubt supernatural events and who deny Jesus' divinity.

WHAT ABOUT US?

We can see how historical and cultural factors influenced theologians of the past. But what about us? Are we more objective? To consider this question, look at three common perspectives of "justice." One can speak of retributive justice, restorative justice, and covenantal justice. These three views are not exhaustive. While they do not inherently contradict, each potentially leads us to highlight different values or ideas.

How does one's view of justice shape a person's understanding of Christ's work? Whatever our theory of atonement, we can be sure some approach to justice underlies it. For example, retributive justice underscores the necessity of God punishing wrongdoers. By contrast, covenant justice might cause readers to focus more on God's saving faithfulness to his people. Our assumptions about the nature of justice affect our interpretation of Scripture whenever it speaks of justice. Rather than argue for one theory of justice over another, we should consider how these multiple facets of justice interrelate.

Broadly, people agree that "justice" refers to right actions or a right state of affairs. However, what is right or correct? What is right depends on circumstances and relationship. How a judge righteously treats a criminal is not the same as how he righteously treats an innocent person. In different cultures and churches, people emphasize varied aspects of justice. Even within Western philosophy, no single theory of justice exists.

RETRIBUTIVE JUSTICE

Retributive justice lays stress on the punishment and correction of wrongdoing. Justice demands that every single sin receives punishment. Accordingly, God reveals his justice through punishing every sin. In this way, it has a negative connotation. This perspective focuses God's role as judge.

Many Christians hold this view today. Its prominence in the church is in part explained by its emphasis during the Protestant Reformation. Retributive justice reflects the belief that the consequences of evil not only will *but should* catch up with a person.

Several biblical texts affirm this conception of justice. For example, in Matthew 16:27, Jesus says, "For the Son of Man is to come with his angels in the glory of his Father, and then he will repay everyone for what has been done."[7]

---

[7]Cf. Job 34:11; Ps 7:15-16; 28:4; 62:12; 137:8; Jer 17:10; 50:15, 29; Mt 16:27; Rom 2:6; Gal 6:7; Rev 18:6.

Some verses merely speak about a general principle of retribution. Ecclesiastes 10:8 says, "He who digs a pit will fall into it, and whoever breaks through a wall will be bitten by a snake."[8] This principle is creatively applied within a Christian context. Christ suffers although he has no sin. Conversely, God shows them mercy although sinners are the ones who do evil.

Perhaps the most cited passage supporting retributive justice comes from Leviticus 24:17-22:

> Anyone who kills a human being shall be put to death. Anyone who kills an animal shall make restitution for it, life for life. Anyone who maims another shall suffer the same injury in return: fracture for fracture, eye for eye, tooth for tooth; the injury inflicted is the injury to be suffered. One who kills an animal shall make restitution for it; but one who kills a human being shall be put to death. You shall have one law for the alien and for the citizen: for I am the LORD your God.[9]

Of course, scholars dispute this passage's interpretation. Some people argue that this command expresses mercy, not severity. Why? In ancient society, people received different penalties based on group identity, social status, and so on. Accordingly, this tooth-for-a-tooth principle eliminates or minimizes injustice.[10]

If we subscribe to this interpretation, what would it mean for our view of justice and the atonement? One could conclude that advocates of retributive justice misunderstand the point of Leviticus and so overemphasize the role of punishment. Specifically, justice would not necessarily require punishment, but rather mercy.[11]

RESTORATIVE JUSTICE

Restorative justice offers an alternative approach. This conception of justice has positive connotations. It emphasizes God as Creator, the one who will set the world right. Its goal is not simply the absence of evil. It also highlights the existence of goodness. Obviously, restorative justice and punishment have no contradiction.[12]

I will list a couple of biblical texts that typify this view of justice. First, Isaiah 45:8 exalts God's righteousness ($ṣĕdāqâ$, "justice"): "Shower, O heavens,

---

[8]Cf. Prov 24:12; 26:27.
[9]Cf. Deut 19:18-21; Mt 5:38-40.
[10]Christopher Marshall, *Beyond Retribution: A New Testament Vision for Justice, Crime, and Punishment* (Grand Rapids, MI: Eerdmans, 2002).
[11]Cf. Is 30:18; Zech 7:9.
[12]For example, in the Bible, God often rescues his people through punishing evil.

from above, / and let the skies rain down righteousness; / let the earth open, that salvation may spring up, / and let it cause righteousness to sprout up also; / I the LORD have created it." Similarly, Psalm 89:11-14 proclaims,

> The heavens are yours, the earth also is yours;
>> the world and all that is in it—you have founded them.
> The north and the south—you created them;
>> Tabor and Hermon joyously praise your name.
> You have a mighty arm;
>> strong is your hand, high your right hand.
> Righteousness and justice are the foundation of your throne;
>> steadfast love and faithfulness go before you.

Each passage depicts God as the Creator who establishes righteousness in the world. Not surprisingly, this approach to justice marks the ideal reign of a king.[13]

COVENANT JUSTICE

Finally, biblical writers speak of what may be called covenant justice. In essence, if people keep their covenant obligations, they are considered righteous. In modern terms, a covenant is similar to a contract or treaty. This kind of justice is relationship dependent. What is just or right depends on one's relationship to another person. Accordingly, Nehemiah 9:8 says, "You found his heart faithful before you, and made with him a covenant to give to his descendants the land of the Canaanite, the Hittite, the Amorite, the Perizzite, the Jebusite, and the Girgashite; and you have fulfilled your promise, for you are *righteous* [*ṣadîq*, just]."[14] Nehemiah reckons God as "just" because he is faithful to keep his covenant promises.

Genesis 38 offers a shocking illustration of covenant justice. The narrative first notes the death of Tamar's husband. Genesis 38:11 says, "Then Judah said to his daughter-in-law Tamar, 'Remain a widow in your father's house until my son Shelah grows up'—for he feared that he too would die, like his brothers. So Tamar went to live in her father's house." However, Judah never made Shelah marry Tamar.

Much later, Judah sees Tamar but doesn't recognize her. He thinks Tamar is a prostitute and impregnates her. When the people accuse Tamar of immorality,

---

[13]Cf. Ps 72:1-2; 99:4; 122:5; Prov 29:4; Is 9:7; 11:3-4; 32:1; Jer 23:5.
[14]Scriptural emphases here and throughout this book are the author's.

notice what Judah says. In Genesis 38:26, "Then Judah identified them and said, 'She is more *righteous* [*ṣadîq*, just] than I, since I did not give her to my son Shelah.' And he did not know her again" (ESV). Although Tamar behaved like a prostitute, Judah calls her just. Why? Even after many years, Tamar fulfills her obligation by never remarrying.

All relationships have certain expectations or conditions. Most are unspoken. Today, many people mistakenly think a righteous person is equivalent to a perfect person. Righteous people in the Bible are not perfect. God calls Noah, Abraham, and David "righteous," but they all sin. They were righteous ultimately because they gave their allegiance to the Creator God (however imperfect their faith was).

THREE TYPES OF JUSTICE

Each of the above views on justice have a different orientation or scope. Retributive justice focuses on punishing specific wrong actions. Restorative justice has a broader, constructive scope. Covenant justice concerns people inside a covenant. Which view is right? Depending on the context, each view contains some aspect of biblical truth. Justice cares about removing evil, establishing good, and keeping relational commitments. The biblical writers concentrate on diverse aspects in different circumstances.

When interpreting Scripture, we must not forget the maxim "Context is king." We do not want merely to assume one kind of justice. We should avoid making false distinctions, pitting one approach to justice against another. Rather, depending on context, we want to lay stress on what the Bible emphasizes. My point here concerns emphasis, not right and wrong.

Although these three views of justice all convey some degree of truth, we tend to highlight one kind of justice according to our background and culture. Traditionally, evangelicals assume biblical justice primarily concerns punishment, that is, retributive justice. They rarely consider other views. Why? Because the stress on retributive justice is traditional. Perhaps tradition is right; perhaps not. Whatever the case, readers ought not merely assume one conception of justice over against another.

Our understanding of justice subtly influences our doctrine of the atonement. For example, if we always assume the priority of retributive justice, regardless of the biblical text, we affirm PSA yet overlook certain aspects of the cross. Likewise, an isolated stress of restorative justice can lead us to ignore the relationship between God's wrath and sin. Our theology of atonement inevitably shapes how we present God to others. We should ask ourselves, *In passages that speak of atonement, what type of justice do we see?*

ATONEMENT AS CONTEMPORARY SHIBBOLETH

In Judges 12, Jephthah gathers the men of Gilead to fight against Ephraim. Verses 5-6 say,

> Then the Gileadites took the fords of the Jordan against the Ephraimites. Whenever one of the fugitives of Ephraim said, "Let me go over," the men of Gilead would say to him, "Are you an Ephraimite?" When he said, "No," they said to him, "Then say Shibboleth," and he said, "Sibboleth," for he could not pronounce it right. Then they seized him and killed him at the fords of the Jordan. Forty-two thousand of the Ephraimites fell at that time.

The distinction between "shibboleth" and "sibboleth" is subtle but significant for those being asked. In effect, the test pronounced death for the average Ephraimite. In some circles, the doctrine of atonement serves as a contemporary shibboleth. This is particularly true in evangelical circles. If a person doubts the truth or primacy of a certain atonement theory, such as PSA, they bear a scarlet letter of shame in the eyes of many evangelical ministries and churches.

This trend is troubling. The recent increase in books trying to reconcile various atonement theories gives witness to this growing concern. Taking a both/and approach to the debate is helpful but limited. Even attempts to relate disparate views devolve into arguments about which theory is most "central." Meanwhile, distrust and disunity persist.

How might we rethink this debate? First, we recognize the plain truth that the Bible never constructs atonement theories in the likeness of those surveyed above. They are valuable contextualizations. They attempt to interpret and communicate biblical truth for certain contexts. Second, we should examine the explicit ways that the Bible portrays Christ's sacrificial death. After all, if we begin by comparing atonement theories, we lose at the starting line.

What happens if we bring down this theological wall of hostility? The church will have new eyes to see the significance of the cross. We will discern new ways to apply the atonement to our lives and ministry. Fresh reflection on the atonement can open surprising opportunities to contextualize the message of salvation for cultures around the world.

"You're a Christian, Right?"

Before his passing, John McDermott was the world's expert in philosophical pragmatism. He knew the works of William James and John Dewey as well as—or better than—anyone in the world. McDermott had a reputation around his department at Texas A&M University. Tough. No nonsense. Sharp tongued. Astute knowledge in about everything. And he was no fan of Christianity (or so I heard).

He was one of my professors during my time at Texas A&M, where I earned a master's degree in philosophy. I took his course as a first-year graduate student. It wasn't long before I learned about this legendary personality. I was told he was an atheist, though I'm not sure whether that was accurate. As a young zealous Christian, I mentally lumped anyone who was anti-Christianity into the "atheist" category. I now had a mission. In McDermott's class, I'd show him the folly of his ways and philosophy by demonstrating the superiority of a biblical perspective.

Each week, we submitted papers interacting with the assigned readings, followed by class discussions. I took these opportunities to refute the materialistic, non-Christian worldview of the authors we studied. A third of the way through the semester, McDermott had enough.

At a class break, he rasped, "Come here. Follow me." I obliged, trailing him until we left the building. Turning, he wasted no time. "You are a Christian, right?" he asked. Now I knew why he summoned me outside. I was successful. I had shown him how well a Christian mind could engage God-ignoring philosophers. "Yes," I said, trying not to puff out my chest. "Then shouldn't you be humble?!" He continued, "Why don't you first understand what you're reading and then criticize it?"

This emotional punch in the gut left me without breath to reply. It jarred my ears open to hear his admonition. He did not berate me. Rather, he acted like a mentor, pounding into my head the literal meaning of *philosophy* (the love of wisdom).

I've yet to recover from that conversation outside of Heldenfels Hall. From that point, I began to listen and discover that we can gain insight from anyone, even if they are atheists or heretics. I learned the value of taking another person's perspective.

HUMILITY IN PERSPECTIVE TAKING

With time, I found out that humility does not mean we must skeptically give up our convictions. Nor does it mean stubbornly holding onto long-held teachings in the name of faith. Instead, humility entails the willingness to examine afresh our beliefs, even traditional ones.

Having intellectual humility means we will consider others' ideas with generosity, being quick not only to find common ground. We also want to augment arguments that make sound points yet merely need better support. After all, we should be interested in truth, not convincing others that we are right when we're not.

Crossing cultures is a never ending challenge to one's humility. While learning a second language, highly educated people are reduced to sounding like four-year-olds when shopping for vegetables. The brain tends to judge the unfamiliar as "bad" or "wrong." With a little experience and even more humility, a person will discover who really is wrong.

Instead of dubbing one cultural perspective "good" or "right" and another negative, *the truth is far more uncomfortable and ambiguous than we'd like to admit.* For missionaries, the situation is complicated by the fact that the church has long melded Christianity with Western culture. Specific historical questions and themes have shaped systematic theologies. They lead us to prioritize certain motifs and problems over others. A traditional Western lens can often narrow our perspective such that we overlook or underemphasize aspects of the Bible.

Consequently, interpreters easily become suspicious of whatever is not traditional. They can be quicker to criticize than to consider what they might learn from a fresh perspective. A half-truth is half-wrong. A 90 percent truth is 10 percent wrong. A series of ideas that are 100 percent correct can still misrepresent the truth if shared in an incoherent manner.

If we love the truth, should we be content with settling for only part of the truth? If we settle for what's merely true, we compromise the gospel since we minimize, overlook, or even deny other biblical teachings.[15] Are we aware of

---

[15]For more on this point, see Wu, *One Gospel for All Nations*, 17-26.

our tendency to defend our ideas before listening with humility to contrary views? If so, what are we practically going to do? Knowing we all read the Bible through a cultural lens, should we not become more critical of our assumptions? *Admitting we have blind spots is not the same thing as actively seeking to take a fresh perspective.* We need action steps. This book is one step on that journey. And why not begin at the cross?

CONCLUSION

The Bible presents Christ's death as a sacrifice that brings atonement. What all that statement entails remains a point of dispute. As we've seen, context plays a critical role in shaping our understanding of the atonement. This claim does not relativize biblical truth. After all, theologians have long compared the atonement to a multifaceted diamond with many sides to admire. Accordingly, we might say that various atonement theories are relative perspectives on absolute truth.

While a theory helps simplify ideas, it can also oversimplify them. Conversely, a theory can make a concept feel utterly complex and difficult to understand. We need not settle for one atonement theory over another. We need a different starting point. What if we instead discern the underlying logic of atonement? What are the common metaphors or images used to explain atonement throughout the Bible?

In the following chapters, we'll turn to the Old Testament. Without this biblical context, the atonement makes little sense. The sacrificial system provides the critical framework for interpreting Christ's work. What does it mean that Christ is a "sin offering"? How does Christ "bear our sin"? These are only a couple of questions to be answered in the coming pages.

2

PREPARING A SANCTUARY FOR THE KING

A COMMON CARICATURE PERSISTS concerning Israel's sacrificial system. Like countless other ideas that stick in the mind, it contains a measure of truth. In popular evangelical theology, ancient sacrifices served as a transaction between God and individual sinners. A person brought an animal to God, who punished it instead of the offender. Once God extinguished his wrath on the sacrifice, the worshiper was purified from sin.

This conception of sacrifice omits a vast amount of critical background needed to make sense of Israel's rituals. Ancient Israelites viewed the world quite differently than we do. They even categorized space, time, people, and objects around them in ways we'd think odd. Lacking this framework, our theology of atonement collapses under the stress of oversimplification. It becomes reductionistic. We sacrifice a biblical understanding of atonement when we substitute our assumptions in place of those held by ancient Israelites.

In this chapter, we explore the function of Israel's sacrifices. What problem do they address? Why did they make their offerings in a sacred space, such as a tabernacle or temple? What does the temple signify? Also, how do we distinguish terms like "clean" and "unclean," "holy" and "common"? Without this context, we will have difficulty understanding the significance of atonement.

SETTING APART SACRED SPACE

While some people might not realize it, we all understand the idea of sacred space. We treat churches, memorials, and certain landmarks with special regard. In daily life, we might like to sit by the fireplace with a book. Perhaps, a person visits a certain coffee shop or park to free up their mind in a special way. Without using the word *sacred*, we set apart the place we got married or engaged as uniquely significant. Indeed, this is one reason people place markers and wreaths at a loved one's gravesite.

For ancient Israel, the tabernacle and, eventually, the temple were more than places people went to "take care of their business with God." The tabernacle represented more than a mere half of the sacred-secular divide assumed by most Westerners today. The tabernacle visually expressed ancient Israel's worldview. It symbolically pointed to God's holiness and design for the world.

Put simply, the tabernacle was a microcosm for the world as God intended it. It was a kind of mobile temple, the place where God dwells with his people. By grasping the significance of the temple, we perceive God's purpose in creation and the role of atonement in God's cosmic plan.[1]

We find many similarities between the creation story and the tabernacle or temple. For example, the building of the tabernacle repeatedly echoes creation language.[2] Likewise, the creation account and the tabernacle's construction both consist of seven commands.[3] Just as God "rested" on the seventh day of creation, so the Lord says of the temple, "This is my resting place forever; here I will reside, for I have desired it" (Psalm 132:14).[4] In the ancient world, temple dedications often lasted seven days.[5] Naturally, an image of the god resided inside the sanctuary.[6] The parallels with Genesis 1 are apparent.

Biblical writers even depict the Garden of Eden as the world's first temple, which humanity was to expand to fill the earth. Humans are told to "work" and

---

[1]The number of scholarly books and articles on this topic is enormous. I simply survey key ideas.

[2]Greg Beale expands on the following discussion in *The Temple and the Church's Mission* (Downers Grove, IL: IVP Academic, 2004). Key observations are summarized by Lindsay Kennedy, "Parallels Between Creation and the Temple," mydigitalseminary.com/parallels-between-creation-and-the -temple. He highlights parallels in Gen 1:31 and Ex 39:43; Gen 2:1 and Ex 39:32; Gen 2:2 and Ex 40:33.

[3]Beale compares Gen 1:3, 6, 9, 14, 20, 24, 26 with Ex 25:1; 30:11, 17, 22, 34; 31:1, 12.

[4]Cf. Ps 132:8; 1 Chron 28:2; 2 Chron 6:41; Is 66:1.

[5]Cf. 2 Chron 7:8; 1 Kings 6:37-38.

[6]John Walton, *The Lost World of Genesis One* (Downers Grove, IL: IVP Academic, 2009), chaps. 7–9; Beale, *Temple and the Church's Mission*, 29-80.

"keep" the garden. These precise verbs describe the priests' work in the sanctuary.[7] One writer concisely captures Beale's idea.

> Israel's temple was separated into three parts of increasing holiness: the outer court where all were welcome, the holy place where the priests worked, and the holy of holies where God Himself dwelt. . . . The Garden of Eden could be seen similarly. The garden itself was not Eden, but a river flowed out of Eden to provide the garden with water (Gen 2:10). Later in Ezekiel a river flowed from the holy of holies (Ezek 47:1), and in Revelation a river flowed from the very *"throne of God and of the Lamb"* (Rev 22:1). Eden could represent the place where God Himself dwelt. . . . Therefore we can identify the world that Adam was to cultivate (Gen 1:28) with the outer court, the garden with the holy place where Adam was to work (Gen 2:15), and Eden with the Holy of Holies.[8]

God dwells in the tabernacle-temple. Here he manifests his presence in unique ways. These include God's displaying his glory and walking among his people.[9] Likewise, readers of the Bible should understand God's design for the world. It is to be sacred space where he dwells with his people. What is the nature of this dwelling place?

GOD'S TEMPLE THRONE

In the Bible, the temple is depicted as God's heavenly throne room. Psalm 11:4 says, "The LORD is in his holy temple; the LORD's throne is in heaven." Isaiah adds, "In the year that King Uzziah died, I saw the Lord sitting on a throne, high and lofty; and the hem of his robe filled the temple" (Isaiah 6:1; cf. Zechariah 6:12-14). The word *theocracy* has fallen out of favor due to some extremists; yet it accurately brings together two aspects of God's plan for creation. The Creator is the one true king of the cosmos.[10] His kingdom will fill the earth. Fittingly, biblical writers draw from this temple and kingdom imagery to portray God's people. God says to Israel, "You shall be for me a priestly kingdom and a holy nation" (Exodus 19:6; cf. 1 Peter 2:9).

---

[7]Cf. Num 3:7-8; 18:7.

[8]Lindsay Kennedy, "Was the Garden of Eden the First Temple?," October 3, 2012, mydigitalseminary .com/was-the-garden-of-eden-the-first-temple/. He draws from Greg Beale, *The Temple and the Church's Mission*, 75-76. For a shorter work, see Beale, "Eden, the Temple and the Church's Mission in the New Creation," *JETS* 48, no. 1 (2005): 5-32.

[9]Cf. Gen 3:8; Deut 23:14.

[10]Cf. 1 Sam 8:7; Is 43:15; Ps 96:10.

Even the "mercy seat" serves as a symbolic throne for God.[11] This point is obscured by common translations in the New Testament, such as "propitiation," "expiation," and "place of atonement." This word refers to the cover atop the ark, which resided in the tabernacle's innermost and holiest room. God tells Moses, "You shall put the mercy seat on the top of the ark; and in the ark you shall put the covenant that I shall give you. There I will meet with you, and from above *the mercy seat*, from between the two cherubim that are on the ark of the covenant, I will deliver to you all my commands for the Israelites" (Exodus 25:21-22).

Various descriptions of the ark reinforce this imagery. God is the one "enthroned on the cherubim."[12] After defeating the Philistines, David arose "to bring up from there the ark of God, which is called by the name of the LORD of hosts who is enthroned on the cherubim" (2 Samuel 6:2). Ezekiel 10:1 says, "Then I looked, and above the dome that was over the heads of the cherubim there appeared above them something like a sapphire, in form resembling a throne." Keil and Delitzsch summarize,

> The ark of the covenant together with the capporeth [mercy seat] became the throne of Jehovah in the midst of His chosen people, the footstool of the God of Israel (1 Chron. 28:2, cf. Ps. 132:7; 99:5; Lam. 2:1). The ark, with the tables of the covenant as the self-attestation of God, formed the foundation of this throne. . . . The gold plate upon the ark formed the footstool of the throne for Him, who caused His name, i.e., the real presence of His being, to dwell in a cloud between the two cherubim above their outspread wings.[13]

Numerous scholars echo this perspective by underscoring the royal dimension of the ark.[14]

Hebrews similarly entwines royal imagery with that from the tabernacle. The writer presents Christ as "a high priest, one who is seated at the right hand of the throne of the Majesty in heaven, a minister in the sanctuary and the true

---

[11]*kapporath; hilastērion* (LXX). Others think it represents the footstool of God's throne. See Laszlo Gallusz, *The Throne Motif in the Book of Revelation* (New York: Bloomsbury, 2013), 21-23; Luther calls it "throne of grace" in *The Complete Works of Martin Luther*, vol. 6 (Harrington, DE: Delmarva Publications, 2015).

[12]A few examples include 1 Sam 4:4; 2 Kings 19:15; 1 Chron 13:6; Is 37:16; Ps 80:1; 99:1. Cf. Mt 5:34-35.

[13]C. F. Keil and F. Delitzsch, "Exodus 25–31," in the *Commentary on the Old Testament*, Logos Edition (Peabody, MA: Hendrickson, 1857).

[14]Examples include Daegeuk Nam, "The 'Throne of God' Motif" (ThD diss., Andrews University, 1989), 1-58; John E. Hartley, *Leviticus*, WBC 4 (Grand Rapids, MI: Zondervan, 1992), 234-35; Gallusz, *Throne Motif*, 21-23.

tent that the Lord, and not any mortal, has set up" (Hebrews 8:1-2). Likewise, Hebrews 4:15-16 says, "For we do not have a high priest who is unable to sympathize with our weaknesses. . . . Let us therefore approach the *throne of grace* with boldness." The writer quotes several Old Testament passages that refer to Israel's king, David's royal offspring.[15] These texts are applied to Christ, a royal figure who makes "purification for sins," having been appointed high priest.

In the ancient world, the reverence shown to kings could be characterized as worship. Famously, the Lord prohibits the worship of other gods and images saying, "You shall not *bow down* to them or worship them" (Deuteronomy 5:9). This same wording describes the honor given to David (1 Kings 1:15) and Joash (2 Chronicles 24:17).

The clothing of the high priest is also noteworthy. His turban and other adornment evoke royalty. In effect, Scripture depicts the high priest as wearing a crown.[16] In Exodus 28:36-37, the Lord describes what Aaron will wear on his head: "You shall make a rosette of pure gold, and engrave on it, like the engraving of a signet, 'Holy to the LORD.' You shall fasten it on the turban with a blue cord; it shall be on the front of the turban." Similarly, in Zechariah 6:11, "Take the silver and gold and make a crown, and set it on the head of the high priest Joshua son of Jehozadak."

Ezekiel both sums up our findings and makes a remarkable connection. He portrays the temple as "the place of my throne and the place for the soles of my feet, where I will reside among the people of Israel forever. The house of Israel shall no more *defile* [*tm'*] my holy name, neither they nor their kings, by their whoring, and by the corpses of their kings at their death" (Ezekiel 43:7). While interpreters often link defilement with the sanctuary, some people are slower to associate such language with royal imagery. On reflection, the connection is not surprising. We would expect those who go before a king to wash themselves and even wear their most splendid garments. Accordingly, Isaiah's response is natural. The prophet says, "In the year that King Uzziah died, I saw the Lord sitting on a throne, high and lofty; and the hem of his robe filled the temple. . . . And I said: 'Woe is me! I am lost, for I am a man of unclean lips, and I live among a people of unclean lips; yet my eyes have seen

---

[15]For example, Heb 1:5-8, 13; 5:5 use 2 Sam 7:14; Ps 2:7; 45:6-7; 89:27; 110:1.

[16]Cf. Ex 28:4, 31, 36-37; 29:6; 39:22, 30; Lev 8:9; 21:12; Zech 6:9-14. Also, Sir 45:12. See D. Kellermann, " 'ātar," *TDOT*, 26; K. A. Kitchen, "Crown," *TNBD*, 247.

the King, the LORD of hosts!'" (Isaiah 6:1, 5). In short, (im)purity language applies to both the sanctuary and the sovereign, because the former served as the king's court.

A PRIESTLY PERSPECTIVE OF THE WORLD

We all mentally divide the world into parts. Our behavior reflects our perspective. At my alma mater, Texas A&M University, the Memorial Student Center honors students who have died while serving in the military. Everyone who enters the building is expected to remove his hat promptly. If he does not, he will certainly incur the loud and persistent wrath of those around him. Even the grass around the building is treated with reverence.

Similarly, the people of ancient Israel divide and subdivide the world into four categories or spheres.[17] This view of the world is fundamental to understanding the Bible's teaching on atonement. The first distinction separates the "holy" from the "common." Second, what is "common" is classified either as "clean" or "unclean." See figure 2.1.

Holy	Common	
Clean		Unclean

Figure 2.1. Four categories in the ancient Israelite world

What do these terms mean? The meaning of *holy* (*qdš; hagios*) includes several ideas. Wenham explains that "holiness" is "intrinsic to God's character" and "is exemplified by completeness."[18] It suggests an otherness beyond the ordinary state of created things. Israel's God is separate in essence from creation.

As we'll see later, holiness conveys unique honor. People call "holy" that which they think has utmost value. Therefore, a person honors what one regards as holy. As a result, people worship God because they see him as holy. To set apart something as "holy" entails giving it honor. While holiness expresses

---

[17]Gordon Wenham, *Leviticus* (Grand Rapids, MI: Eerdmans, 1979), 19; Jay Sklar, *Sin, Impurity, Sacrifice and Atonement: The Priestly Conceptions* (Sheffield: Sheffield Phoenix, 2005), 105n2; likewise, Matthew Thiessen, *Jesus and the Forces of Death: The Gospels' Portrayal of Ritual Impurity Within First-Century Judaism* (Grand Rapids, MI: Baker Academic, 2021), 8-20. Cf. Lev 10:10 with 1 Sam 21:5-6; Ezek 48:15.
[18]Wenham, *Leviticus*, 22, 24.

honor, honor does not necessarily express holiness. After all, people honor or respect parents, teachers, and leaders daily; yet we rarely regard such authorities as holy.

Besides God, the Bible also says the temple, certain utensils within it, and God's people are holy. Why? People and things can have a derived holiness. Because the temple and its furniture, for example, have a special relationship with God, they are considered holy. They are objects used for worshiping God and ushering in his presence. In this respect, their holiness derives from God. Furthermore, "holiness does not [necessarily] mean moral purity."[19] A significant function of holiness language is to delimit boundaries. Accordingly, "the label 'most holy,' then, establishes the most serious boundaries of divine space and appropriately mediates contact between Israel and the deity."[20]

Whereas holiness connotes specialness, its opposite is common or ordinary. Observe the distinction in 1 Samuel 21:4: "The priest answered David, 'I have no *ordinary* bread at hand, only *holy* bread.'" What is common includes normal, ordinary, everyday things. *Common* does not necessarily have negative connotations in Scripture. Certain land is designated "for ordinary use" (Ezekiel 48:15). In addition, this category further divides into two types—clean and unclean. Leviticus 10:10 highlights these fundamental distinctions. The Lord tells Aaron, "You are to distinguish between the holy and the common, and between the unclean and the clean." While "holy" things are "clean," what is clean is not necessarily holy.

Ezekiel 44:23 reinforces the point from Leviticus 10. It says, "They shall teach my people the difference between the holy and the common, and show them how to distinguish between the unclean and the clean" (cf. Ezekiel 22:26). How does one become unclean or impure? Many possible reasons exist.[21] Philip Jenson differentiates "minor impurities" and "major impurities."[22] Jay Sklar summarizes,

> These poles are determined based on the type of rite for cleansing, the duration of the impurity, and the degree of its contagion. Minor defilements are those

---

[19] For example, objects and places have no "moral purity" as if they could sin. Doug Kennard, "Hebrew Metaphysic: Life, Holy, Clean, Righteousness, and Sacrifice," *Answers Research Journal* 1 (2008): 178.

[20] Michael Hundley, "Objects, Offerings, and People in the Priestly Texts: A Reappraisal," *JBL* 132, no. 4 (2013): 764.

[21] Cf. Jonathan Klawans, *Impurity and Sin in Ancient Judaism* (Oxford: Oxford University Press, 2000).

[22] Philip Peter Jenson, *Graded Holiness: A Key to the Priestly Conception of the World*, JSOTSup 106 (Sheffield: Sheffield Academic, 1992), 46.

which are typically cleansed via bathing and/or laundering, which last one day, and which are not contagious. . . . Major defilements require several more rites for cleansing. . . . Most importantly, the cleansing of a major impurity always involves sacrifice, something that is never found with a minor impurity.[23]

The following gives examples of each type of impurity.

Minor:

• Touching unclean carcass	Leviticus 11:24-28
• Eating in a contaminated house	Leviticus 14:46-47
• Sexual intercourse	Leviticus 15:16-18
• Touching a corpse	Numbers 19:22

Major:

• Giving birth	Leviticus 12
• Skin disease	Leviticus 13–14
• Discharge (male or female; menstruation)	Leviticus 15:13-15, 28-30

What does impurity or uncleanness entail?[24] I'll highlight a few reasons that language about purity and impurity is significant. First, various cultures use purity language to demarcate boundaries. Impurity is regarded as dangerous, whereas purity signifies safety and goodness. *Cleanness* indicates health, wholeness, and rightness. Accordingly, purity language can distinguish insiders and outsiders. Societies exclude those deemed unclean; yet groups treat clean people as insiders. In the Bible, sick people or other nonconformists are reckoned outsiders. Such exclusion is physical and social.

Second, purity language concerns order and disorder. By distinguishing clean and unclean, people indicate order in the world. As Mary Douglas explains, "Pollution beliefs of a culture are related to its moral values, since these form part of the structure of ideas for which pollution behavior is a protective device."[25] Naturally, symbolic boundaries establish relationships in

---

[23]Sklar, *Sin, Impurity, Sacrifice*, 127-28.

[24]Mary Douglas, *Purity and Danger: An Analysis of Concepts of Pollution and Taboo* (London: Routledge, 1966); Tova Ganzel, "The Defilement and Desecration of the Temple in Ezekiel," *Biblica* 89, no. 3 (2008): 369-79.

[25]Mary Douglas, "Symbolic Classification," in *International Encyclopedia of Social and Behavioral Sciences*, ed. James Wright (Oxford: Elsevier, 2015), 199. Originally published as Mary Douglas, "Pollution," in *International Encyclopedia of Social Sciences*, vol. 12, ed. David L. Sills (Springfield, OH: Crowell Collier and Macmillan, 1968), 335-41.

keeping with the perceived moral order of the world.[26] Those who are clean and have access to sacred places can enjoy higher social status. Among biblical scholars, there is much agreement that ancient Israelites in some way correlated purity and impurity with life and death.[27]

Third, impurity can carry a sense of shame.[28] An unclean person suffers the stigma of being different and excluded. The community may think unclean people, in some sense, lack social worth and therefore social status. Naturally, purity and honor are related. By protecting purity, we protect honor. For example, how do people honor God's temple? They preserve its purity and so avoid impurity. They don't treat God's sacred space like ordinary places, such as bathrooms or play areas. Those serving inside the temple have honor within society. Anyone who cannot enter the temple could have some degree of shame.

This brief overview highlights major threads that make up the worldview of ancient Israel. With this lens, we can better appreciate the context in which the biblical writers speak of impurity as a theological problem.

The Problem of Impurity

What is reckoned unclean? The sanctuary? People? What's the relationship between the Holy Place and the people's uncleanness and transgressions? This is a much-debated question. Sklar and others contend that impurities defiled the sanctuary.[29] While some interpreters suggest that impurity and sin pollute the inner sanctuary itself, this impression appears mistaken. Greenberg points out several inconsistencies with the claim that impurities are stored inside the Holy Place.[30] Whatever the case, impurity dishonors God, as we'll see, when people disregard it and so treat God as ordinary and unworthy of honor.

---

[26]Michele Lamont, Sabrina Pendergrass, and Mark Pachucki, "Symbolic Boundaries," in Wright, *International Encyclopedia of Social and Behavioral Sciences,* 23:15341-47.

[27]Thiessen, *Jesus and the Forces of Death,* 8-20.

[28]Impurity does not necessarily evoke shame. For example, circumstances like touching the dead body of a loved one, menstruation, and sexual emissions are not likely to cause shame.

[29]Sklar, *Sin, Impurity, Sacrifice,* 129; following Jacob Milgrom, "Israel's Sanctuary: The Priestly 'Picture of Dorian Gray,'" *Revue Biblique* 83 (1976): 394.

[30]See James Greenberg, *A New Look at the Atonement in Leviticus: The Meaning and Purpose of Kipper Revisited* (University Park: Penn State University Press, 2020), 32, 53-54, 65, 94, 169-70. For example, how can the inner sanctuary be holy and unclean simultaneously and consistently? If impurity and sin are stored in the sanctuary, what do the daily offerings accomplish if the Day of Atonement ritual remains necessary? If one suggests that the sin or reconciliation offering transfers impurity or sin into the sanctuary (where it collects until the Day of Atonement), why would the sin or reconciliation offering then remove impurity or sin on the Day of Atonement?

Sin is never described as something that is contagious and spreads like impurity. Greenberg says,

> While sins may affect the land, they are still associated with the people who created them. For example, in Lev 18:24-30 (Holiness School), the land is defiled because of its inhabitants. Once these inhabitants are removed, the land is no longer defiled. Thus, the sinful acts that defiled the land are on the people (18:1-23) and do not appear to become some type of substance that polluted the land.[31]

Accordingly, sin appears to be connected to people, not sacred objects. Sinners defile what is sacred.

What about uncleanness in Leviticus 20:2-5? Leviticus 20:3 says, "I myself will set my face against them, and will cut them off from the people, because they have given of their offspring to Molech, *defiling* [*ṭmʾ*] my sanctuary and *profaning* [*ḥll*] my holy name."

While *ṭmʾ* often means "unclean," Greenberg says, "The verb and noun derivatives of *ṭmʾ* may also act as a synonym of the verb and noun derivatives of *ḥll*, having the sense of dishonor or profane."[32] Since impurity and holiness should be separated, the language of uncleanness aptly conveys the dishonor shown to God by Molech worship.[33] To treat the sanctuary with disregard shows contempt toward God.

People become unclean and need cleansing. The sanctuary is cleansed when uncleanness and sin are removed from the people who enter it. If God's people do not remedy their uncleanness, they profane God. They dishonor him by treating him as common. Several texts make this logic explicit.[34] Leviticus 15:31 warns, "Thus you shall keep the people of Israel separate from their uncleanness, so that they do not die in their *uncleanness by defiling* my tabernacle that is in their midst."[35] Likewise, "any who are unclean but do not purify themselves, those persons shall be cut off from the assembly, for they have defiled the sanctuary of the LORD. Since the water for cleansing has not been dashed on them,

---

[31]Greenberg, *New Look*, 155n10.

[32]Cf. Num 5:27-28; Ezek 43:7-8. Greenberg, *New Look*, 57. In 2 Kings 23:8, 13, the king defiles (*ṭmʾ*) the places of false worship that are set up in opposition to the Lord. The writer hardly implies that such places of idolatry were previously clean.

[33]Greenberg, *New Look*, 58.

[34]Among others, see Lev 22:1-9; Num 19:13; Mal 2:12.

[35]The piel stem of *ḥll* routinely connotes dishonor or desecration. Cf. Gen 49:4; Lam 2:2; see Greenberg, *New Look*, 55-61.

they are unclean" (Numbers 19:20). In Ezekiel, the Lord will cleanse the people of their uncleanness by which they "defiled" the land and "profaned" God's name (Ezekiel 36:16-18, 22-27).

At times, the language of impurity and defilement expresses contempt or dishonor toward a king and his people. The Lord God says to the prince of Tyre, "Because you compare your mind / with the mind of a god, / therefore, I will bring strangers against you, / the most terrible of the nations; / they shall draw their swords against the beauty of your wisdom / and defile your splendor" (Ezekiel 28:6-7). Isaiah adds, "The LORD of hosts has planned it— / to defile the pride of all glory, / to shame all the honored of the earth. . . . He has stretched out his hand over the sea, / he has shaken the kingdoms" (Isaiah 23:9, 11). Similarly, "And the houses of Jerusalem and the houses of the kings of Judah shall be defiled like the place of Topheth" because of their unfaithfulness (Jeremiah 19:13).[36]

It is striking that this imagery even applies to the Lord as well. Malachi 1:6-8 says,

> A son honors his father, and a servant his master. If then I am a father, where is my honor? And if I am a master, where is my fear? says the LORD of hosts to you, O priests, who despise my name. But you say, "How have we despised your name?" By offering polluted food upon my altar. But you say, "How have we *polluted you* [*gēalnûkā*]?" By saying that the LORD's table may be despised. When you offer blind animals in sacrifice, is that not evil? (ESV)

The priests despise God's name by offering polluted food at the altar, which is tantamount to polluting God himself! The prophet then adds, "Cursed be the cheat who has a male in the flock and vows to give it, and yet sacrifices to the Lord what is blemished; for I am a great King, says the LORD of hosts, and my name is reverenced among the nations" (Malachi 1:14). Ezekiel shares a similar message. The Lord says, "Its priests have done violence to my teaching and have profaned my holy things; they have made no distinction between the holy and the common, neither have they taught the difference between the unclean and the clean, and they have disregarded my sabbaths, so that *I am profaned* [*ḥll*] among them" (Ezekiel 22:26). The label "common" is not inherently derisive. It is in treating what is holy as though it were common that one "profanes" the Lord.[37] A person dishonors God by acting as though what is holy were unholy

---

[36]In the day of Israel's salvation, they shall have one king, a united kingdom, and will be cleansed from their defilement (Ezek 37:22-23).

[37]This explanation clarifies how "profane" can mean "common" yet still have negative connotations.

(i.e., something common or profane). Likewise, being indifferent about impurity is one way a person dishonors what is holy.

In these texts, the people not only profane God's name, but God himself. Profaning God's holy things and disregarding his Sabbaths are equivalent to profaning God. In short, how we treat holy things reflects our regard for God.

DIVINE INTOLERANCE

God does not tolerate impurity. The above discussion provides important background for understanding why Leviticus and other books give a common explanation: impurity can defile the sanctuary, God's dwelling place. Even if an Israelite was not in the sanctuary, his impurities can dishonor the sanctuary. When ignored, they profane God's presence.

As we've seen, impurity is not necessarily the result of sin. In Leviticus 15, the people become unclean from natural phenomena, such as discharges from disease (Leviticus 15:1-15), seminal emissions (Leviticus 15:16-18), as well as menstruation (Leviticus 15:19-33). Each cause of impurity is physiological, not immoral. Nevertheless, the writer adds, "Thus you shall keep the people of Israel separate from their uncleanness, lest they die in their uncleanness by defiling my tabernacle that is in their midst" (Leviticus 15:31).

The fact that one becomes unclean does not by itself imply a person commits sin. God even *allows* people to become unclean for certain reasons. For example,

> They shall not *defile* [*ṭm '*] themselves by going near to a dead person; for father or mother, however, and for son or daughter, and for brother or unmarried sister they may *defile* [*ṭm '*] themselves. After he has become clean, they shall count seven days for him. On the day that he goes into the holy place, into the inner court, to minister in the holy place, he shall offer his reconciliation offering, says the Lord GOD. (Ezekiel 44:25-27)

How do we understand God's seeming ambivalence toward people's uncleanness?

God does not regard uncleanness as inherently sinful.[38] Instead, he takes issue with people *not* addressing the problem. This is when God shows wrath. Numbers 19 is a case in point. Numbers 19:13 says, "All who touch a corpse, the body of a human being who has died, *and do not purify themselves, defile the tabernacle of the LORD*; such persons shall be cut off from Israel. Since water for

---

[38]Interestingly, the Lord says, "When you come into the land of Canaan, which I give you for a possession, and I put a leprous disease in a house in the land of your possession" (Lev 14:34).

cleansing was not dashed on them, they remain unclean; their uncleanness is still on them." In Numbers 19:14-19, a person touches a dead body, human bone, or a grave. Numbers 19:20 then says, "Any who are unclean but do not purify themselves, *those persons shall be cut off* from the assembly, *for they have defiled the sanctuary of the* LORD. Since the water for cleansing has not been dashed on them, they are unclean." The basic moral transgression that evokes punishment or retribution is not impurity. Greenberg summarizes,

> The negative act that has disrupted the relationship is contracting an unclean substance. Even though the contraction of this unclean substance may be involuntary, it still reflects a negative act, as evidenced by the fact that the individual is barred from the sanctuary and may be isolated from the community. In some cases, the unclean person may unintentionally not perform the required purification rituals but still be allowed to make a sacrificial remedy (Lev 5:2-3). However, if the unclean person intentionally rejects the priestly ritual for handling impurity, then being cut off and death result (compare Lev 15:31; Num 19:13, 20).[39]

The real issue is their not solving the problem of impurity. A person is responsible to cleanse himself.

Anyone with kids or a professional job can grasp the point. We ask our kids to wear nice clothes and brush their hair before attending a wedding. We'd never bring them directly from playing in the mud to the ceremony without having them clean up.

What about passages that seem to connect being unclean and bearing sin? Leviticus 22 is helpful. Leviticus 22:4-8 address priests who become unclean by an emission of semen, touching anything unclean, and the like. The Lord tells them how to become clean (Leviticus 22:5-7). Finally, Leviticus 22:9 says, "They shall therefore keep my charge, lest they bear sin for it and die thereby when they profane it: I am the LORD who sanctifies them" (ESV).

A few verses later, we better discern what the writer means by "bear sin." Leviticus 22:14-16 states, "And if anyone eats of a holy thing unintentionally, he shall add the fifth of its value to it and give the holy thing to the priest. They shall not profane the holy things of the people of Israel, which they contribute to the LORD, and so cause them to bear iniquity and guilt, by eating their holy things: for I am the LORD who sanctifies them" (ESV). In context, the passage

---

[39]Greenberg, *New Look*, 91.

prohibits a layperson or the priest's married daughter from eating holy things. The person unintentionally eats the holy food in Leviticus 22:14, yet he still faces consequences (Leviticus 22:15-16). Even unintentional actions pose a threat. However, pay careful attention to the context. Whether touching something unclean or unintentionally eating something holy, the Lord gives instruction about how to rectify the problem. It is only when one does *not* address the problem that a person "bears sin."

In summary, indifference to uncleanness threatens the life of God's people. He requires purification. Impurity places an obligation on the unclean person. Purification becomes a duty. As we'll see later, the requirement that one be cleansed essentially functions like a debt. From this perspective, purification pays the debt. This observation will prove helpful when we connect the various biblical metaphors for atonement.

Why Does God Care About Uncleanness?

Why is God so concerned with people being unclean? Is God uptight or ill-tempered? What's the rationale behind the prohibitions in Leviticus 11 against touching an animal carcass and eating unclean foods? The writer explains in Leviticus 11:44-45, "For I am the Lord your God; sanctify yourselves therefore, and be holy, for I am holy. You shall not defile yourselves with any swarming creature that moves on the earth. For I am the Lord who brought you up from the land of Egypt, to be your God; you shall be holy, for I am holy." The first Hebrew word in Leviticus 11:45, "because" (*kî*), helps us understand the problem with impurity. Since God's people belong to him, they should not have impurity.

Other passages shed more light on the issue. Leviticus 22, studied above, addresses the person who touches unclean things or unintentionally eats holy food. In each case, the writer gives the same reason why God's people should not act profanely: "For I am the Lord; I sanctify them" (Leviticus 22:9, 16).

We return to the matter of sacred space. It is the presence of God their king that sets Israel apart. His people must show him proper honor, not behaving as though he was not with them. In Numbers 5:1-3, "The Lord spoke to Moses, saying: 'Command the Israelites to put out of the camp everyone who is leprous, or has a discharge, and everyone who is unclean through contact with a corpse; you shall put out both male and female, putting them outside the camp; they must not defile their camp, *where I dwell among them.*'" Various sorts of people symbolically defile their camp. So, they are put outside the community for a time. Deuteronomy 23:9-14 reveals similar logic:

> When you are encamped against your enemies you shall guard against any impropriety. If one of you becomes unclean because of a nocturnal emission, then he shall go outside the camp; he must not come within the camp. When evening comes, he shall wash himself with water, and when the sun has set, he may come back into the camp. You shall have a designated area outside the camp to which you shall go. With your utensils you shall have a trowel; when you relieve yourself outside, you shall dig a hole with it and then cover up your excrement. *Because the LORD your God travels along with your camp*, to save you and to hand over your enemies to you, *therefore your camp must be holy, so that he may not see anything indecent among you and turn away from you.*

Such efforts to remove uncleanness from the camp serve to publicly recognize the Lord's presence among them. They must not treat him as any ordinary person. He is worthy of unique honor.

In Ezekiel, notice what happens when Israel disregards the Lord. Ezekiel 5:11 says, "Therefore, as I live, says the Lord GOD, surely, because you have defiled my sanctuary with all your detestable things and with all your abominations— therefore I will cut you down; my eye will not spare, and I will have no pity."[40]

In light of these severities, one might question whether God's presence is a blessing. If his presence brings calamity, why would Israel want him near? We have ample evidence that biblical writers did not think this way. God's presence is celebrated (Psalm 16:11; 21:6; 100:2). It gives assurance of protection (Psalm 46). His people should "seek his presence continually!" (1 Chronicles 16:11; Psalm 105:4). Being cast away from the Lord's presence entails judgment or exile (2 Kings 17:18-23; 24:20; Jeremiah 52:3; Ezekiel 8–10).

By analogy, fire is not bad. In the presence of fire, we enjoy good meals and warmth during a frigid winter snow. On the other hand, fire in the forests of California during drought season causes destruction. While fire is a blessing, we must respect its power to bring both life and death.

---

[40]Multiple texts reinforce the point that God's people must not profane or defile sacred space or things (e.g., Lev 10:6-7; Num 3:5-10; Ezek 23:38).

THE IMPURITY OF SIN

Thus far, we've primarily looked at ordinary causes of uncleanness. Such reasons include giving birth, menstruation, skin diseases, touching unclean things, and various bodily discharges. What about unambiguous cases of sin (e.g., premeditated murder)?[41] Sin disrupts or disconnects people's relationship with God.[42] The Bible uses several metaphors to depict sin, including impurity, debt, and burden. Richard Beck explains the significance of metaphors for our thinking. He says, "Each metaphor comes with specific entailments, implications that are intuitively suggested by the dominant metaphor. The entailments create a 'logic' that is governed and made available by the metaphor."[43] Naturally, understanding these images will help us understand how atonement acts as a solution for sin.

Sin causes impurity. Leviticus 18:24-27 says,

> Do not make yourselves unclean by any of these things, for by all these the nations I am driving out before you have become unclean, and the land became unclean, so that I punished its iniquity, and the land vomited out its inhabitants. But you shall keep my statutes and my rules and do none of these abominations, either the native or the stranger who sojourns among you (for the people of the land, who were before you, did all of these abominations, *so that the land became unclean*). (ESV)

Iniquity is regarded as uncleanness worthy of punishment. In Numbers 5, sexual infidelity defiles the adulterous. Likewise, murder pollutes the land in Numbers 35:33-34. The Lord warns, "Cast away the detestable things your eyes feast on, every one of you, and do not defile yourselves with the idols of Egypt; I am the LORD your God" (Ezekiel 20:7).

Other passages reinforce this perspective. David prays, "Wash me thoroughly from my iniquity, and cleanse me from my sin" (Psalm 51:2). Implicitly, David describes sin as impurity. He adds, "Purge me with hyssop, and I shall

---

[41] Along with others, I acknowledge how little the Levitical system explicitly addresses "ordinary, everyday sins," like losing one's temper or jealousy. The Mosaic law is more like wisdom literature and far more casuistic than some modern readers prefer. See John Walton and J. Harvey Walton, *The Lost World of the Torah: Law as Covenant and Wisdom in Ancient Context* (Downers Grove, IL: IVP Academic, 2019). Thus, we shouldn't be surprised that it is not overtly exhaustive as we might like. The New Testament, however, does speak to a wider variety of sins yet clearly affirms Christ saving us from all such sin.

[42] The next chapter revisits this aspect of sin when looking at the meaning of *ḥ 't.*

[43] Richard Beck, *Unclean: Meditations on Purity, Hospitality, and Mortality* (Eugene, OR: Cascade, 2011), 35.

be clean; wash me, and I shall be whiter than snow" (Psalm 51:7). Isaiah's plea is hardly subtle, "Wash yourselves; make yourselves clean; / remove the evil of your doings / from before my eyes; / cease to do evil" (Isaiah 1:16). Isaiah 64:6 is especially vivid, "We have all become like one who is unclean, / and all our righteous deeds are like a filthy cloth [literally, menstrual rag]. / We all fade like a leaf, / and our iniquities, like the wind, take us away" (cf. Isaiah 24:5).

THE DEBT AND BURDEN OF SIN

Due to impurity, people have a debt before God. The link between impurity and debt language might not be obvious. The following explanation clarifies why those who are unclean incur a debt. First, the Bible often portrays sin as a debt. Jesus tells his disciples to pray, "Forgive us our debts, as we also have forgiven our debtors. And do not bring us to the time of trial, but rescue us from the evil one. For if you forgive others their trespasses, your heavenly Father will also forgive you, but if you do not forgive others, neither will your Father forgive your trespasses." (Matthew 6:12-15). Luke's version of the prayer underscores the point: "And forgive us our sins, for we ourselves forgive everyone *indebted* to us" (Luke 11:4). Sin and trespasses are clearly equated to debt needing forgiveness.

Jesus' parables also compare sin and debt. In Matthew 18, Peter asks, "Lord, if another member of the church sins against me, how often should I forgive? As many as seven times?" (Matthew 18:21). Jesus then tells of a servant who was heavily indebted to his master. He says,

> And out of pity for him, the lord of that slave released him and forgave him the debt. But that same slave, as he went out, came upon one of his fellow slaves who owed him a hundred denarii; and seizing him by the throat, he said, "Pay what you owe." Then his fellow slave fell down and pleaded with him, "Have patience with me, and I will pay you." But he refused; then he went and threw him into prison until he would pay the debt. When his fellow slaves saw what had happened, they were greatly distressed, and they went and reported to their lord all that had taken place. Then his lord summoned him and said to him, "You wicked slave! I forgave you all that debt because you pleaded with me. Should you not have had mercy on your fellow slave, as I had mercy on you?" And in anger his lord handed him over to be tortured until he would pay his entire debt. *So my heavenly Father will also do to every one of you, if you do not forgive your brother or sister from your heart.* (Matthew 18:27-35)

Matthew 18:35 is an unambiguous answer to Peter's question. Just as the master forgave the servant's debt, so also we should forgive others' sin.

When a woman anoints Jesus, the Pharisees object, "If this man were a prophet, he would have known who and what kind of woman this is who is touching him—that she is a sinner" (Luke 7:39). Jesus responds, "'A certain creditor had two debtors; one owed five hundred denarii, and the other fifty. When they could not pay, he canceled the debts for both of them. Now which of them will love him more?' Simon answers, 'I suppose the one for whom he canceled the greater debt.' And Jesus tells him, 'You have judged rightly'' (Luke 7:41-43). He then concludes, "'Therefore I tell you, her sins, which are many, are forgiven—for she loved much. But he who is forgiven little, loves little.' And he said to [the woman], 'Your sins are forgiven'" (Luke 7:47-48 ESV).

Paul too depicts sin as debt. He writes, "And you, who were dead in your trespasses and the uncircumcision of your flesh, God made alive together with him, having forgiven us all our trespasses, by *canceling the record of debt* that stood against us with its legal demands. This he set aside, nailing it to the cross" (Colossians 2:13-14 ESV). "Record of debt" is a fitting translation of *cheirographon*.[44] The typical use of this document was to publicly acknowledge one's debt.[45] In the ancient world, the declaration also stipulated the conditions for repayment.

Finally, sin is characterized as a burden.[46] This point is implicit in several texts. The following verses use the verb "bear," which translates the Hebrew *naśa*. Elsewhere, *naśa* is translated as "carry," "lift up," or "take."[47] Two verses are representative of many others. Leviticus 5:1 says, "If anyone sins in that he hears a public adjuration to testify, and though he is a witness, whether he has seen or come to know the matter, yet does not speak, he shall bear his iniquity" (ESV). Also, Leviticus 16:22, "The goat shall bear on itself all their iniquities to a barren region; and the goat shall be set free in the wilderness."[48]

---

[44]Although nowhere else in the New Testament, it is found in Tob 5:3; 9:5.

[45]Col 2:13 uses *aphiēmi*, a common term when speaking of the forgiveness of a debt (for example, Mt 6:12; 18:27, 32; LXX Deut 15:2); cf. Roy Yates, "Colossians 2:14: Metaphor of Forgiveness," *Biblica* 71, no. 2 (1990): 248-59. Challenging the majority view, see Kyu Seop Kim, "The Meaning of *cheirographon* in Colossians 2:14 Revisited," *TynBul* 68, no. 2 (2017): 223-39. He suggests that Colossians merely refers to "declaration to observe the religious regulations taught by the false teaching" (238).

[46]Gary Anderson, *Sin: A History* (New Haven, CT: Yale University Press, 2009).

[47]The Hebrew word appears over 650 times in the Old Testament. A few examples include Ex 25:27-28; Lev 10:4-5; Is 41:16.

[48]Similarly, see Lev 5:7; 22:9; Num 9:13; 18:22.

In summary, biblical writers depict sin as a debt. Such debt weighs on people like a heavy burden. Consequently, sinners need the debt to be repaid. The one who makes repayment ineffective bears or takes away the burden of debt.

WHY IS SIN CONSIDERED A DEBT?

Sin is considered a debt, but why? If we don't understand the logic behind this language, we can't fully unpack its implications. This imagery can shape our theology and open doors for contextualization in various ways. I'll list five circumstances where someone becomes a debtor.

First, we borrow things from other people. For instance, in Matthew 18:23-25, Jesus says, "For this reason the kingdom of heaven may be compared to a king who wished to settle accounts with his slaves. When he began the reckoning, one who owed him ten thousand talents was brought to him; and, as he could not pay, his lord ordered him to be sold, together with his wife and children and all his possessions, and payment to be made." Borrowing is probably the most familiar scenario in which one incurs debt.

Second, we are indebted to others when we receive something from a person under the expectation that we should give something else in return. In human relationships, this is simply reciprocity. The "something" that we exchange could be anything from material goods to favors.

We should not necessarily think of reciprocity as merely paying back, such as a business transaction. To some degree, all close friendships have this dynamic. We help one another, expecting that they too will be there for us one day. Americans often reply with, "I owe you one," when somebody does them a favor. I'm not suggesting that we all calculate how we will barter favors. However, people understand that relationships require give-and-take.

With respect to God, he graciously gives us many things. Such gifts are obviously not preconditioned on our obedience. However, it is a moral expectation that we respond with gratitude and honor.[49]

Third, if we damage someone's property, we owe them compensation. On my sixteenth birthday, I backed my parent's van into the side of brand-new Chevy stepside pickup. It still had paper plates. In addition to my humiliation, I now had a debt. I owed money for damages. Even in an accident, we are liable. Exodus 21:35 illustrates this principle: "If someone's ox hurts the ox of another,

---

[49]John Barclay elaborates on this point in *Paul and the Gift* (Grand Rapids, MI: Eerdmans, 2015).

so that it dies, then they shall sell the live ox and divide the price of it; and the dead animal they shall also divide."

Fourth, certain responsibilities are inherent to relationships. We might owe a person some sort of affection, concern, or respect. Such relationships include parents and children, husbands and wives, and close friends. This principle is implicit to Malachi 1:6, which says, "A son honors his father, and servants his master. If then I am a father, where is the honor due me?"

Fifth, we all have duties or obligations within various contexts. This kind of debt applies to relationships between authorities and their subordinates, whether a king, an employer, and so on. Paul tells the Romans, "Pay to all what is due them—taxes to whom taxes are due, revenue to whom revenue is due, respect to whom respect is due, honor to whom honor is due. Owe no one anything, except to love one another; for the one who loves another has fulfilled the law" (Romans 13:7-8). It is noteworthy that the word "owe" (*opheilō*) belongs to the same family of words that convey the idea of debt.

The significance of these observations will become apparent later in this book. We will see how atonement repays a person's debt. Naturally, certain images speak more strongly to certain people. As interpreters, we need to understand the why behind biblical metaphors. By grasping the internal logic of various themes, we can more clearly communicate the Bible's message. Accordingly, when it comes to contextualization, we can know both our freedom and our limits.

THE CONSEQUENCES OF SIN

Scripture does not minimize sin by describing it with metaphors. Humans cannot help but use metaphorical language. We understand what is meant by the "fall" of Rome or a stock market's "crash."

The Bible is unequivocal when describing sin's consequences. Because of sin, we deserve God's wrath. In Isaiah 13:9, the prophet warns, "See, the day of the LORD comes, / cruel, with wrath and fierce anger, / to make the earth a desolation / and to destroy its sinners from it." Likewise, Romans 1:18 states, "For the wrath of God is revealed from heaven against all ungodliness and wickedness of those who by their wickedness suppress the truth." Paul adds, "Put to death, therefore, whatever in you is earthly: fornication, impurity, passion, evil desire, and greed (which is idolatry). On account of these the wrath of God is coming on those who are disobedient" (Colossians 3:5-6).

Sin not only elicits God's wrath; it brings death. This was promised in Genesis 2:16-17, "You may freely eat of every tree of the garden; but of the tree of the knowledge of good and evil you shall not eat, for in the day that you eat of it you shall die." Jeremiah warns rebellious Israel, "All shall die for their own iniquity" (Jeremiah 31:30). Paul's summary is concise: "The sting of death is sin" (1 Corinthians 15:56).[50]

CONCLUSION

This chapter covers much ground. It introduces the basic worldview of ancient Israel. This background provides the essential context for understanding the Bible's teaching on atonement.

Israel's tabernacle and then the temple signify the intersection of earth and heaven, God's throne room. The ark of the covenant not only rests in Israel's most sacred space; it symbolizes the place where God reigns. The priests are called to guard against every impurity that threatens God's honor and the life of his people. Uncleanness itself is not necessarily a moral failure; however, ignoring it is a problem. Certainly, sin and transgression profane the temple and defile the land. The Bible depicts impurity as both a debt and burden.

Why do I highlight these three metaphors rather than others? As we'll see, when the Bible speaks of the atonement, it most often uses these three metaphors. Atonement concerns the problems of impurity, debt, and burden.[51] If we misunderstand a problem, we'll likely misunderstand its solution.

---

[50]Cf. 1 Sam 2:25; 2 Kings 14:6; Rom 5:12-14; 6:23; 7:5.

[51]Of course, the use of these controlling metaphors does not exclude notions of guilt or transgression, just as it does not prohibit the use of other metaphors.

3

OFFERING A WAY TO GOD

THIS CHAPTER LOOKS AT THE MAJOR FUNCTIONS of the sacrificial system in the Old Testament. One of its purposes was to address the problem of impurity, including sin. The New Testament, however, underscores the insufficiency of the sacrifices.

In Hebrews 10:1-4, the writer explains,

> Since the law has only a shadow of the good things to come and not the true form of these realities, it can never, by the same sacrifices that are continually offered year after year, make perfect those who approach. Otherwise, would they not have ceased being offered, since the worshippers, cleansed once for all, would no longer have any consciousness of sin? But in these sacrifices there is a reminder of sin year after year. For it is impossible for the blood of bulls and goats to take away sins.

The broader context in Hebrews unambiguously uses the sacrificial system to elucidate the significance of Christ's death. Ironically, to understand Christ's atonement, we first need to see the Mosaic law's insufficiency. Furthermore, this text seems to pose problems for readers. On the one hand, God established a law to deal with sin. On the other hand, no animal sacrifice sufficiently atones for sin. These two facts seem to contradict.

COMING NEAR TO GOD

The Mosaic law established the sacrificial system to atone for sin. While some people are uncomfortable with my plain statement, the basic idea is undeniable. Various offerings brought about atonement. Whatever the law's limitations, its sacrifices in some way inform our view of Christ's death on the cross.

We need first to define our terms. Although people routinely speak of "sacrifices," problems arise when we import our own meaning into the term or oversimply its significance. A sacrifice is more than something one gives up. The word *qrb*, or "offering," sheds light on the significance and purpose of various sacrifices. Its root word appears 462 times in the Old Testament. It consistently conveys the act of coming near, to approach, and to be near.

The following texts give examples where *qrb* clearly expresses the idea of "coming near."[1]

> When they went into the tent of meeting, and when they *approached* the altar, they washed, as the LORD commanded Moses. (Exodus 40:32)

> Then Moses *brought* Aaron and his sons forward, and washed them with water. (Leviticus 8:6)

> None of you *shall approach* anyone near of kin to uncover nakedness. I am the LORD. (Leviticus 18:6)

These verses should open our minds to the broader implications of the Israelite sacrifices. They raise questions about what Israelites thought they were doing with their offerings.

In Leviticus, we see how *qrb* is used in contexts that explicitly concern sacrificial offerings. Leviticus 1:2-3 uses the verb form four times. The noun appears another three times. God says to Moses, "Speak to the people of Israel and say to them: When any of you *bring* an *offering* of livestock to the LORD, you shall *bring* your *offering* from the herd or from the flock. If the offering is a burnt *offering* from the herd, you shall *offer* a male without blemish; you shall *bring* it to the entrance of the tent of meeting, for acceptance in your behalf before the LORD."[2] For the Israelites, an "offering" referred to the way they came near holiness. Ultimately, their sacrifices enabled people to come near to God. Sacrifices are a primary way that people interact with God. For ancient Israel, sacrifices were the means by which people maintain covenant relationship with God.[3]

---

[1] Each passage uses the same word, *qrb*, not merely the root.

[2] Cf. Lev 1:14; 2:1; 3:1-2; Num 31:50.

[3] As David Moffitt argues in several places, including "Atonement at the Right Hand: The Sacrificial Significance of Jesus' Exaltation in Acts," *NTS* 62 (2016): 549-68.

As we'll see, an Israelite's offering conveyed honor to God. By analogy, if we enter an honored person's home, we will bring a gift. The gift is not a bribe. It merely expresses respect and acknowledges the person's status. Gifts are a way of coming near to honored people. Next, I'll briefly introduce the major sacrificial offerings. The following survey underscores the diversity within the sacrificial system. It also highlights key terms that will affect our understanding of atonement.

BURNT OFFERINGS

Leviticus 1 and 6:8-13 focus on the burnt offering. The worshipers slaughter an animal (e.g., a bull, sheep, goat, or bird) and cut it in pieces. Finally, the people burn the entire animal at the altar. A few observations are noteworthy.

- The worshiper is to lay his hand on the head of the animal (Leviticus 1:4).

- It appears to belong to a process that effects atonement (Leviticus 1:4).

- It is an aroma pleasing to Yahweh (Leviticus 1:9, 13, 17).

- As a result, it changes God's attitude toward people (Genesis 6:5; 8:21).

In the first century, Philo, an Alexandrian Jewish philosopher, highlights another significant aspect of the burnt offering. Philo says,

> It conduces to *the honour of God*, which ought to be aimed at not for the sake of any other reason, but for itself alone, as being both *honourable* and necessary. . . . The law has assigned the whole burnt offering as a sacrifice adequate to that *honour which is suited to God* . . . the whole burnt offering being sacrificed for God himself alone, who must be *honoured for his own sake*, and not for that of any other being or thing; and the others for our sake.[4]

Dan Reid summarizes, "Philo regards the burnt offering as rendering honor (*timē*) to God apart from any other motive or self-interest (Philo Spec. Leg. 1.195-97)."[5]

GRAIN OFFERING

The grain offering (*minḥâ*) is the subject of Leviticus 2 and 6:14-23. Worshipers salt unleavened fine flour, mixing it with oil and frankincense (Leviticus 2:1-13).

---

[4]1.195-97 quoted from Philo of Alexandria. *The Works of Philo: Complete and Unabridged,* trans. Charles Duke Yonge (Peabody, MA: Hendrickson, 1995).
[5]See D. G. Reid, "Sacrifice and Temple Service," *DNTB,* 1,038.

After a portion is burned up as "a food offering with a pleasing aroma to the LORD. . . . The rest of the grain offering shall be for Aaron and his sons; it is a most holy part of the Lord's food offerings" (Leviticus 2:2-3 ESV). This offering is unique because it does not involve animals.

This Hebrew word *minḥâ* routinely refers to a gift. It is a means of seeking favor. A *minḥâ* is often used as a gift to a superior. Gideon says to the Lord, "Do not depart from here until I come to you, and bring out my *present*, and set it before you" (Judges 6:18). Elsewhere, this same word is rendered "gift" or "tribute."[6] Psalm 45:12 says, "The people of Tyre will seek your favor with *gifts*, the richest of the people." The king of Babylon "sent envoys with letters and a *present* to Hezekiah, for he had heard that Hezekiah had been sick" (2 Kings 20:12).

PEACE OFFERING

The peace offering of Leviticus 3 and 7:11-21 is sometimes called a "fellowship offering." Leviticus 3:11, 16 explicitly describe this offering as *leḥem*, "food" or "bread."

> Then the priest shall turn these into smoke on the altar as a *food offering* by fire to the LORD. (Leviticus 3:11)

> Then the priest shall turn these into smoke on the altar as a *food offering* by fire for a pleasing odor. All fat is the LORD's. (Leviticus 3:16)

The priest eats most of the meat. However, the fat, the best part of the offering, is burnt on the altar. This sacrifice is one of the few instances where "lay worshippers are allowed to share in the sacred meal, normally a priestly privilege."[7] Beckwith expands our picture of the peace or fellowship offering:

> Nor do they just share the food of priests; they share the food of God. The tabernacle and temple symbolize the court of a king; indeed, the same word in Hebrew (*hêykāl*) is used for a temple and a palace. The altar of burnt offering is the king's table (Mal. 1:7, 12), and the regular sacrifices there are accompanied by cereal offerings and drink offerings (Exod. 29:38-41; Num. 15:1-12) because the table of a king must have not only flesh on it but also bread and wine. The sacrifices are described as his bread or food (Lev. 3:11; 21:6, 8, 17, 21; 22:25; Num. 28:2; Ezek. 44:7).[8]

---

[6]1 Kings 4:21; 2 Kings 17:3.
[7]Roger T. Beckwith, "Sacrifice," *NDBT*, 758.
[8]Beckwith, "Sacrifice," 758.

The Bible often depicts a peace offering as food. This correlation might cause concern or confusion for some readers. So, we will return to this subject later.[9]

PURIFICATION, SIN, OR RECONCILIATION OFFERING?

The "sin offering" (*ḥaṭṭā 't*) is particularly important for the purposes of this book (Leviticus 4:1–5:13; 6:24-30). People generally hear the word *sin* and assume this sacrifice mainly deals with moral offenses. Not necessarily. Sin offerings even affect the altar. They sanctify the altar and can bring ritual cleansing to worshipers. Some interpreters translate *ḥaṭṭā 't* as "purification offering." Because of its pervasive influence, scholars do not agree on a single translation. As we'll see, a reasonable suggestion is "reconciliation offering."[10]

In Leviticus 4, worshipers slaughter either a bull, goat, or lamb.[11] Contrary to the impression of some readers, the blood from the sacrifice is not applied to people; instead, it is sprinkled or poured out on the sanctuary or altar. The priest eats the meat offered by the worshipers (Leviticus 6:26). Otherwise, it must be burned outside the camp. Finally, fat is burned on the altar.

Scholars debate the precise mechanics of the reconciliation offering. The discussion is complex; yet, understanding certain aspects of the reconciliation offering clarifies how several texts speak about atonement. For example, the related verb (*ḥṭ'*) is translated differently depending on the Hebrew grammar. Sometimes, it is translated as "sin." Elsewhere, however, Bibles render it as "purify" or "cleanse."[12] The NRSV renders Leviticus 8:15, "Moses took the blood [of the reconciliation offering] and with his finger put some on each of the horns of the altar, *purifying* the altar; then he poured out the blood at the base of the altar. Thus he consecrated it, to make atonement for it."[13]

---

[9]Also noteworthy is Lev 22:23, which allows people to offer an imperfect animal if the peace offering is a freewill offering though not in fulfillment of a vow.

[10]James Greenberg, *A New Look at the Atonement in Leviticus: The Meaning and Purpose of Kipper Revisited* (University Park: Penn State University Press, 2020), 71. Alternatively, John Nolland proposes "deficiency offering" since the scope of the *ḥaṭṭā 't* extends beyond cases of sin and impurity. See John Nolland, "Sin, Purity, and the *ḥṭ't* Offering," *VT* 65 (2015): 606-20. For consistency, I'll use reconciliation offering in cited translations that use "sin offering."

[11]Lev 5:7, 11 mentions "two turtledoves or two pigeons" and "a tenth of an ephah of fine flour" for those who are poor.

[12]The qal stem of *ḥṭ'* is generally translated "sin." However, Bibles typically translate the piel stem as "purify" or "cleanse."

[13]Other examples include Ex 29:36; Lev 14:49, 52; Ezek 43:20, 22, 23; 45:18.

Greenberg's important study adds nuance to the term.[14] He examines an array of critical texts that befuddle interpreters. Some scholars argue that *ḥṭ'* indicates "removing," "cleansing," or "purging." Greenberg shows why these translations cannot be applied consistently throughout Scripture. He suggests an underlying meaning for *ḥṭ'* that works across texts yet accounts for the perception that the word conveys removing, cleansing, and purging. According to Greenberg, its basic meaning concerns binding. This binding usually involves blood.

In Leviticus 14 and Numbers 19, "absorbing materials" are used in conjunction with blood, which acts as a "binding agent."[15] Leviticus 14 describes the process by which the priest cleanses a leprous person or house. In the prescribed ritual, a bird is killed in an earthenware vessel over fresh water. Someone will "take the living bird with the cedarwood and the crimson yarn and the hyssop, and dip them and the living bird in the blood of the bird that was slaughtered over the fresh water" (Leviticus 14:6; cf. 14:51).[16] The priest then sprinkles the mixture on either the house seven times or the person who needs cleansing from leprosy. Finally, the live bird is released outside of the city.

What does the blood do? It binds and transfers the leprosy to the water and absorbing materials.[17] The live bird carries the leprosy into the open field, away from Israel. Only at this point is the house deemed clean. While blood is used to remove leprosy, it plays a particular role within a larger mechanism of cleansing.[18]

Normally, the reconciliation offering does not use "absorbing materials." In Leviticus 8:15 and Exodus 29:36, blood and oil are used to consecrate the altar and the priests. Unlike with the normal reconciliation offering, both the

---

[14]Greenberg, *New Look*. What follows draws from his work.

[15]Greenberg, *New Look*, 66-79.

[16]Greenberg notes, "Cedar wood and scarlet string are often used in the ancient Near Eastern rituals to attracts gods and absorb impurities" (68). He cites Yitzhaq Feder, *Blood Expiation in Hittite and Biblical Rituals: Origins, Context, and Meaning* (Atlanta: Society of Biblical Literature, 2011), 129n57, and Volkert Haas, *Materia et Medica Hethitica* (Berlin: De Gruyter, 2013), 640-41.

[17]While Noam Zohar does not mention binding, he suggests "the basic meaning of חטא to be replace /displace/transfer." See "Repentance and Purification: The Significance and Semantics of *ḥṭ't* in the Pentateuch," *JBL* 107, no. 4 (Dec 1988): 616.

[18]Inasmuch as *ḥṭ'* binds and facilitates absorbing, it is natural that one could regard the purpose of this offering as purification. We must be careful, however, because the idea of cleansing is not always present where *ḥṭ'* is used, whereas some sort of binding process does appear.

altar and priests are yet to be reckoned holy. Since these texts describe an ordination ceremony, "the priests do not need forgiveness (Leviticus 4:1-5:26) or to be made clean (Leviticus 12-15)."[19] Prior to the ritual, the altar and Aaron are merely considered common. In these texts, the altar is the direct object of the verb *ḥṭ'*. Thus, the blood of the offering binds Aaron and his sons to the altar. Greenberg translates Exodus 29:36 in this way: "And you shall bind the altar [with Aaron and his sons] when you are making removal for it, and you shall anoint it in order to consecrate it."[20] The altar and Aaron become holy together.

A typical reconciliation offering does not use absorbing materials (Leviticus 4:1-5:13; 6:25-30).[21] Also, it presumes the offerer is either unclean or commits an unintentional sin.[22] The worshiper

> shall bring the bull to the entrance of the tent of meeting before the LORD and lay his hand on the head of the bull and kill the bull before the LORD. And the anointed priest shall take some of the blood of the bull and bring it into the tent of meeting, and the priest shall dip his finger in the blood and sprinkle part of the blood seven times before the LORD in front of the veil of the sanctuary. And the priest shall put some of the blood on the horns of the altar of fragrant incense before the LORD that is in the tent of meeting, and all the rest of the blood of the bull he shall pour out at the base of the altar of burnt offering that is at the entrance of the tent of meeting. (Leviticus 4:4-7 ESV)

In this instance, the blood binds the worshiper with the altar and, symbolically, the Lord.[23] In both the standard and nonstandard uses of this offering, the *ḥṭ'* binding leads to atonement. Accordingly, it plays a key role in removing the separation between God and people.[24]

---

[19]Greenberg, *New Look*, 83. In English Bibles, Lev 5 only has nineteen verses. Drawing from the Hebrew MT, Greenberg's reference to Lev 5:26 includes Lev 6:1-7 (the burnt offering).

[20]Greenberg, *New Look*, 84. Drawing from Ex 29:35, he infers the link to "with Aaron and his sons."

[21]We see this offering applied in Lev 12–15.

[22]The term "unintentional" is misleading. The related Hebrew words translated as "intentional" include *šĕgāgâ*, *šgg*, and *šgh*. In Leviticus 5:1-6; 6:1-7, the reconciliation offering addresses sins that are inherently intentional, such as swearing falsely and not giving testimony as one ought. Perhaps, the notion of "unintentional" implies sin due to weakness or negligence.

[23]The idea of binding also clarifies the use of the verb *ḥṭ'* in Gen 31:39; Ps 51:7; Lev 6:26 and Num 19:18-19; Job 41:25 (using hitpael of *ḥṭ'*).

[24]Depending on who needs atonement (e.g., priest, lay worshiper), certain differences exist in how the reconciliation offering works. See figure 3.1.

Figure 3.1. Ḥaṭṭā't offering

Status	Offerer	Uses Absorbing Materials	No Absorbing Materials
Clean	Priest	N/A	Blood binds people to the altar (God) Consecration with oil Ordination of priests Leviticus 8:15; Exodus 29:36 Only God eats offering (burned)
Unclean or Unintentional Sin	Priest	Blood binds and transfers contamination (compare Numbers 19)	Blood binds offerer to the altar (God) Blood applied to tent of meeting (altar of incense) Leviticus 4:3-12 Only God eats offering; Leviticus 6:30 (burned)
Unclean or Unintentional Sin	Non-Priest		Blood binds offerer to the altar (God) Blood application varies from tent of meeting (altar of incense) to altar of burnt offering Leviticus 4:13-5:13 Priest eats offering; Leviticus 6:25-29
Unclean or Unintentional Sin	Objects	Blood binds and transfers leprosy (compare Leviticus 14)	N/A

Understanding the meaning of the verb *ḥṭ'* sheds light on the meaning of sin. At this point, our discussion could become overly technical for most readers, so I'll quickly attempt to capture a few essential ideas while relegating technical details to the footnotes. First, the meaning of a Hebrew word depends on its stem (its grammatical form). One stem (i.e., piel) negates, undoes, or removes the idea conveyed by another (qal) stem.[25] Now consider the meaning of verb *ḥṭ'*. While one stem translates "sin," another (piel) stem conveys the idea of *de*-sinning or *un*-sinning. Yet, we saw above that the latter stem of *ḥṭ'* somehow entails binding. Accordingly, Greenberg says, the *ḥaṭṭā't* "contributes to the reconciliation between the offender and YHWH by means of 'binding.' In this view, the act of sinning (*qal* of *ḥṭ'*) disrupts relationship, and the *piel* of *ḥṭ'* 'binds' and, thus, with flesh burning, repairs relationship."[26] His analysis

---

[25]The qal stem of *ḥṭ'* is typically translated "sin." The piel *ḥṭ'* acts as the privative of the qal *ḥṭ'*. A privative effectively negates, undoes, or removes a word's meaning. So, the piel privative of the qal *ḥṭ'* conveys the idea of de-sinning or un-sinning.

[26]Greenberg, *New Look*, 71. He adds, "Following these assertions, it may be concluded that the *piel* of *ḥṭ'* 'to bind,' that is, repair relationship, is the privative of the *qal* of *ḥṭ'* where 'to sin' has the sense 'to disconnect,' break relationship. Furthermore, the *piel* of *ḥṭ'* is a denominative of the noun *ḥaṭṭā't*, where 'sin' is the act that causes a relationship disconnect. Finally, the *piel* of *ḥṭ'* is a component of

helpfully elucidates the meaning of sin and the *ḥaṭṭā 't* offering. In the Bible, sin is whatever breaks or disconnects relationship with God. Fittingly, the *ḥaṭṭā 't* offering is not merely the "sin offering" or "purification offering." It reconnects the worshiper to God. Therefore, it is a "reconciliation offering."

One final comment is needed to correct a popular impression concerning the reconciliation offering. People commonly think that sins of the worshiper are placed on the sacrificed animal, who then becomes a substitute suffering the sinner's punishment. This reading is more often assumed and asserted than rigorously defended from the Bible. In addition, scholars observe several short-comings with this view.[27] For example, Csilla Saysell says, "The transfer of sins is problematic because these would defile the animal, whereas we are told that is flesh is holy (Lev. 6:22). Further, ritual impurities and inadvertent or ignorant sins (for which *ḥaṭṭā 't* is offered) do not require the death penalty."[28] While the simplicity of this popular model is attractive, it does not reckon with what we find in the ancient biblical text.

REPARATION OR GUILT OFFERING

"Reparation offering" is a better translation for what people commonly call the guilt offering.[29] Some consider it a subset of the sin or purification offering. The term "reparation offering" expresses its function.[30] A sacrificed animal is cut in pieces before the fat is burned on the altar. Only priests eat the reparation offering. Also, "Leviticus 1-7 do not mention any blood application rite for the guilt [reparation] offering."[31]

The reparation offering deals with two problems. First, it provides restitution for offenses against holy things (Leviticus 5:15-16). When people desecrate or defile the Lord's holy place or name, they need to make reparation. Possible examples include not bringing tithes to the sanctuary, people other than priests eating sacred food, and breaking a Nazarite vow or perhaps an oath made

---

the *ḥaṭṭā 't* offering, which, as a result, should be rendered 'reconciliation offering' where binding to YHWH is an integral part of reconciliation."

[27]For a list of substantial critiques, see Csilla Saysell, "The Blood Manipulation of the Sin Offering and the Logic of Defilement," in *Holding Forth the Word of Life: Essays in Honor of Dr. Timothy Meadowcroft*, ed. Csilla Saysell and John de Jong (Eugene, OR: Wipf & Stock, 2020), 67.

[28]Saysell, "Blood Manipulation," 46. He cities August Dillman, *Die Bücher Exodus und Leviticus* (Leizig: Hirzel, 1897), 439; Jacob Milgrom, *Leviticus 17–22* (New York: Doubleday, 2000), 1,475.

[29]For consistency, I'll use "reparation offering" in cited translations that use "guilt offering."

[30]See Lev 5:14–6:7; 7:1-7.

[31]Christian Eberhart, "A Neglected Feature of Sacrifice in the Hebrew Bible," *HTR* 97, no. 4 (2004): 488.

before the Lord. Second, the reparation offering deals with harm committed against others. It atones for a person's sin, enabling them to receive forgiveness (Leviticus 5:16, 18; 6:7).

One can easily confuse the reparation offering and the reconciliation offering. The two sacrifices often seem paired. A reparation offering assumes the need for a reconciliation offering. Various transgressions require a reconciliation offering; only certain types of those offenses require a reparation offering. Whatever the case, the arguments in this book do not depend on this distinction.

OFFERING TRIBUTE AND GIFTS

The symbolism of the sacrifices illumines their significance. Readers sometimes overlook not so subtle aspects of these offerings. For instance, they can act as figurative gifts. Israel's sacred offerings serve as symbolic tribute to God their king. To offer tribute is an act of submission, a way to express honor. Numerous texts use the same word (*minhah*) that signifies a grain offering to express the idea of tribute or gift. In Scripture, to whom is *minhah* paid?

Kings. After Saul is proclaimed king, 1 Samuel 10:27 reports, "But some worthless fellows said, 'How can this man save us?' And they despised him and brought him no *present*. But he held his peace." Referring to Israel's king, Psalm 72:10 says, "May the kings of Tarshish and of the isles render him *tribute*; may the kings of Sheba and Seba bring gifts!" Numerous other passages could be listed.[32]

The Lord or angel of the Lord. In Judges 6, the angel of the Lord visits Gideon, who says, "'Do not depart from here until I come to you, and bring out my *present*, and set it before you.' And he said, 'I will stay until you return'" (Judges 6:18).

To prophets. "Elisha went to Damascus while King Ben-hadad of Aram was ill. When it was told him, 'The man of God has come here,' the king said to Hazael, 'Take a *present* with you and go to meet the man of God. Inquire of the LORD through him, whether I shall recover from this illness.' So Hazael went to meet him, taking a *present* with him, all kinds of goods of Damascus, forty camel loads" (2 Kings 8:7-9).

To Esau (from Jacob). In Genesis 32–33, Jacob anticipates his reunion with Esau, whose blessing Jacob previously stole. Therefore, he prepares to send Esau a "present" (*minhah*) in Genesis 32:13, 18, 20-21. When Esau initially turns the

---

[32]For example, Judg 3:17-18; 2 Sam 8:2, 6; 1 Kings 4:21; 10:25; 2 Kings 17:3-4 (king-to-king); 1 Chron 18:2, 6; 2 Chron 9:24; 17:5, 11; 26:8; Hos 10:6; Ezra 4:13; 7:24.

gift away, Jacob said, "No, please; if I find favor with you, then accept my *present* from my hand; for truly to see your face is like seeing the face of God—since you have received me with such favor" (33:10).

Joseph. Israel's sons prepare a gift for Joseph when they want to secure his favor in Genesis 43. The sons initially balk at the idea of returning to Egypt:

> Then their father Israel said to them, "If it must be so, then do this: take some of the choice fruits of the land in your bags, and carry them down as a present to the man—a little balm and a little honey, gum, resin, pistachio nuts, and almonds. . . ."
>
> They made the *present* ready for Joseph's coming at noon, for they had heard that they would dine there. When Joseph came home, they brought him the *present* that they had carried into the house, and bowed to the ground before him. (Genesis 43:11, 25-26; cf. 43:15)

In the above passages, *minhah* is not a temple sacrifice. They are gifts. In a royal context, they are seen as tribute. The giver uses them to entreat or seek the recipient's favor. These gifts express honor or even loyalty. Giving God offerings expresses honor and allegiance. The offering indicates that the giver submits to God.

SACRIFICING THE FOOD OF GOD

The sacrifices can symbolically give food to God. They act as food gifts.[33] Above we saw Leviticus 3:11, 16, which explicitly regard the peace offerings as "food" (*lehem*). It makes sense that sacrificial offering might be seen as food. In that ancient culture, sharing meals marked one's relational network. It distinguished insiders from outsiders. Meals were a way that people fostered mutual trust. God certainly does not need food. Nevertheless, the practice of people sharing food with God signifies and sustains relationship.

When addressing the priests directly, Leviticus several times calls the sacrificial offerings "bread" or "food."

> Speak to Aaron and say: No one of your offspring throughout their generations who has a blemish may approach to offer the *food* of his God. . . . No descendant of Aaron the priest who has a blemish shall come near to offer the LORD's offerings by fire; since he has a blemish, he shall not come near to offer the *food* of his God. He may eat the *food* of his God, of the most holy as well as of the holy. (Leviticus 21:17, 21-22; cf. 21:8; 22:25)

---

[33]Cf. William K. Gilders, "Sacrifice in Ancient Israel," *SBL Newsletter*, www.bibleodyssey.org/en /passages/related-articles/sacrifice-in-ancient-israel.

"Food" is a better translation than "bread" (ESV, KJV) since the word *lehem* regularly refers to meat. In Leviticus 24:5-9, the food seems to be offered to God but eaten by priests.

In Leviticus 7:14-17, the bread is regarded as a "gift to the LORD." The priest first eats the offering. Then, God seems to consume the meal in 7:17.

> From this you shall offer *one cake* from each offering, as a *gift* to the LORD; it shall belong to the priest who dashes the blood of the offering of well-being. And the flesh of your thanksgiving sacrifice of well-being shall be eaten on the day it is offered; you shall not leave any of it until morning. But if the sacrifice you offer is a votive offering or a freewill offering, it shall be eaten on the day that you offer your sacrifice, and what is left of it shall be eaten the next day; but what is left of the flesh of the sacrifice shall be burned up on the third day.

Leviticus 21:6 says of the priests, "They shall be holy to their God, and not profane the name of their God; for they offer the LORD's offerings by fire, the *food* of their God; therefore they shall be holy." The Lord's "food" in Leviticus 21:6 is equated to the Lord's "fire" (*'iššе*). In Leviticus, the term describes each of the five offerings above and is equated with the bread elsewhere.[34] Why use the fire imagery? In effect, the burning fire transforms the sacrifice, lifting it to God. Therefore, God and people could have fellowship. Where did they eat this meal? In God's dwelling place, his temple, or simply God's "house."[35]

These observations run contrary to modern sensibilities. Still, God explicitly commands Israel to give him food. The Lord tells Moses, "Command the Israelites, and say to them: My offering, the *food* for my *offerings by fire* [*'iššе*], my pleasing odor, you shall take care to offer to me at its appointed time" (Numbers 28:2). Ezekiel even appears to represent blood as a kind of drink given to God. Ezekiel 44:7 rebukes Israel's leaders for "admitting foreigners, uncircumcised in heart and flesh, to be in my sanctuary, profaning my temple when you offer to *me my food, the fat and the blood*. You have broken my covenant with all your abominations."[36]

---

[34]Cf. Lev 24:7; Num 28:2, 24. Also, see the burnt offering (Lev 1:9, 13, 17), grain offering (Lev 2:2, 3, 9-11, 16), peace offering (Lev 3:16), reconciliation offering (Lev 5:12), and reparation offering (Lev 7:5).

[35]See 2 Sam 7:13. The term for "house" (*bayit*) can signify a palace. In some passages, God's temple is regarded as God's palace; cf. Ezra 5:14-15; Ps 5:7. This comment reinforces a key point from the previous chapter, where the temple was presented as God's throne room.

[36]Cf. Num 18:17.

To be clear, these offerings are symbolic gifts. Scripture does not claim that God needs food. In fact, Psalm 50:7-15 rejects the suggestion. The psalmist says,

Hear, O my people, and I will speak,
    O Israel, I will testify against you.
    I am God, your God.
Not for your sacrifices do I rebuke you;
    your burnt offerings are continually before me.
I will not accept a bull from your house,
    or goats from your folds.
For every wild animal of the forest is mine,
    the cattle on a thousand hills.
I know all the birds of the air,
    and all that moves in the field is mine.

If I were hungry, I would not tell you,
    for the world and all that is in it is mine.
Do I eat the flesh of bulls,
    or drink the blood of goats?
Offer to God a sacrifice of thanksgiving,
    and pay your vows to the Most High.
Call on me in the day of trouble;
    I will deliver you, and you shall glorify me.

The fact that Israel could misunderstand the sacrifices like this further confirms the above interpretation, that is, sacrifices served as symbolic food. Hendel says, "These meals dramatize the bonds of intimacy and distance that relate Israel to God. Table and altar are analogous in various ways, implicitly foregrounding the Israelites' closeness to God."[37]

This book attempts to understand the internal logic of Israel's sacrificial system and its implications for atonement. How do sacrifices function? Many readers know that these atoning sacrifices purify people of uncleanness and act as payments of restitution. Not only do they work to cleanse and make compensation, but these offerings establish communion with God. How is this

---

[37]Ronald Hendel, "Table and Altar: The Anthropology of Food in the Priestly Torah," in *To Break Every Yoke: Essays in Honor of Marvin L. Chaney*, ed. R. B. Coote and N. K. Gottwald (Sheffield: Sheffield Phoenix Press, 2007), 145.

accomplished? The sacrificial rituals symbolically present God with the gift of a meal. But how is the food given to God?

An Atoning Aroma

Christian Eberhart's keen observations provide valuable insight. He explores a simple question: What is common to every type of sacrifice? His answer will surprise people. He says, "Rather than the slaughter of animals, the burning rite on the altar is the element common to all types of sacrifice, as well as the feature that distinguishes the sacrifice as an 'offering for Yhwh. . . .' Indeed, it is the burning rite that accomplishes the goal of biblical sacrifice—namely, communication with God."[38]

The grain offering is the most obvious exception to the suggestion that shedding blood is the common thread uniting the sacrificial system. For each offering, worshipers burn the sacrificial gift on the altar. As a result, the smoke produces a "pleasing aroma." This is illustrated in following passages.

- burnt offering (Leviticus 1:9, 13, 17)
- grain offering (Leviticus 2:2, 12; 6:15, 21)
- peace offering (Leviticus 3:5, 11, 16)
- reconciliation offering (Leviticus 4:19-20, 26, 31, 35)
- reparation offering (Leviticus 7:2-7; "burned" but no mention of "pleasing aroma")

Outside of Leviticus, Eberhart notes, the Bible presents burning as the "climax" of the sacrifice.[39] The Lord says of Eli, "I chose him out of all the tribes of Israel to be my priest, to go up to my altar, to *offer incense*, to wear an ephod before me; and I gave to the family of your ancestor all my *offerings by fire* from the people of Israel" (1 Samuel 2:28). Likewise, in 2 Chronicles 2:4, "I am now about to build a house for the name of the LORD my God and dedicate it to him for *offering fragrant incense* before him, and for the regular offering of the rows of bread, and for *burnt offerings* morning and evening, on the sabbaths and the new moons and the appointed festivals of the LORD our God, as ordained forever for Israel."[40] Deuteronomy 4:28 contrasts the Lord and false gods, who

---

[38]Eberhart, "Neglected Feature," 485-93. What follows largely traces Eberhart's work.
[39]Eberhart, "Neglected Feature," 492.
[40]Cf. Deut 33:10; Jer 33:18; Rev 8:3-4.

are "made by human hands, objects of wood and stone that neither see, nor hear, nor eat, nor smell."

"Devoted" Gifts

The above sacrifices are all considered "devoted." What is a devoted gift? In the Bible, a holy thing that cannot be redeemed for ordinary use is called "devoted." Leviticus 27:28-29 says, "Nothing that a person owns that has been devoted to destruction for the LORD, be it human or animal, or inherited landholding, may be sold or redeemed; every devoted thing is most holy to the LORD. No human beings who have been devoted to destruction can be ransomed; they shall be put to death." Accordingly, only God or priests can use the devoted sacrifice.

With respect to the Lord, a devoted gift is "most holy." In Leviticus 27:21, 28-29, a field is consecrated to the Lord and so becomes a "devoted" gift. As a result, only priests can use it: "This shall be yours from the most holy things, reserved from the fire: every offering of theirs that they render to me as a most holy thing, whether grain offering, reconciliation offering, or reparation offering, shall belong to you and your sons. . . . Every devoted thing in Israel shall be yours" (Numbers 18:9, 14 NRSV, author's adaptation). The firstborn cow, sheep, or goat cannot be redeemed in Numbers 18:17.

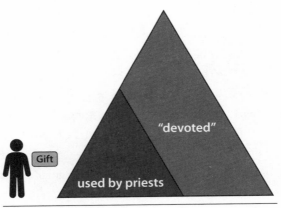

Figure 3.2. Devoted gift

Why is a "devoted thing" irredeemable? Because it cannot be given to others. Since it is God's alone, it is holy. No one else can use it. People then must destroy the devoted thing. Doing so prevents others from using it. Otherwise, someone would treat it as common, not holy. In burning the fat of a firstborn cow, for example, Israel symbolically gives a gift to God.

Accordingly, if a devoted thing is alive, it must be killed, hence the shedding of blood. In this sense, its life is entirely given to God. The devoted thing literally gives its life for God. Death is merely a method whereby people devote something to God. Consider a sacrificed animal. If a person did not kill the devoted animal, people could then use the animal for common purposes. In that case, the animal is not totally or exclusively given over to God.

What about God's people? They belong to God yet are not killed. However, they are never reckoned devoted things. Later, we will return to this question to explain why Israel's firstborn need redemption. Those who belong to God must be redeemed through substitutes that are perpetually devoted to God. In this way, the concept of a devoted gift proves surprisingly helpful for understanding Christ's atonement.

In the remainder of this chapter, we look at two applications that follow from what's been said. First, we'll consider whether Christ is a devoted sacrifice and substitute. Second, we explore one potential way of contextualizing the Israelite concept of an offering whereby worshipers draw near to God, a fundamental goal of atonement.

CHRIST, THE DEVOTED SUBSTITUTE?

Is Christ a devoted substitute? Yes. And this is a significant point. We've noted that a devoted thing is a gift given to God that cannot be redeemed by people. If a devoted thing is a living creature, it must die (i.e., shedding blood). In this sense, its life is entirely given to God. The devoted thing literally gives its life for God. How might these observations apply to Christ? We can better discern why blood is necessary for interpreting Leviticus 17:11, Hebrews 9:22, and the atonement. We owe God our entire lives. Due to sin, we essentially have robbed God. We are in debt and have an obligation to bring compensation via sacrifice. Otherwise, we should die.

For redemption, we need atonement (thus freedom or release from debt). God wants us holy, that is, uniquely his, wholly given to him. If we cannot be redeemed, we will be destroyed. God requires a holy gift as a substitute. Christ, in giving his perfect life, offers himself as a gift to God. He wholly gives himself as a reconciliation offering. He is utterly holy and effectively becomes a devoted gift. By shedding his blood, he atones for us.

In short, Christ utterly giving himself to God, even unto death, forsaking sin, is him devoting himself only to God just as a devoted thing belongs to him alone.[41] In this way, Christ's death is that same death that constitutes his being a devoted thing. *The cross is the place where Christ finally and utterly devotes himself to God.* This is the sacrifice that pleases the Father.

IS GOD NEAR OR FAR?

Drawing near to God is a fundamental purpose of atonement. Yet, other religions do not necessarily share this assumption. If we're honest, this might not even be the conscious goal of many average churchgoers, who merely want to avoid eternal punishment. Matthew Bennett says, "Since the Qur'an portrays God as wholly transcendent . . . then fellowship with him will not factor into the ultimate purpose of life."[42] For Visistadvaitic Hindus, the theological pendulum swings to the other extreme. Salvation is a liberation from ignorance; it is conceived of as recognizing the union between Brahman, the self, and all matter.[43]

Each of these views creates a formidable challenge to contextualization. The Bible forges an uncompromising distinction between God and creation. At the same time, the definitive end of history is the union between heaven and earth. How might we bridge this difference in perspectives?

Perhaps, Eastern Orthodoxy offers a way forward, even if it cannot entirely overcome the chasm. Eastern Orthodox theologians lay greater weight on subjective aspects of atonement. The Orthodox concept of *theosis* is often described as "deification." This terminology creates confusion, seeming to suggest that people become gods themselves. Eve Tibbs's comments clarify how Orthodox Christians conceive of atonement.

> Salvation in Orthodox theology is seen primarily in terms of freedom from death through union with Christ, rather than release from death through substitutionary atonement as in the primary Western metaphor. . . . *Theosis* is the process of growing in holiness in increasing communion with God. The Orthodox take

---

[41]This point also accounts for the need that Christ be without sin.

[42]Matthew A. Bennett, *Narratives in Conflict: Atonement in Hebrews and the Qur'an* (Eugene, OR: Pickwick, 2019), 179.

[43]See Godfrey Kesari, *The Atonement Creating Unions: An Exploration in Inter-Religious Theory* (Eugene, OR: Pickwick, 2019).

seriously the promise of becoming "participants of the divine nature" (2 Pet 1:4) and hold that human beings were created for glorification to become by grace what God is by nature (cf. Jn 10:34-35; Rom 5:2). St. Athanasius the Great of Alexandria put it this way: "Christ became human so that human beings may become divine."[44]

"At-one-ment" with God consists in reflecting the glorious nature of God. Compared to Christ's death, his resurrection appears more prominent in an Orthodox view of atonement.[45]

This perspective draws from the paradoxical nature of Christ's incarnation, the hypostatic union between divine and human. As beings created in God's image, we are most fully human when we reflect the divine. In a sense, Orthodox theology maintains God's transcendence while claiming that Christ brings us into union with God. It is important to distinguish union from identification. We do not become God; rather, the Spirit animates our life to embody his holiness in the world.

Union with Christ is a pervasive biblical motif that may help some readers who are less familiar with Orthodox theology.[46] What is true of Christ becomes true of those who are "in Christ," who give their allegiance to him. Accordingly, Paul writes,

> Do you not know that all of us who have been baptized into Christ Jesus were baptized into his death? Therefore we have been buried with him by baptism into death, so that, just as Christ was raised from the dead by the glory of the Father, so we too might walk in newness of life. For if we have been united with him in a death like his, we will certainly be united with him in a resurrection like his. (Romans 6:3-5)

By emphasizing the above themes, we can improve how we contextualize the atonement for diverse audiences. No single model or metaphor captures the totality of this message. Still, we can help people understand the purpose of atonement even while we reach for images to explain it more fully.

---

[44] Eve Tibbs, "Eastern Orthodox Theology," *GDT*, 245.

[45] An Orthodox theology of atonement most resembles the recapitulation theology and the moral exemplar theory. See appendix A. For a recent proposal, see Khaled Anatolios, *Deification Through the Cross: An Eastern Christian Theology of Salvation* (Grand Rapids, MI: Eerdmans, 2020).

[46] Helpful works include Grant Macaskill, *Living in Union with Christ: Paul's Gospel and Christian Moral Identity* (Grand Rapids, MI: Baker Academic, 2019); Constantine Campbell, *Paul and Union with Christ: An Exegetical and Theological Study* (Grand Rapids, MI: Zondervan, 2012).

Conclusion

This chapter highlights several important conclusions that shape a biblical understanding of the atonement. A basic purpose of sacrifices was to enable people to draw near to God. They were meant to honor God. Certain offerings function as tribute or gifts, even serving symbolically as food.

We also saw that the *ḥaṭṭā 't* offering, traditionally known as the sin offering or purification offering, is better translated "reconciliation offering." The reconciliation offering frequently appears in contexts where atonement is made. Whereas sin disrupts relationship with God, the reconciliation offering connects people to God. Blood serves as a "binding agent." When used with absorbing materials (e.g., hyssop), it binds and transfers uncleanness away from the person or object receiving atonement. When the reconciliation offering does not use absorbing materials (e.g., as part of a consecration ritual), blood binds a person to the altar (and, symbolically, God).

Finally, we focused on two insights that will play a key role in chapters ahead. First, we identified the characteristic common to each of the atoning sacrifices. It is not the shedding of blood; it is a burning rite that yields a pleasing aroma to God. Second, a devoted gift is most holy and therefore cannot be redeemed. It belongs to God alone. In the coming chapters, we will apply these observations to interpret key passages.

4

ATONEMENT AND THE
SIGNIFICANCE OF BLOOD

So FAR, I've not fully defined *atonement*. Doing so with precision is not easy. We would do better to *describe* atonement as Scripture portrays it. What basic imagery do biblical writers use in contexts that explicitly speak of atonement?

WHAT IS ATONEMENT?

We begin by looking at key biblical terms. What does the Hebrew verb *kpr* mean? The verb is often found in contexts where purification or cleansing occurs. Thus, scholars frequently suggest that *kpr* means something like "purge," "erase," or "wipe away." The noun *kpr* also seems to indicate a ransom or compensation (as we'll see later). Accordingly, one gains redemption, release, and freedom through atonement. People use a ransom to save slaves. Nevertheless, purification and redemption are implications of *kpr*, not the meaning of the term itself.[1]

It is widely thought that *kpr* means "cover." This idea stems from scholars who suggest this Hebrew term is related to the Arabic word *kafara*. If so, the word's basic meaning *perhaps* includes "covering."[2] This view is problematic, and scholars increasingly argue against it.[3]

---

[1]Cleansing (purging) is not a synonym with *kpr* but the "result of an action, that is, a status change." See James Greenberg, *A New Look at the Atonement in Leviticus: The Meaning and Purpose of Kipper Revisited* (University Park: Penn State University Press, 2020), 171. People or objects are purified inasmuch as uncleanness is removed through the overall *kpr*-process, which may include the binding achieved via blood in the reconciliation offering.

[2]Oft cited is Gen 6:14, which says, "Make yourself an ark of cypress wood; make rooms in the ark, and cover [*kpr*, verb] it inside and out with pitch [*kpr*, noun]." The verb uses qal *kpr*, not the more common piel.

[3]Jay Sklar, *Sin, Impurity, Sacrifice and Atonement: The Priestly Conceptions* (Sheffield: Sheffield Phoenix, 2005), 44-45; Baruch Levine, *Presence of the Lord: A Study of Cult and Some Cultic Terms in Ancient*

Greenberg's proposal is helpful. In his view, *kpr* is "to repair or create a new protective connection" between the worshiper and the Lord. Therefore, it "reflects [the Lord's] acceptance of the priestly offering."[4] This meaning makes sense of several passages that don't fit common interpretations of atonement. For instance, *kpr* is necessary when consecrating the altar and the priests (Exodus 29; cf. Leviticus 16:15-19). In Exodus 30:11-16, people must pay a census tax to prevent future plagues. Exodus 30:15-16 say,

> The rich shall not give more, and the poor shall not give less, than the half shekel, when you bring this offering to the LORD to *make atonement* for your lives. You shall take the *atonement money* from the Israelites and shall designate it for the service of the tent of meeting; before the LORD it will be a reminder to the Israelites of the *ransom* given for your lives.

It is also needed when preparing the Levites for service in the sanctuary (Numbers 8). In short, *kpr* bestows the beneficiary with special favor and honor.

In Genesis 32:20, Jacob wants to gain Esau's favor. He sends his brother a gift and a message, "'Moreover, your servant Jacob is behind us.' For he [Jacob] thought, 'I *may appease* [*kpr*] him with the present that goes ahead of me, and afterward I shall see his face; perhaps he will accept me.'"[5] A wooden translation of the Hebrew is "atone *his face*." How do we interpret his meaning? The last phrase—"he will accept me"—says, "He will lift my face" in Hebrew. If Esau accepts Jacob, he will lift Jacob's face.[6]

To better grasp the meaning of *kpr*, we need to look elsewhere. The most common Greek verb in the Septuagint (LXX) for *kpr* is *exilaskomai*. How does the Old Testament use this word? Though some people translate it "atone" or "propitiate," a simpler, more consistent translation is "entreat."[7]

Israel (Leiden: Brill, 1974), 57-63, 123-27; Yitzhaq Feder, "On *kuppuru*, *kippēr* and Etymological Sins that Cannot Be Wiped Away," *Vetus Testamentum* 60 (2010): 537. Notably, *BDB* says, "Cover over sin: the older explan. cover, lid has no justification in usage." See *"kpr,"* in *The Enhanced Brown-Driver-Briggs Hebrew and English Lexicon* (Oak Harbor, WA: Logos, 2000).

[4]Greenberg, *New Look*, 45, 48.

[5]Noteworthy, he sends a present to gain atonement. Also, in Hebrew, the word "present" is the same word for "grain offering" (*minhah*).

[6]For a similar idiom in the LXX, see Mal 1:9, *"exilaskesthe to prosōpon tou theou."* We can imagine a person kneeling before a king. If that king treats you graciously, he will lift up your face. The imagery of the verse also makes the translation "to cover his face" unlikely. After all, Jacob immediately hopes to "see his face." The act of covering and seeing his face seem to conflict, especially in light of the final phrase, "He will lift my face" (in Hebrew).

[7]Dictionary definitions of *propitiate* refer to one's gaining of favor or making peace with someone; yet many contemporary readers could mistakenly infer that *propitiate* necessitates anger on the part of the one receiving propitiation.

In Malachi 1:9, the prophet writes, "And now *implore the favor* of God, that he may be gracious to us. The fault is yours. Will he show favor to any of you? says the LORD of hosts." If we used a conventional rendering of the word, Malachi urges the people to "atone" God's face.[8] Rather, this passage evokes different imagery, where people bow down before an authority. If the authority (e.g., God) accepts the gift-giver, the authority will then lift the head of the lower-status person. Thus, to see a king's face indicates his acceptance.[9]

At this point, I'll respond to an assumption latent in the mind of some readers. Theologians often claim that *atone* implies appeasing wrath. This is a half-truth. In the following passages, *atone* indicates "entreat" or "seek favor." The contexts do not necessarily imply wrath. To "entreat the Lord" could entail appeasing God's wrath, but not necessarily. Nor do they clearly speak about punishment. In short, appeasing God's wrath implies seeking his favor; however, seeking God's favor does not necessarily imply appeasing his wrath.[10] We will return to these claims later.

One way to confirm this interpretation of *kpr* and *exilaskomai* is to observe how the Old Testament interweaves the same narrow set of Hebrew and Greek terms. To see evidence, we'll take a brief dive into the biblical languages. I add the following excursus merely to reinforce the point that we can better understand a concept—that is, atonement—by examining the network of words and ideas that surround it.

Compare Zechariah 7:2, which says, "Now the people of Bethel had sent Sharezer and Regem-melech and their men, to *entreat the favor* of the LORD." Then we read in Zechariah 8:21-22, "The inhabitants of one city shall go to another, saying, 'Come, let us go to *entreat the favor of the LORD* [lit. "seek out the face of the Lord"], and to seek the LORD of hosts; I myself am going.' Many peoples and strong nations shall come to seek the LORD of hosts in Jerusalem, and to *entreat the favor of the LORD.*" In 8:22, the Greek word again is *exilaskomai*. However, the corresponding Hebrew word is not *kpr* but *ḥlh*. As with *exilaskomai*, biblical authors routinely conjoin *ḥlh* with *pāne* (face).

---

[8] This sentence does not advocate for the conventional rendering (atone). I simply point out how awkward it would be for us to speak of atoning for God's face.

[9] The head and face signify one's honor. They often appear in idiomatic expressions such that lifting of the head or face concern respect, having or showing favor, etc; cf. Gen 19:21; Lev 19:15; Deut 10:17; 28:50; 2 Sam 2:22; 2 Kings 5:1; Job 11:15; 32:21; Prov 6:35; Is 3:3; 9:14.

[10] Since one definition includes the other, I go with the broader meaning that includes both. Thus, "entreat" favor (= propitiation) does not exclude "appease wrath."

Idiomatically, *ḥlh* and *exilaskomai* both convey the idea of seeking favor. Accordingly, in Job 11:19 it reads, "You will lie down, and no one will make you afraid; many *will court your favor*" (cf. Psalm 119:58).

How does one seek favor? The psalmist writes, "The people of Tyre will *seek your favor* with gifts, the richest of the people" (Psalm 45:12).[11] Likewise, Saul tells Samuel, "I said, 'Now the Philistines will come down upon me at Gilgal, and I have not entreated the favor of the LORD'; so I forced myself, and offered the burnt offering" (1 Samuel 13:12). In presenting the burnt offering, Saul seeks the Lord's favor. He offers a gift to the Lord to gain atonement. The verb *ḥlh* consistently expresses the desire to please someone, especially an authority, in order to gain acceptance.[12]

In international relations, politicians are sensitive to the protocols of gift-giving that might help them gain favor in the eyes of other national leaders. Cubans like to hand out cigars while the French routinely give wine to visiting diplomats. Some gifts cause us to scratch our heads, as when Marquis de Lafayette provided John Quincy Adams with an alligator. Other presents can send the wrong signal, such as giving a clock, which symbolizes death in some East Asian cultures. Whatever the effect, the intention is clear: foster a good relationship.

One does not need to be an academic to grasp the main idea. A consistent web of terms sheds light on the underlying function of *kpr*. While people seek atonement, they might desire to appease God's wrath, but not necessarily. But in every case, they entreat the Lord's favor.

This point is evident to any reader of the Pentateuch. We see a basic sequence of thought. Whether for moral or nonmoral reasons, people become unclean. Therefore, they need atonement. If they don't seek atonement, they remain unclean. Such negligence profanes God and provokes his anger. However, the fact that God threatens to bring punishment on those people does not imply that God is angry with *all* unclean people prior to their making atonement. Rather, God's anger is reserved for those who neglect or reject his provision for making atonement.

Atonement removes whatever obstacle impedes one's having a right relationship with another. Intentional sin is not the only thing that destroys friendships. What else gets in the way of fostering good relationships? Lack of

---

[11]*Gifts* here is the same word for "grain offerings" (*minḥa*).
[12]See "*ḥlh*" (piel) in *HALOT*.

awareness. Disparities in social status. Accidents of the past. Misinformation and suspicions inherited from one's family also undermine social harmony.

A person can feel neither prejudice nor hatred toward another person yet feel separation between them. Once that invisible wall becomes visible, however, one is responsible to tear it down. Otherwise, that person effectively approves of its existence. They reinforce the barrier.

Steven Adams, center for the Oklahoma City Thunder, learned this lesson in 2016. During the NBA finals, he said the guards for the Golden State Warriors were "quick little monkeys." Outrage followed since the Warriors' guards are Black and the term *monkeys* is widely recognized as a racial slur in the United States. Yet Adams is from New Zealand, where the word carries no such connotation. He said,

> "I was just trying to express how difficult it was chasing those guys around. . . . It's just different, mate," Adams told USA Today Sports. "Different words, different expressions, and stuff like that. But they obviously can be taken differently, depending on which country you're in. I'm assimilating, mate, still trying to figure out the boundaries. But I definitely overstepped them tonight."[13]

Adams intended nothing malicious by his remarks; in fact, he tried to compliment the Warriors on their athleticism. Still, once he discovered his comments caused offense, he quickly sought to apologize and rectify the problem. Although he had no ill motive, he needed to set things right.

Atonement refers to the biblical process of making things right. It is how people seek God's favor. As we'll see more in coming chapters, biblical writers highlight three primary metaphors of atonement. It cleanses, ransoms, and removes a burden. These metaphors are entwined. Atonement saves people from impurity and the burden of debt that ensues. It entreats God's favor. The end result is reconciliation.

BURNING AND ATONEMENT

Why do so many atonement passages emphasize burning? Eberhart highlights an important but overlooked observation.[14] The Pentateuch routinely mentions

---

[13]"Thunder's Steven Adams Apologizes for 'Monkeys' Comment," *USA Today* (May 17, 2016), www .usatoday.com/story/sports/nba/2016/05/17/thunders-steven-adams-apologizes-for-monkeys -comment/84479448/.

[14]Christian Eberhart, "A Neglected Feature of Sacrifice in the Hebrew Bible," *HTR* 97, no. 4 (2004): 491.

a sacrifice and then says, "The priest shall make atonement for them, and they shall be forgiven."[15] The pattern is consistent: *atonement follows closely after burning.*

Interestingly, this declaration is not made after the shedding of blood; rather, forgiveness and atonement follow after the offering is burned on the altar.[16] A typical example comes from Leviticus 4:19-21, 25-26:

> He shall remove all its fat and *turn it into smoke on the altar*. He shall do with the bull just as is done with the bull of the reconciliation offering; he shall do the same with this. *The priest shall make atonement for them, and they shall be forgiven*. He shall carry the bull outside the camp, and *burn it as he burned the first bull*; it is the reconciliation offering for the assembly.

> The priest shall take some of the blood of the reconciliation offering with his finger and put it on the horns of the altar of burnt offering, and pour out the rest of its blood at the base of the altar of burnt offering. All its fat he shall turn into smoke on the altar, like the fat of the sacrifice of well-being. *Thus the priest shall make atonement on his behalf for his sin, and he shall be forgiven.* (NRSV, author's adaptation)

Numerous other passages could be mentioned.[17]

In Numbers 16:44-48, Aaron burns incense rather than use blood. In so doing, he makes atonement for the people.

> And the LORD spoke to Moses, saying, "Get away from this congregation, so that I may consume them in a moment." And they fell on their faces. Moses said to Aaron, "Take your censer, *put fire on it* from the altar and *lay incense on it*, and carry it quickly to the congregation and *make atonement for them*. For wrath has gone out from the LORD; the plague has begun." So Aaron took it as Moses had ordered, and ran into the middle of the assembly, where the plague had already begun among the people. *He put on the incense, and made atonement for the people.* He stood between the dead and the living; and the plague was stopped.

---

[15]Cf. Lev 4:20, 26, 31, 35.

[16]Later, we'll discuss Lev 17:11.

[17]We should note the implicit contrast in Lev 26:31-32. God says, "And I will lay your cities waste, will make your sanctuaries desolate, and I will not smell your pleasing aromas. I will devastate the land, so that your enemies who come to settle in it shall be appalled at it." God's *not* smelling pleasing aromas correlates with his condemnation of Israel. See Lev 4:31, 35; 5:12-23; 8:32, 34; 16:24-25, 27; Num 15:24-25, 28. Outside the Pentateuch, note Is 6:6-7.

The writer twice links lighting incense with atonement. The effect of the incense is atonement. The passage never mentions blood; yet it does repeat the act of burning.[18] As a result, the burning of incense appeases God's wrath.

Greenberg suggests a further distinction. He states,

> The burning of flesh on the altars appears to convey two possible results. If sin or bodily impurity are in view, then flesh burning seems to reflect YHWH's removal of the effects of sin or bodily impurity that have separated the offerer from YHWH. . . . If there is no sin or bodily impurity, then burning flesh seems to reflect a dedication, or relationship confirmation, between the offerer and YHWH, for example, the burnt offering.[19]

We've already seen how burning flesh can "reflect a dedication, or relationship confirmation, between the offerer and YHWH." Burning appears to be the mechanism that Israel used to present gifts to God. The fire produces smoke, which visually carries the meal or incense upward to God.

Today, many people don't feel comfortable using food imagery when teaching the sacrifices. They fear it leads to confusion and perhaps encourages idolatrous notions of God. The problem with this thinking is apparent. Biblical writers use these metaphors even though they could *and did* confuse people. If so, shouldn't we be willing to follow the Bible's example?

Culture is another reason some readers are less likely to accept or even notice this imagery. In traditional, non-Western cultures, meals are often regarded as near-sacred events. They establish binding connections. Eating with another person is an implicit approval of them. In other cultures, eating with another person redefines a relationship and even resets certain moral expectations. For example, among the Moose of Burkina Faso, West Africa, "eating is an intimate act that helps to define familial and sexual relations. Moose culture accepts extramarital sex unless it involves sex between a man and the wife of someone with whom the man eats."[20]

What happens when meals become little more than tolerated interruptions or biological necessities? When interpreters live in cultures where people

---

[18]The point here is not to deny the importance of blood but to highlight where the text lays explicit emphasis. The shedding of blood is often implicit, left unstated; however, writers repeatedly underscore the link between atonement and burning.

[19]Greenberg, *New Look*, 74.

[20]Lisa Miller, Paul Rozin, and Allan Page Fiske, "Food Sharing and Feeding Another Person Suggest Intimacy: Two Studies of American College Students," *European Journal of Social Psychology* 28 (1998): 425.

routinely eat alone, on-the-go, and in quick fashion, they can hardly grasp the significance of this biblical imagery.

Greenberg's conclusion is consistent with our earlier observations concerning the reconciliation offering and atonement. In the context of uncleanness or sin, the reconciliation offering binds and removes the obstacle that hinders relationship with God. With respect to the altar and the priests, blood binds the priest to the altar, representative of God. In both circumstances, atonement is accomplished. A "positive, protective connection" is made between the worshiper and God.[21]

OBJECTS OF ATONEMENT

The primary goal of this chapter is to discern how the Bible describes atonement. Studying the meaning of *kpr* is key to that task. So, we next consider the object of atonement. In other words, what receives atonement? In what follows, I'll survey the Hebrew and Greek Old Testament to identify the direct object of *kpr* or *exilaskomai*, that is, the objects that receive atonement.

The most common objects receiving atonement include the Holy Place, tent of meeting, and the altar. For example, Leviticus 16:20 says, "When [Aaron] has finished atoning for the holy place and the tent of meeting and the altar, he shall present the live goat." Likewise, in Ezekiel 43:26, the prophet writes, "Seven days shall they make atonement for the altar and cleanse it, and so consecrate it" (cf. Ezekiel 43:20). Ezekiel adds, "You shall do the same on the seventh day of the month for anyone who has sinned through error or ignorance; so you shall make atonement for the temple" (Ezekiel 45:20; via the reconciliation offering, Ezekiel 45:18-19).

Contrary to popular belief, the primary object of atonement is *not* people. Although atonement is made on behalf of people, the priests make atonement for sacred objects and space. When impurity threatens to defile the temple, atonement cleanses the sacred space by removing the uncleanness that belongs to people. In so doing, unclean people are protected from God's anger that would otherwise fall on them. Even land receives atonement. Moses says of the Lord, "He will repay those who hate him and *cleanse* [*kpr*] the land for his people" (Deuteronomy 32:43).[22] In this sense, *kpr* bestows honor on the land or altar. In short, *atonement restores a proper relationship between the sacred object and people.*

---

[21]Greenberg, *New Look*, 42.
[22]Earlier in Deut 21:8, innocent blood or "bloodguilt" (ESV) is atoned.

ATONEMENT AND DEATH

Many interpreters assume that atonement somehow entails a judicial death sentence. Popular versions of penal substitutionary atonement (PSA) suggest that our atonement is due to God's punishing Christ. Yet, atonement in the Old Testament does not *inherently* imply a death sentence. Several passages undermine this supposition.

In Leviticus 10:17, the Lord asks, "Why have you not eaten the reconciliation offering in the place of the sanctuary, since it is a thing most holy and has been given to you that you may *bear the iniquity of the congregation, to make atonement for them* before the LORD" (ESV, author's adaptation)? Leviticus 10:17 says "that you may bear." Who is the "you"? The priests. Originally, it was through a reconciliation offering that priests "bore" people's sin. Yet, the design of the sacrificial system is not that priests would be executed whenever they "bear the iniquity of the congregation." Even though the priests make atonement by bearing the congregation's sin, they are not killed in place of the people.

In Leviticus 5:11-13, *choice flour* atones for sin:

> But if you cannot afford two turtledoves or two pigeons, you shall bring as your offering for the sin that you have committed one-tenth of an ephah of choice flour for a reconciliation offering; you shall not put oil on it or lay frankincense on it, for it is a reconciliation offering. You shall bring it to the priest, and the priest shall scoop up a handful of it as its memorial portion, and turn this into smoke on the altar, with the offerings by fire to the LORD; it is a reconciliation offering. Thus the priest shall *make atonement* [*kpr*] on your behalf for whichever of these sins you have committed, and you shall be forgiven. Like the grain offering, the rest shall be for the priest. (NRSV, author's adaptation)

This passage causes some readers to scratch their head. A tenth of an ephah of fine flour could count as a reconciliation offering. Why? Because the people who offer the sacrifice are poor. We should not miss a seemingly trivial detail. This reconciliation offering is *not* living. Obviously, "a tenth of an ephah of fine flour" does not receive a death sentence. Nevertheless, the reconciliation offering is able to atone for sin. God forgives sin through the reconciliation offering, which consists of a tenth of an ephah of fine flour. Leviticus 5 contradicts the idea that atoning sacrifices, such as reconciliation offerings, receive a death sentence in the place of the worshiper. In this text, however, that suggestion is impossible.

Furthermore, incense appeases God's wrath in Numbers 16:44-50.

> And the LORD spoke to Moses, saying, "Get away from the midst of this congregation, that I may consume them in a moment." And they fell on their faces. And Moses said to Aaron, "Take your censer, and put fire on it from off the altar and lay *incense* on it and carry it quickly to the congregation and *make atonement* for them, for *wrath* has gone out from the LORD; the plague has begun." So Aaron took it as Moses said and ran into the midst of the assembly. And behold, the plague had already begun among the people. And he put on the *incense* and *made atonement for the people*. And he stood between the dead and the living, and the plague was stopped. Now those who died in the plague were 14,700, besides those who died in the affair of Korah. And Aaron returned to Moses at the entrance of the tent of meeting, when the plague was stopped. (ESV)

The congregation sins. God in wrath is ready to "consume them" and even begins to condemn the congregation via a plague. What atones for the people's sin? According to Numbers 16:46-47, Aaron offers incense, not blood, nor a person's life. Apparently, atonement does not inherently require someone receiving a judicial death sentence.

In Numbers 31:48-51, gold and jewelry bring atonement.

> Then the officers who were over the thousands of the army, the commanders of thousands and the commanders of hundreds, approached Moses, and said to Moses, "Your servants have counted the warriors who are under our command, and not one of us is missing. And we have brought the LORD's offering, what each of us found, articles of gold, armlets and bracelets, signet rings, earrings, and pendants, to *make atonement* for ourselves before the LORD." Moses and Eleazar the priest received the gold from them, all in the form of crafted articles.

We again find evidence that atonement does not have an *inherent* requirement of punishment. Exodus 32:30-32 likewise is striking.[23] It says,

> On the next day Moses said to the people, "You have sinned a great sin. But now I will go up to the LORD; perhaps I can *make atonement* for your sin." So Moses returned to the Lord and said, "Alas, this people has sinned a great sin; they have made for themselves gods of gold. But now, if you will only forgive their sin—but if not, blot me out of the book that you have written."

---

[23]Christopher J. H. Wright, "Atonement in the Old Testament," in *The Atonement Debate: Papers from the London Symposium on the Theology of Atonement*, ed. Derek Tidball, David Hilborn, and Justin Thaker (Grand Rapids, MI: Zondervan, 2008), 74.

Although Moses wants to make atonement for them, he doesn't offer a sacrifice. He merely prays. Exodus 32:32 does not refute the point, as though Moses offered himself. In fact, the verse reinforces our point. Notice the contrast. If God does not forgive their sin, Moses wants to die. Moses' death assumes God will not forgive. Therefore, we cannot say that Moses' death somehow would atone for their sin.

These passages provide overwhelming evidence that atonement does not have an inherent requirement of capital punishment. This observation challenges a latent assumption held by many readers. No doubt, it raises many questions about other biblical texts and the way atonement functions in Scripture. Some people will be alarmed. Still, I assure you that the following chapters will answer many, if not most, of the common questions that arise when readers see these verses.

FROM UNCLEAN TO CLEAN TO HOLY

The process of atonement brings about at least two kinds of transformation. First, atonement transitions an object from being unclean to becoming clean.[24] For instance,

> The priest shall offer the reconciliation offering, to make atonement for the one to be cleansed from his uncleanness. Afterward he shall slaughter the burnt offering; and the priest shall offer the burnt offering and the grain offering on the altar. Thus the priest shall make atonement on his behalf and he shall be clean. (Leviticus 14:19-20 NRSV, author's adaptation)

> For on this day atonement shall be made for you, to cleanse you; from all your sins you shall be clean before the LORD. (Leviticus 16:30)

This transition is one reason why atonement and purification are frequently linked.

Second, atonement can transform an object *from a state of being clean to being holy*. In short, this is what it means to consecrate or sanctify. Note the following examples. In each case, the biblical authors explicitly link atonement and *qdš* (consecration). Exodus 29:33-37 is especially illustrative:

> They themselves shall eat the food by which *atonement* is made, to ordain and *consecrate* them, but no one else shall eat of them, because they are holy. If any of the flesh for the ordination, or of the bread, remains until the morning,

---

[24]Cf. Lev 12:7, 8; 14:18, 19, 20, 29, 31, 53; 15:30; 16:16, 30; Num 8:21; Ezek 43:26.

then you shall burn the remainder with fire; it shall not be eaten, because it is *holy*. Thus you shall do to Aaron and to his sons, just as I have commanded you; through seven days you shall ordain them. Also every day you shall offer a bull as a reconciliation offering for *atonement*. Also you shall offer a reconciliation offering for the altar, when you make *atonement* for it, and shall anoint it, to *consecrate* it. Seven days you shall make *atonement* for the altar, and *consecrate* it, and the altar shall be most holy; whatever touches the altar shall *become holy*. (NRSV, author's adaptation)

Atonement is made for the priests (Exodus 29:33) and the altar (Exodus 29:36-37). Thus, they are holy or consecrated. Likewise, Leviticus 8:15, "And [the bull of the reconciliation offering] was slaughtered. Moses took the blood and with his finger put some on each of the horns of the altar, purifying the altar; then he poured out the blood at the base of the altar. *Thus he consecrated it, to make atonement for it.*" Finally, compare Leviticus 16:19-20, which says, "He shall sprinkle some of the blood on it with his finger seven times, and cleanse it and hallow it from the uncleannesses of the people of Israel. When he has finished atoning for the holy place and the tent of meeting and the altar, he shall present the live goat." Leviticus 16:20 clearly summarizes the cleansing or consecration process in Leviticus 16:19 as making atonement for "the holy place and the tent of meeting and the altar."[25]

In short, what atonement accomplishes depends on the initial state of its object. If it is unclean, then atonement makes it become clean. If already clean, then atonement makes the object become holy. The figure below provides a visual summary.[26]

Figure 4.1. How atonement makes an object holy

[25]Nazarites (Num 6) appear to undergo a two-step process, being made pure before being consecrated. Perhaps Lev 5:16 shows an instance where restitution is given for defiling a holy thing, thus implying reconsecration.

[26]The figure is adapted from Sklar, *Sin, Impurity, Sacrifice*, 125.

CLEANSING THE LEVITES

Numbers 8 illustrates much of what has been said. Numbers 8:5-6 say, "The LORD spoke to Moses, saying: Take the Levites from among the Israelites and cleanse them." How should Moses cleanse the Levites? The answer immediately follows in Numbers 8:7-15.

> Thus you shall do to them, to cleanse them: sprinkle the water of purification on them, have them shave their whole body with a razor and wash their clothes, and *so cleanse themselves*. Then let them take a young bull and its grain offering of choice flour mixed with oil, and you shall take another young bull for a reconciliation offering. You shall bring the Levites before the tent of meeting, and assemble the whole congregation of the Israelites. When you bring the Levites before the LORD, the Israelites shall lay their hands on the Levites, and Aaron shall present the Levites before the LORD as an elevation offering from the Israelites, that they may do the service of the LORD. The Levites shall lay their hands on the heads of the bulls, and he shall offer the one for a reconciliation offering and the other for a burnt offering to the LORD, to *make atonement* for the Levites. Then you shall have the Levites stand before Aaron and his sons, and you shall present them as an elevation offering to the LORD. Thus you shall *separate* the Levites from among the other Israelites, and the Levites shall be mine. Thereafter the Levites may go in to do service at the tent of meeting, *once you have cleansed them* and presented them as an elevation offering. (NRSV, author's adaptation)

In Numbers 8:14, we see the separation between holy and common.[27] God singles them out for service to himself.[28]

Why does he do this? Numbers 8:16-19 shows the inner logic.

> *For* they are unreservedly given to me from among the Israelites; I have taken them for myself, in place of all that open the womb, the firstborn of all the Israelites. For all the firstborn among the Israelites are mine, both human and animal. On the day that I struck down all the firstborn in the land of Egypt I *consecrated* [*qdš*] them for myself, but I have taken the Levites in place of all the firstborn among the Israelites. Moreover, I have given the Levites as a gift to Aaron and his sons from among the Israelites, to do the service for the Israelites at the tent of meeting, and *to make atonement* for the Israelites, *in order that* there may be no plague among the Israelites for coming too close to the sanctuary.

---

[27]Cf. Ex 26:33; Lev 10:10; 11:47; Ezek 22:26.

[28]This separation resembles Num 16:9; 1 Kings 8:53; Ezra 8:24. It is a complete separation, as in severing of an animal's body (Lev 1:17; 5:8). These texts share the common verb *bdl*.

God consecrates the Levites because he consecrated the firstborn of Israel. The separation of Numbers 8:14 is rooted in Numbers 8:17 ("consecrating them"). The symbolic act in the passage seems to consummate what God already did in Numbers 8:17. The Levites' consecration is due to God consecrating all of Israel's firstborn in Egypt. Because God consecrates the Levites (Numbers 8:14, 17), they need atonement (Numbers 8:12). As a result, they assist the priests and so "make atonement for the Israelites, in order that there may be no plague among the Israelites for coming too close to the sanctuary" (Numbers 8:19).

Numbers 8:16 is noteworthy. It begins with "for," indicating the reasons for which the Levites need atonement. They need atonement *not because* of the Levites' sin; it's because God consecrates all of Israel's firstborn (Numbers 8:16-18). In this passage, atonement is God's method of consecration.

In Numbers 8:20-22, Israel obeys the commands of Numbers 8:5-19. The Levites *purified themselves* and Aaron made *atonement* for them to cleanse them. The atonement mentioned in Numbers 8:12, 21 sanctifies the Levites through purification. Purifying a clean thing makes it become holy. For example, making atonement for the temple and altar does not imply they were previously defiled or bad. They simply were *common*. Likewise, apart from atonement, the Levites would merely be clean in the same sense as any common person.

Numbers 8 is very similar to Numbers 3:5-13. Numbers 3:10 seems to imply levels of purity. God specifically consecrates the Levites as holy. But outsiders do not have the same degree of purity. Outsiders are merely common, not holy.[29] Why does God treat the Levites in this way? Numbers 3:11-13 explain:

> Then the LORD spoke to Moses, saying: "I hereby accept the Levites from among the Israelites as substitutes for all the firstborn that open the womb among the Israelites. The Levites shall be mine, for all the firstborn are mine; when I killed all the firstborn in the land of Egypt, I *consecrated* for my own all the firstborn in Israel, both human and animal; they shall be mine. I am the LORD."

In essence, God repeats the logic of Numbers 8:16-19.

LEVITICUS 17:11 IN CONTEXT

How does the above discussion relate to Leviticus 17:11? What does the context of Leviticus 17:11 teach concerning the function of blood? It says, "For the life

---

[29]Cf. Num 1:51; 3:38.

of the flesh is in the blood; and I have given it to you for making atonement for your lives on the altar; for, as life, it is the blood that makes atonement."[30]

At least two things complicate our effort to interpret this verse. First, Leviticus 17:11 does not primarily develop a theology of atonement. The writer only mentions atonement in the larger context of prohibiting people from eating blood. Still, the immediately preceding paragraph does address the proper place where one should offer a sacrifice. Second, Leviticus 17:11 was something of a dictum or axiomatic in rabbinic literature.[31] Its wide, nonspecific usage muddies the historical lens through which we read Leviticus 17:11.

To understand the relationship between atonement and blood in Leviticus 17, we'll first revisit the concept of a devoted gift. Something is *devoted* if it cannot be redeemed because it is most holy to the Lord (Leviticus 27:28-29). Perhaps wedding rings are a close contemporary analogy. They are expensive, often made of gold and sometimes crowned with a diamond. More importantly, a ring belongs exclusively to one's spouse.

Why is a devoted thing considered irredeemable? Because it cannot be given to others. Since it is God's alone, it is most holy. Others cannot use it; otherwise, people would treat it as common, not holy. Accordingly, people must destroy living things that are devoted to God. Doing so prevents people from using it. Even when a field is consecrated to the Lord, it becomes a devoted gift. It is not destroyed since a field is not a living thing. As a result, only priests may use it (Leviticus 27:21). The firstborn cow, sheep, and goat cannot be redeemed and thus become a devoted gift to the Lord (Numbers 18:8-17). By implication, the reconciliation offering is reckoned a "devoted thing." Burning it symbolically gives the gift to God.

Figure 4.2. Nature of a devoted thing

---

[30]The ESV inconsistently translates *nepeš* as "souls" rather than "lives" (as it does in the final clause).
[31]Jacob Milgrom, "Prolegomenon to Leviticus 17:11," *JBL* 90, no. 2 (1971): 156n34. He lists *Yoma,* 5a; cf. *Sifra, Vay. Ned.,* 4:9; *Zeb.,* 6a; *Men.,* 93b; *Pesik. R.,* 194b; perhaps *Jub.* 6:2. Also see William Johnsson, "Defilement and Purgation in the Book of Hebrews" (PhD diss., Vanderbilt University, 1973), 329.

In summary, if a devoted thing is a living creature, it must die (i.e., shedding blood). In this sense, its life is entirely given to God. The devoted thing literally gives its life for God. If one were not to kill a devoted animal, people could use it. In that case, the animal is not given to God *alone*. (From this perspective, we glimpse the significance of Paul's exhortation in Romans 12:1, "to present your bodies as a living sacrifice, holy and acceptable to God.")

This insight is consistent with Leviticus 17:11. The significance of blood is in the life. The passage emphasizes *life*, not death. Death is one way of being devoted to God. The blood given to God represents an entire life given to God. Therefore, consecration requires blood because the life of the flesh is in the blood.[32]

The above explanation sheds light on why Israel's firstborn need redemption. The firstborn (of men and unclean animals; Numbers 18:15) are God's but are not devoted things because they can be redeemed. Rather, a devoted gift (such as a reconciliation offering) serves as a substitute and redeems a person's life. It redeems those who belong to God.

God consecrates and redeems   **Firstborn**

substitution

Israel consecrates and redeems   **Levites**
via burnt offering and reconciliation offering
(i.e., "devoted" things)

Figure 4.3. Consecrating and redeeming

Again, Numbers 8 helpfully connects blood with redemption, atonement, and sanctification (or holiness). First, God consecrates the firstborn, therefore they are his. Numbers 8:16-18 says,

> For they are unreservedly given to me from among the Israelites; I have taken them for myself, in place of all that open the womb, the firstborn of all the

---

[32]This statement does not negate the use of oil or other components involved in consecration (Ex 40:9; Lev 8:12). Also, a similar set of features mark Deut 15:19-23. The people consecrate the firstborn of the flock. They are told, "You shall do no work with your firstling ox nor shear the firstling of your flock. You shall eat it. . . . Its blood, however, you must not eat" (Deut 15:19-20, 23).

Israelites. For all the firstborn among the Israelites are mine, both human and animal. On the day that I struck down all the firstborn in the land of Egypt I *consecrated* them for myself, but I have taken the Levites in place of all the firstborn among the Israelites. (cf. Numbers 3:13)

God allows the Levites to substitute for Israel's firstborn (Numbers 8:18). Therefore, he tells Aaron to make atonement for them to purify them. Numbers 8:21 says, "The Levites purified themselves from sin and washed their clothes; then Aaron presented them as an elevation offering before the LORD, and Aaron *made atonement* for them to cleanse them." Accordingly, the reconciliation offering and burnt offering are given. "The Levites shall lay their hands on the heads of the bulls, and he shall offer the one for a reconciliation offering and the other for a burnt offering to the LORD, to *make atonement* for the Levites" (Numbers 8:12 NRSV, author's adaptation).

In effect, these actions are the means of consecrating the Levites. Numbers 8:14 says, "Thus you shall separate the Levites from among the other Israelites, and the Levites shall be mine." What if the number of firstborn exceeds that of the Levites? According to Numbers 3:44-49, Israel must pay a redemption price. Without Levites acting as substitutes for Israel's firstborn, God's wrath would destroy Israel (Numbers 1:53; 8:19; 18:3-5, 21-23).

How do we summarize the above sequence? Recall what distinguishes the Levites. It comes from God's consecrating (or sanctifying) Israel's firstborn. What is the underlying logic? It seems to be something like the following summary: being holy is tantamount to belonging to God (Numbers 8:16-17; 3:13). If an animal is the Lord's (i.e., it is holy), then it must die (Numbers 18:17; Exodus 34:19-20; Leviticus 27:26, 28-29). However, God does not want the firstborn of Israel to die. So, Israel consecrates the Levites such that they become the Lord's and thus redeem Israel's firstborn (Numbers 3:9, 41, 45; cf. 8:14). Furthermore, because God does not want the Levites to die, the priests give a reconciliation offering, making atonement for the Levites (Numbers 8). The reconciliation offering is "most holy" (Exodus 30:10; Leviticus 6:17, 25; 10:17; 14:13; Numbers 18:9). In effect, the reconciliation offering is a substitute that serves as a devoted gift (which is holy) in place of the Levites and firstborn.

Perhaps, Abraham's offering of Isaac is a fitting analogy (Genesis 22). In laying his only son on the wood and raising his knife to slaughter Isaac,

Abraham in essence gives the boy over to God utterly and completely. However, God did not want Isaac to die. He after all was the child of promise. So, God himself provides a ram as a substitute to ransom Isaac. Through sacrifice, Abraham gives the ram in place of the son, whom he intended to devote to God.

The atonement of the Levites helps us to understand the significance of several interrelated concepts. That which is holy belongs to the Lord. A devoted thing is most holy to the Lord. Accordingly, it becomes a substitute that is able to redeem his people. This review of Levite consecration is no meandering through the intellectual wilderness. Instead, it illustrates one sphere in which Israel applied the concept of a devoted thing. In coming chapters, we'll see more clearly how Jesus also serves as a devoted sacrifice on our behalf.

LIFE IS IN THE BLOOD

What then is the significance of blood in light of Leviticus 17:11? I suggest a few answers to this much-debated question. First, blood is *primarily* about life (*nepeš*), not death. Observe the context of the chapter and the explicit logic of Leviticus 17:11.

> If anyone of the house of Israel or of the aliens who reside among them eats any blood, I will set my face against that person who eats blood, and will cut that person off from the people. For the *life* of the flesh is in the blood; and I have given it to you for making atonement for your *lives* on the altar; *for*, as *life*, it is the blood that makes atonement. Therefore I have said to the people of Israel: No person among you shall eat blood, nor shall any alien who resides among you eat blood. (Leviticus 17:10-12)

Blood makes atonement for people's lives because blood is seen to contain life.

The biblical writers repeatedly underscore the relationship between blood and life. Just a few verses later, Leviticus 17:14 says, "For the life of every creature—its blood is its life; therefore I have said to the people of Israel: You shall not eat the blood of any creature, for the life of every creature is its blood; whoever eats it shall be cut off." Deuteronomy 12:23 adds, "Only be sure that you do not eat the blood; for the blood is the life, and you shall not eat the life with the meat."

The symbolism and prohibition against eating blood precede the Mosaic law. Genesis 9:4 states, "But you shall not eat flesh with its life, that is, its blood." The symbolism ("life is in the blood") in Leviticus 17:11 goes back to Genesis 9:4. Its emphasis on blood is not rooted in its representing punitive death via the

Mosaic law. Leviticus 17:11 is not based on the fact that the law demands the death of sinners as represented by blood. In context, blood does not signify death *by punitive measures*. Instead, it represents life. Even if death is required to extract blood, the emphasis remains on life. The blood is not about punitive death but rather a life given to God. We will return to this point when we look at how Hebrews applies Leviticus 17 and consider the significance of Christ shedding his blood.

BLOOD AS A GIFT TO GOD

The significance of the blood above parallels that of the fat burned during a sacrificial offering. The prohibition against eating blood in Leviticus 17:10, 12 resembles the similar prohibition on eating the fat of oxen, sheep, and goats (Leviticus 3:16-17; 7:22-27).[33] That portion is always offered to the Lord.

In fact, the Bible consistently links the application of blood and burning of fat. For example, Leviticus 17:6 says, "The priest shall dash the blood against the altar of the LORD at the entrance of the tent of meeting, and turn the fat into smoke as a pleasing odor to the LORD."[34] In only a few places, writers prohibit eating blood *but* do not mention fat.[35]

Why then does the Lord prohibit the eating of blood? A blood offering represents the giving of life, which effectively treats blood as sacred and thus not for common use. Blood is reserved exclusively for God. This suggestion is consistent with our observations concerning gifts "devoted" to God.[36] Likewise, Ezekiel reinforces this interpretation when presenting blood as part of a meal. In Ezekiel 44:6-7, the Lord says, "O house of Israel, let there be an end to all your abominations in admitting foreigners, uncircumcised in heart and flesh, to be in my sanctuary, profaning my temple when you offer to me *my food, the fat and the blood*. You have broken my covenant with all your abominations"

---

[33]This fat (*ḥēleb*) specifically refers to "the whole broad tail, which shall be removed close to the backbone, the fat that covers the entrails, and all the fat that is around the entrails; the two kidneys with the fat that is on them at the loins, and the appendage of the liver, which you shall remove with the kidneys" (Lev 3:9-10).

[34]Also, see Ex 29:12-13, 22-22; Lev 1:1-15; 3; 4; 7; 8; 9; Num 18:17.

[35]Lev 17:10, 12; 19:26; Deut 12:16, 23; 15:23. These texts tend to be brief, as though concise restatements of previous passages.

[36]Andrew Rillera observes that worshipers may eat nonatoning sacrifices, but "if a sacrifice has an atoning function, then the offerer cannot eat from it." Andrew Rillera, "Paul Does Not Have a Kippēr Theology: Understanding Paul's Sacrificial Imagery Applied to Jesus" (paper, Society of Biblical Literature Annual Conference, San Antonio, TX, November 21, 2021).

(cf. Numbers 18:17). In short, blood signifies a gift reserved for God alone. It can even symbolize part of a meal shared with God.

Although I addressed a common concern in the last chapter, it's worth reiterating here. Linking blood with a meal does *not* suggest that God needs food, nor that he drinks blood. Rather, as symbolic food, blood represents a precious gift that binds worshipers and God in relationship just as people are knit together when they share a meal.

CONCLUSION

This chapter began with the question, "What is the atonement?" The biblical writers use multiple images when speaking of atonement. In particular, cleansing, carrying, and compensation are among the most significant. However, these ideas do not capture what is fundamentally achieved by atonement. Atonement removes whatever barrier exists between the worshiper and God. Such obstacles include uncleanness and sin. When making atonement, people seek God's favor. This perspective accords with our observations concerning the reconciliation offering, which repairs or restores a positive connection between God and the worshiper.

Other consistent patterns also emerged. For example, forgiveness and atonement follow after an offering is burned on the altar, not the shedding of blood. Furthermore, atonement brings about two types of transformation. First, atonement can make what is unclean become clean. Second, atonement is used for the sake of consecrating people and places (i.e., making what is clean become holy or sacred).

Finally, we considered the role of blood in effecting atonement. This study adds to observations made in the previous chapter. Death is not always necessary for atonement, yet Leviticus 17:11 raises questions about the relationship between blood and atonement. In context, Leviticus 17:11 primarily explains the rationale for not eating blood. Blood makes atonement for people's lives because blood is seen to contain life. It represents the giving of one's life to God.

5

SEEKING GOD'S FACE THROUGH SACRIFICE

WARS EXPOSE THE WORST IN NATIONS. In some ways, the period after a conflict reveals the best in countries. Since World War 2, Germany has never fatigued in expressing grief and shame over the atrocities of the Nazi regime. Monuments and museums abound across the country that testify to the Holocaust. Commemorating the seventy-fifth anniversary of Auschwitz's liberation, the German prime minister expressed a "deep sense of shame for the barbaric crimes that were here committed by Germans."[1] Japan's response is more controversial. Some condemned the Japanese prime minister's decision to visit Tokyo's Yasukuni Shrine, "a memorial to Japanese war dead that critics say honors war criminals and the country's past militarism."[2] Furthermore, the Korean government in April 1948 violently crushed protests on the island of Jeju, killing about 10 percent of the population. In April 2018, President Moon Jae issued an official apology, promising to "address the grievances of the victims and restore their honor."[3]

What do these testimonies illustrate? Reconciliation entails a recognition of reality. To atone for one's actions, a person must acknowledge the problem. Our response can serve as a confession. We are weak and flawed. More important

---

[1]Jacob Eder, "Germany Is Often Praised for Facing Up to Its Nazi Past. But Even There, the Memory of the Holocaust Is Still Up for Debate," *Time Magazine*, January 27, 2020, time.com/5772360/german-holocaust-memory/.

[2]Greg Rienzi, "Other Nations Could Learn from German Effort to Reconcile After WWII," *Johns Hopkins Magazine*, Summer 2015, accessed April 21, 2020, hub.jhu.edu/magazine/2015/summer/germany-japan-reconciliation/.

[3]Kim Rahn, "Moon Vows Fact-Finding for Jeju Massacres," *The Korea Times*, April 3, 2018, accessed April 21, 2020, koreatimes.co.kr/www/nation/2018/04/356_246662.html.

is the need to give honor to those whom we dishonored. Our words and actions have power to disrespect and shame. Atonement, however, seeks to "address the grievances of the victims and restore their honor."

SACRIFICING GOD'S HONOR

How might honor and shame shed light on the saving significance of sacrifices in the Bible? One's understanding of the sacrificial system greatly influences our view of atonement. For some, this chapter could fundamentally reorient how they understand the purpose of biblical sacrifices. For this reason, I'll preview a few key ideas.

To begin, what function do the sacrificial offerings have? How do they work? In a word, *sacrifices work by vindicating God's honor*. Sin spits in God's face. Our words and deeds defame his name. In contrast, sacrifices are regarded as gifts to vindicate God's honor. By offering valuable gifts, the giver sets aside his own "face" and "gives God face." The worshiper acknowledges God's higher position and confesses our lower position and sin. In short, sacrifices honor God as glorious.

What is the overall argument presented in this chapter? First, giving the offerings prescribed in the Mosaic law sets God apart as holy (i.e., it "sanctifies" God). Second, sanctifying God means giving him unique honor, regarding him as uniquely glorious. Thus, only when God's honor is vindicated is sin atoned for. This chapter offers a positive, constructive argument. It does not explicitly critique or oppose other views. Accordingly, the present proposal and other views are not necessarily mutually exclusive.

HOLINESS AND PURITY AS HONOR LANGUAGE

The biblical writers often use honor-shame language to clarify the meaning and significance of concepts like holiness, sanctification, and purity. Obviously, these terms are inextricably tied to the practice of sacrifice.

Stated plainly, holiness expresses unique honor. If someone sets apart as holy (sanctifies) people, places, or things, one bestows on them unique honor. People regard as holy that which they think has utmost value. We honor what we regard as holy. To be clear, *holiness expresses honor, but honor does not necessarily express holiness*.

People worship God because they regard him as holy. He has unique worth. The Bible says the temple, certain temple utensils, and God's people are holy.

Why? People and things can have derived holiness. Because the temple and people have a special relationship *with God*, they are reckoned holy or sanctified. In some respect, they reflect God's unique honor, that is, his holiness. If people live in a holy manner, their lives reflect God's honor. As a result, a holy person is worthy of praise precisely because God's holiness and honor deserve praise.[4]

Several passages illustrate the point. For example, God responds to the sin of Nadab and Abihu in Leviticus 10:3 saying, "Among those who are near me I will be *sanctified*, and before all the people I will be *glorified*" (ESV). To "be glorified" restates and clarifies the significance of being sanctified. Leviticus 10:10 elaborates on what is required for God to be glorified, "You are to distinguish between *the holy* and *the common*, and between *the unclean and the clean*."

How does God sanctify the tabernacle? In Exodus 29:43-44, he says, "I will meet with the Israelites there, and it shall be *sanctified by my glory*; I will *consecrate* the tent of meeting and the altar; Aaron also and his sons I will *consecrate*, to serve me as priests." It is God's glory that is distinctive in sanctifying the tabernacle, its altar, and the priests.[5]

Glory belongs to the nature of holiness. Holiness inherently has honor connotations. Hence, Isaiah exclaims, "Holy, holy, holy is the LORD of hosts; the whole earth is full of his glory" (Isaiah 6:3). In Ezekiel 28:22, God's "glory" and "holiness" are mutually explanatory. John Hartley explains,

> When Yahweh manifests himself, his holiness is visible as glory. Vriezen defines כבוד, "glory," as "the radiant power of His Being" (*An Outline*, 150). In the words of van Imshoot (*Theology of the OT*, 47), "Glory is not identical with holiness; it stresses power which is included in holiness; furthermore glory is often the exterior manifestation of power and holiness or of Yahweh Himself, while holiness always denotes Yahweh's intimate nature and has often a moral aspect which is not formally included in the concept of glory." "Holiness" thus refers to Yahweh's inner nature and "glory" to his outward appearing.[6]

---

[4]To use a colloquial Chinese expression, sanctifying a person essentially means giving them "face" above all else.

[5]This tabernacle is finally made holy in Ex 40:34-35, "Then the cloud covered the tent of meeting, and the glory of the LORD filled the tabernacle. Moses was not able to enter the tent of meeting because the cloud settled upon it, and the glory of the LORD filled the tabernacle." The holiness of the sanctuary comes from God's glory.

[6]John E. Hartley, *Leviticus*, WBC, vol. 4 (Grand Rapids, MI: Zondervan, 1992), lvi. He cites Th. C. Vriezen, *An Outline of Old Testament Theology* (Newton Centre, MA; Branford, 1966); Paul van

God says, "I am against you, O Sidon, / and I *will gain glory* in your midst. / And they shall know that I am the LORD / when I execute judgments in it, / and *manifest my holiness* in her" (Ezekiel 28:22 NRSV, author's adaptation).[7]

Because God ties his own honor to a people who behave shamefully, it is necessary for God to sanctify or cleanse them, lest God suffer dishonor. God explains why he brings Israel out of Egypt.

> But I acted *for the sake of my name*, that it should not be profaned in the sight of the nations among whom they lived, in whose sight I made myself known to them in bringing them out of the land of Egypt. . . . I gave them my statutes and showed them my ordinances, by whose observance everyone shall live. Moreover I gave them my sabbaths, as a sign between me and them, *so that they might know* that I the LORD sanctify them. (Ezekiel 20:9, 11-12)

Sanctification, that is, setting his people apart as holy, is how God both restores his honor and removes their shame.

In Ezekiel 36:22-32, God emphasizes that he will sanctify himself. This does not mean he makes himself holy in an objective sense. Rather, he displays the holiness that makes him worthy of honor.[8] God's name has been dishonored. Therefore, God's solution in Ezekiel 36:22-23 is to sanctify himself.

> Therefore say to the house of Israel, Thus says the LORD God: It is not for your sake, O house of Israel, that I am about to act, but *for the sake of my holy name*, which you have profaned among the nations to which you came. I will *sanctify my great name*, which has been *profaned* among the nations, and which you have *profaned* among them; and the nations shall know that I am the LORD, says the Lord GOD, when through you I *display my holiness* before their eyes.

Because the people profane God's name, they are "unclean," worthy of "disgrace" and "shame" (Ezekiel 36:24-25, 29-30, 32-33). However, God will sanctify himself by "cleansing" his people, granting them a new heart and his Spirit (Ezekiel 36:26-27).

A number of passages use honor-shame language to explain the holiness of God's people. The Lord says to Israel that he will "set you high above all nations

---

Imschoot, *Theology of the Old Testament*, vol. 1, *God*, trans. K. Sullivan and F. Buck (New York: Desclee, 1954).

[7]Thus, God will be honored when "they shall know that I am the Lord GOD" (Ezek 28:24). God's holiness signifies the fact that unique honor is due his name; cf. Ps 29:2.

[8]Thus, even people "sanctify" God. See Is 8:13-14, "But the LORD of hosts, him you shall regard as holy [or "him you shall sanctify"]. . . . He will become a sanctuary." Likewise, compare 1 Pet 3:15, "In your hearts *sanctify* [*hagiasate*] Christ as Lord."

that he has made, *in praise and in fame and in honor*; and for you to be a people *holy* to the LORD your God, as he promised" (Deuteronomy 26:19).[9] God foretells of his salvation in Isaiah 61 when "you shall be called priests of the LORD" and will enjoy "glory" instead of "shame" and "dishonor" (Isaiah 61:6-7).[10]

The New Testament likewise uses honor to explain holiness language. Hebrews overtly depends on and interprets the Old Testament sacrificial system. Therefore, it is quite significant that Hebrews 2:9-11 states,

> But we do see Jesus, who for a little while was made lower than the angels, now *crowned with glory and honor* because of the suffering of death, so that by the grace of God he might taste death for everyone. It was fitting that God, for whom and through whom all things exist, in *bringing many children to glory*, should make the pioneer of their salvation perfect through sufferings. For the one who *sanctifies* and those who are *sanctified* all have one Father. For this reason Jesus is not ashamed to call them brothers and sisters.

The phrase in Hebrews 2:10, "bringing many children to glory," is interpreted as "sanctified" in Hebrews 2:11.

John's Gospel, which draws heavily on temple imagery, entwines sanctification and honor language. In John 17:19, Jesus speaks about sanctification, "And for their sakes I *sanctify* myself, that they also *may be sanctified* in truth." John 17:22, 24 suggest how this happens: "The glory that you have given me I have given to them, so that they may be one, as we are one [such that they will] see my glory, which you have given me." By granting Christ's glory to his people, God makes them holy.

Paul also interlinks honor-shame language with holiness-purity imagery in Romans 1. Those who did not honor God (as in Romans 1:21) "exchanged the glory of the immortal God for images resembling mortal man and birds and animals and creeping things. Therefore, God gave them up in the lusts of their hearts *to impurity, to the dishonoring* of their bodies among themselves" (Romans 1:23-24 ESV). Impurity is explained in terms of dishonor.

---

[9]In Ezek 37:28, God receives honor as the one who will "sanctify Israel, when my sanctuary is among them forevermore"; cf. Is 60:7, 9, 13 where God will glorify or "beautify" (ESV) his sanctuary and "will glorify where [his] feet rest." Less direct is Is 55:3, 5, where God demonstrates that he is "the Holy One of Israel, for he has glorified you" in keeping with his covenant promises.

[10]By contrast, in Jer 51:51, observe the sign that leads Israel to say, "We are put to shame, for we have heard insults; dishonor has covered our face." Jeremiah adds, "For aliens have come into the holy places of the LORD's house."

Idol worship is the quintessential act of profaning God's name (Ezekiel 20:39). So, in Romans, "they exchanged the glory of the immortal God for images resembling a mortal human being or birds or four-footed animals or reptiles" (Romans 1:23). Furthermore, their idolatrous, impure hearts produce "dishonorable passions" (ESV) and "shameless acts" by those who "did not see fit to acknowledge God" (Romans 1:25-28).

Second Timothy 2:20-21 unambiguously equates honor and holiness. Paul writes, "Now in a great house there are not only vessels of gold and silver but also of wood and clay, some for *honorable* use, some for *dishonorable*. Therefore, if anyone *cleanses* himself from what is *dishonorable*, he will be a vessel for *honorable* use, set apart as *holy*, useful to the master of the house, ready for every good work" (ESV). Significantly, Paul uses *holy* to express "honorable." Also, it is because of dishonor that one needs cleansing.

Similar language is sprinkled throughout the New Testament. In 1 Thessalonians 4:3-4, Paul writes, "For this is the will of God, your *sanctification*: that you abstain from fornication; that each one of you know how to control your own body in *holiness* and *honor*."[11] Given 1 Thessalonians 4:7, the contrast to honor is "impurity."[12] In 1 Thessalonians 2:3-6, Paul explains the fact that "our appeal does not spring from deceit or impure motives or trickery." After all, they "have been approved by God . . . so we speak, not to please mortals, but to please God." Furthermore, "we never came with words of flattery. . . . Nor did we seek glory from people." In contrast, Paul adds, "You are witnesses, and God also, *how holy* and righteous and blameless was our conduct toward you believers" (2:10 ESV). Throughout the letter, purity and holiness are directly explained using honor-shame language.[13]

Peter extensively uses honor and shame to explain his holiness-purity language, particularly in 1 Peter 1:15-2:17. Quoting Leviticus 11:44, Peter says, "As he who called you is holy, be holy yourselves in all your conduct, for it is written, 'You shall be holy, for I am holy'" (1 Peter 1:15-16). Temple-sacrificial imagery

---

[11]1 Thess 4:7 reinforces the contrast between "impurity" and "holiness."

[12]Also see Col 3:12, 17, where Paul urges readers to live as "holy" people, thus "whatever you do, in word or deed, do everything in the name of the Lord Jesus, giving thanks to God the Father through him."

[13]A parallel between holiness and impurity with honor and shame (not taken up here) is the observation that, like holiness and impurity, both honor and shame can be contagious. For a discussion on the latter, see Gregg ten Elshof, *For Shame: Rediscovering the Virtues of a Maligned Emotion* (Grand Rapids, MI: Zondervan, 2021), 24-26, 88-95.

pervades the passage (1 Peter 1:19, 22; 2:5, 9). Importantly, he increasingly uses clear honor-shame language to develop his thought (1 Peter 2:6-7, 9, 12, 17). Thus, those who are holy will "not be put to shame" but will receive honor as they live honorably for the sake of God's glory.

Honor is a key concept to understanding holiness, purity, and sanctification language. We can apply this observation to Old Testament passages that concern sacrifices. Observe what happens when priests consecrate the altar in Exodus 29:36-37.

> Every day you shall offer a bull as a *reconciliation offering for atonement.* Also you shall offer a reconciliation offering for the altar, when you *make atonement for it,* and shall anoint it, to *consecrate* it. Seven days you shall *make atonement for the altar,* and *consecrate* it, and the altar shall be most holy; whatever touches the altar shall become holy. (NRSV, author's adaptation)

By offering a sacrifice, the priest treats the altar with unique honor. As a result, atonement is made.[14] Similar logic is found in other Old Testament passages. Sacrifices effect atonement inasmuch as they sanctify God as uniquely holy.

SACRIFICES GIVE HONOR TO GOD

In the Pentateuch, one primary function of sacrifice is to sanctify, thus honor God. As a result, atonement is made. In Leviticus 10, Aaron's sons Nadab and Abihu mistake the fundamental purpose of the offering. God's rebuke is illuminating. He says, "I will be sanctified," which is explained by the phrase, "I will be glorified" (Leviticus 10:3).[15]

The following context is significant because it immediately clarifies what the sacrifices intend to achieve. Moses is angered by what seems to be another instance of disregard for the sacrifices. In Leviticus 10:17, he asks, "Why have you not eaten the *reconciliation offering* in the place of the sanctuary, since it is a thing most holy and has been given to you that you may *bear the iniquity* of the congregation, to *make atonement* for them before the LORD?" (ESV, author's adaptation).

---

[14]The reconciliation offering consecrates the altar thus purifying or atoning for it. Likewise, in Lev 8:14-15, "He led forward the bull of reconciliation offering; and Aaron and his sons laid their hands upon the head of the bull of reconciliation offering, and it was slaughtered. Moses took the blood and with his finger put some on each of the horns of the altar, purifying the altar; then he poured out the blood at the base of the altar. Thus he consecrated it, to make atonement for it" (NRSV, author's adaptation; cf. 8:10-13). Similarly, see 2 Chron 30:15; Ezek 43:25-26.

[15]In contrast, Lev 10:10 indicates how priests should sanctify and glorify God, "You are to distinguish between the holy and the common, and between the unclean and the clean."

When does a reconciliation offering bring atonement? When people offer sacrifice in ways that honor God. Note the sequence. First, sacrifice is offered (Leviticus 10:3, 17). Accordingly, the sacrifice sanctifies or glorifies God. Finally, atonement is made before the Lord. Similar connections are made in Leviticus 9:6-7.

> And Moses said, "This is the thing that the LORD commanded you to do, so that the glory of the LORD may appear to you." Then Moses said to Aaron, "Draw near to the altar and sacrifice your reconciliation offering and your burnt offering, and make atonement for yourself and for the people; and sacrifice the offering of the people, and make atonement for them; as the LORD has commanded."

For God's glory to appear, sacrifice must be offered such that atonement is made for the priests and the people. This is precisely the result in Leviticus 9:23.[16]

This understanding of sacrifice is consistent with passages outside the Pentateuch. In 1 Samuel 6:2-5, the Philistines discuss what should be done with the ark of the Lord. The chiasm in 1 Samuel 6:4-5 is significant.

> 4a And they said, "What is *the reparation offering* that we shall return to him?"
>
> 4b They answered, "Five golden tumors and five golden mice, according to the number of the lords of the Philistines, for the same plague was upon all of you and upon your lords.
>
> 5a So you must make images of your tumors and images of your mice that ravage the land,
>
> 5b and *give glory to the God of Israel.*" (NRSV, author's adaptation)

1 Samuel 6:4a suggests they should return to the Lord a reparation offering. The repetitious reply in 1 Samuel 6:4b, 5a specifies how they should do this, that is, by making images of tumors and mice. Finally, 1 Samuel 6:5b completes the chiasm and so expresses the effect of the offering mentioned in 1 Samuel 6:4a, namely, giving glory to God. Though the method of the offering differs from that of the Levitical priests, the purpose is the same—honoring God such that the people are healed and his hand will not be against them (1 Samuel 6:3).

Further evidence is found in Israel's songs of worship. In 1 Chronicles 16:29, praise is given to God.[17]

---

[16]Cf. 2 Chron 7.
[17]Cf. Ps 96:8-9.

> Ascribe to the LORD the glory due his name;
>> bring an offering, and come before him!
> Worship the LORD in holy splendor.

The people worship God due to the glory or splendor of his holiness. By bringing God an offering, they honor him. Psalms makes clear that the natural function of offering a sacrifice is to give glory to God.[18]

The point is vividly demonstrated via contrast. In Malachi 1:6–2:3, Israel gives shameful offerings. The entire passage intertwines honor-shame and purity language. Most significant is Malachi 1:6-8,

> A son honors his father, and a servant his master. If then I am a father, where is my honor? And if I am a master, where is my fear?" says the LORD of hosts to you, O priests, who despise my name. But you say, "How have we despised your name?" By offering polluted food upon my altar. But you say, "How have we *polluted* [*g'l*] you?" By saying that the LORD's table may be despised. When you offer blind animals in sacrifice, is that not evil? (ESV)

How have the people dishonored God and despised his name? By offering shameful sacrifices and polluting the altar; thus, *they even pollute God.*[19] Notice how sacrifice works. How a person gives a sacrifice *represents* how one regards God. In short, offering polluted food is equivalent to polluting God![20]

First Samuel 2:29-30 confirms this interpretation. The Lord speaks to Eli,

> "Why then look *with greedy eye at my sacrifices and my offerings* that I commanded, and *honor your sons more than me* by fattening yourselves on the choicest parts of every offering of my people Israel?" Therefore the LORD the God of Israel declares: "I promised that your family and the family of your ancestor should go in and out before me forever"; but now the LORD declares: "Far be it from me; *for those who honor me I will honor, and those who despise me shall be treated with contempt.*"

In scorning the sacrifices and offerings, Eli honors his sons above the Lord. Yet, 1 Samuel 2:30 makes clear the intent of such sacrifices. Giving sacrifices ought to represent the honor that people give to God.

---

[18]Cf. Ps 50:23. The psalmist says, "The one who brings thanksgiving as their sacrifice honors me; to those who go the right way I will show the salvation of God!" The key part of the verse is the fact the writer chooses a sacrificial metaphor to express how a person honors God.

[19]Similar surprising language is found in Is 63:3, where the LORD says the blood of condemned sinners "stained all my robes."

[20]Also see Mal 1:11-12, 14.

The Lord's comments in Isaiah 43:23-24 succinctly restate the point. Isaiah writes, "You have not *brought me your sheep for burnt offerings, or honored me with your sacrifices.* / I have not burdened you with offerings, / or wearied you with frankincense. / You have not bought me sweet cane with money, / or satisfied me with the fat of your sacrifices." The purpose of the sacrifices is not merely assumed; it is explicitly stated. (NRSV, author's adaptation)

SACRIFICES REMOVE SHAME AND RESTORE HONOR

There is a second way that honor and shame help us understand the meaning of the sacrifices and the reason they bring atonement. Not only do sacrifices sanctify God as uniquely worthy of honor; they also sanctify the giver. In other words, sacrifices remove the sinner's shame and restore human honor.

When the priests rebuke King Uzziah for burning incense to the Lord, they state the implicit assumption of those who gave offerings in the sanctuary. In 2 Chronicles 26:18, "They withstood King Uzziah, and said to him, 'It is not for you, Uzziah, to make offering to the LORD, but for the priests the descendants of Aaron, who are consecrated to make offering. Go out of the sanctuary; for you have done wrong, and *it will bring you no honor from the LORD God.'*" Apparently, one should expect sacrifices to bring honor to the worshiper.

Inasmuch as sacrifices effect atonement, Ezekiel offers direct evidence that atoning sacrifices address the sinner's objective reason for shame: "I will establish my covenant with you, and you shall know that I am the LORD, that you may remember and *be confounded* [or *disgraced*] and never open your mouth again because of your *shame,* when I *atone* for you *for all that you have done* declares the Lord GOD" (Ezekiel 16:62-63 ESV). Their "shame" refers to "all that you have done." Accordingly, the Lord will atone for the shame of Ezekiel's listeners. Because God atones for sinful actions, he thus atones for shame.

Furthermore, sacrifices remove the shame due to ritual impurity. The basic logic of the Pentateuch is this:

1. Uncleanness can cause shame or exclusion.

2. Sacrifices solve uncleanness.

3. Therefore, sacrifices solve a shame problem.

Several passages illustrate the first point: uncleanness can be considered shameful.[21] Leviticus demonstrates the second premise: sacrifice solves the problem of uncleanness. In Leviticus 5, the one who becomes unclean for touching an animal carcass (even unknowingly) must make compensation via a reconciliation offering, which brings about atonement for sin (Leviticus 14:19-20).[22] In this way, sacrifices solve the problem of uncleanness.

A POSSIBLE OBJECTION

Perhaps someone will object by claiming we need to distinguish two kinds of sacrifice. One type is a gift. They glorify God. This is their function. In addition, we might speak of a second kind (like atoning sacrifices) as not being gifts. They are people's duty and therefore have a different function. They serve as compensation.

Biblically speaking, this is a false dichotomy. In Scripture, a sacrifice can be a gift *and* compensation. Therefore, what we call "sacrifice," Jesus calls a "gift." Matthew 8:3-4 says, "He stretched out his hand and touched him, saying, 'I do choose. Be made clean!' Immediately his leprosy was cleansed. Then Jesus said to him, 'See that you say nothing to anyone; but go, show yourself to the priest, and offer the gift that Moses commanded, as a testimony to them'" (alluding to Leviticus 14:2-32). In Scripture, even *obligatory* sacrifices can be regarded as gifts (which are ways of honoring the recipient). The gift or sacrifice mentioned in Leviticus 14 *atones for sin* and *cleanses impurity* (Leviticus 14:19-20). This is a person's duty. Yet, Jesus calls the obligatory sacrifice a "gift."

---

[21]While not all uncleanness is shameful, uncleanness opens a door for shame and exclusion; cf. Deut 23:13-14; Is 47:3; recall Lev 10. By not distinguishing "between the holy and common, and unclean and clean," Nadab and Abihu did not sanctify or glorify the LORD (10:3, 10). In Deut 23, "holy" linguistically contrasts "indecent," which translates *ʿrwt* as "nakedness" in English Bibles. Yet, throughout the Old Testament, uncovering someone's nakedness is regarded as exposing one's shame. The LXX makes this quite clear because the translators consistently translate the phrase by combining the verb *apokalyptō* (expose, reveal) with the noun *aschēmosynē* or *aischynē* (shame). Is 47:3 reinforces the point: "Your nakedness shall be uncovered, and your disgrace shall be seen." Conceptually, multiple passages highlight the shame that may come on someone who is unclean, such as the lepers of Lev 13-14, those with a discharge (Num 5:2), and one with a nocturnal emission (Deut 23:10). Because of uncleanness, they suffer the shame of exclusion from the community. For an introduction to the link between shame and impurity, see Werner Mischke, *The Global Gospel* (Scottsdale, AZ: Mission One, 2014), 127-44.

[22]Lev 14:19-20 indicates that a reconciliation offering and a burnt offering are needed to cleanse first the one who is unclean and then the priest who makes atonement for the one who was unclean.

Contextualization And Christian Practice

Contextualization begins with interpretation then extends to our explanation and application of Scripture. We've seen that honor is central to a biblical view of atonement. To contextualize the atonement for global cultures, we must underscore the ways that atonement brings us into the presence of a king who is worthy of unique honor. Sometimes, we will need to draw from cultural analogies to make our meaning clear. Among Chinese, I've often needed to explain the heart of the gospel; namely, Jesus is king. For many people, *emperor* sufficiently carried the meaning of "king." For others, I compared the gospel to the message "Jesus is Chairman" (*yesu zuo zhuxi*). In communist China, every listener immediately grasped the significance of that claim to authority.

Similarly, Jay Moon shares the meaning of an African proverb, "A human being hides in the feathers of a chicken." According to Kofi, a local pastor,

> "In the life of the Builsa people, chickens are used to hide shame from problems. If someone has money troubles, they sell some chickens at market and then use the money to solve the problem. If someone has sickness, infertility, drought, or famine, the traditional Builsa culture allows the sacrifice of chickens to the ancestors or earth shrines. Growing up, I knew that we were always protected from shame as long as we had chickens, because we could always hide inside their feathers. . . . They also help us initiate friendships," Kofi continued. "If I want to start a friendship with someone, then I offer them a chicken for use to share a meal together, or I give him a chicken to take home. Now that I am a *Kristobiik* [Christian], I feel that *Yezu* [Jesus] is the chicken that I hide under. When problems come, I can run to *Yezu* in prayer and ask him to cover my shame and protect me. He will bear the full impact of the problem that has come upon me, and I can safely rest in his feathers."[23]

The Bible speaks more of goats and bulls than chickens. Still, this account alerts us to ways that people in different cultures use metaphors to convey honor, hide shame, and build relationships. While symbols may vary across cultures, we will likely find similar underlying patterns of thinking. Furthermore, as we become aware of these cultural perspectives, we become more attuned to comparable concerns found in the Bible.

---

[23]Jay Moon, "Chicken Theology: Local Learning Approaches from West Africa," in *Challenging Tradition: Innovation in Advanced Theological Education*, ed. Perry Shaw and Havilah Dharamraj (Carlisle, UK: Langham Global Library, 2018), 384-85.

Finally, I will suggest a few practical applications. The first concerns missions. An honor-shame perspective could help people more easily grasp the meaning and significance of the sacrificial system and ultimately Christ's atonement. In cultures around the world, few things are more important to daily life than one's public reputation or "face."

The interpretation given in this chapter lays the groundwork for a robust and healthy contextualization. It affirms what is foundational without supposing that people must immediately understand the various theories and mechanics of atonement.

A second area of application concerns worship and character. The sacrificial system overturns conventional expectations of honor and shame. Through a sacrificial death, God is glorified, and shame is taken away. Accordingly, God's people are challenged to reevaluate what they regard as praiseworthy and pure, sacred and secular. Repentance, service, and humility become means of glorifying God and getting honor from the Creator King.

The ideas in this chapter also shape ethics. God brings reconciliation through sacrifice (figuratively, via animals; ultimately, in Christ). Thus, he gives us a model for understanding reconciliation and repentance. Each sacrifice requires the offender to admit their lowly condition and acknowledge God's honor. Godliness is not defined by rules or ceremony; rather it is oriented on God's glory. In short, Christ's followers are called to seek God's face by sacrificing their own.

Conclusion

In summary, the passages surveyed above confirm a relationship between honor, shame, and the sacrificial system. Specifically, the sacrificial system (e.g., the process of giving a reconciliation offering) aims to honor God such that he removes our shame by atoning for sin. Next, I'll conclude by briefly answering a question: How does this view of biblical sacrifice relate to other theories of atonement (especially penal substitution)?

One strength of this interpretation is that it draws from the entire biblical canon. As a result, it naturally integrates multiple metaphors used to describe atonement. For instance, we've already seen the seamless interrelationship between honor, holiness, and purity language.

Precisely because God's people are a kingdom of priests, their sacrifices simultaneously affirm their allegiance to the divine king with whom they are bound by covenant. In a sense, the sacrificial system typifies Christ's victory over sin and death in the same way that the sacrificed Passover lamb was God's means of judging the Egyptian gods (Exodus 12:12; Numbers 33:4; cf. Exodus 6:6; 7:4). Just as God won glory over Pharaoh, so Christ's sacrifice ensures that God's name is proclaimed in all the earth (Exodus 14:4, 17, 18).[24]

The proposal offered in this chapter highlights an area of agreement held by those who hold different theories of the atonement: the sacrifices prescribed in the Old Testament should glorify God. Even if people disagree at other points, interpreters can find common ground on the ultimate goal of the sacrificial system.

What about penal substitutionary atonement (PSA)? Someone who accepts PSA can affirm the main ideas of this chapter just as readily as someone who rejects PSA. The difference between those two people would simply be *how* they think Christ's sacrifice upholds God's honor. For example, John Piper, as advocate of PSA, says,

> Thus, if God is to be righteous, he must repair the dishonor done to his name by the sins of those whom he blesses. He must magnify the glory men thought to deny him. . . . In putting Christ forth as a propitiation, God acts for the sake of his glory, i.e., he actively demonstrates inviolable allegiance to the honor of his name . . . in order that he might remain and *be* righteous.[25]

Of course, other people might suppose that PSA amounts to something negative akin to a divine "honor killing." Therefore, they will separate God's honor from his wrath. Instead, they might prefer other positive formulations. For example, one could simply say that the act of sacrifice is a straightforward demonstration of repentance and allegiance. Or they might use more explicit language from the Old Testament, saying that sacrifices sanctify God, that is, set God apart as uniquely worthy of glory.

Finally, this chapter has explained the Bible's sacrificial system from an honor-shame perspective. The offerings function to restore God's honor, which is defamed by human sin. Because God accepts a sacrifice, his people will not be put to shame. This view is reinforced throughout the canon, including the New Testament. As a reconciliation offering, Christ bears our shame by giving to God the glory due his name.

---

[24]Also, see Ex 9:16; 1 Cor 15:28.
[25]John Piper, "The Demonstration of the Righteousness of God," *JSNT* 2, no. 7 (Jan 1980): 28, 31.

In the next section, we explore three fundamental "ingredients" that make up a biblical theology of atonement. These metaphors—purity, debt, and burden—are indispensable for understanding and explaining this doctrine. The following chapters trace how the Bible uses these metaphors to interpret the atoning work of Christ.

INTERPRETING

BIBLICAL METAPHORS

for ATONEMENT

6

WHAT DOES CHRIST PURIFY?

MORALITY HAS LONG BEEN connected with cleanness. Feeling dirty is linked with immorality. Such imagery is ingrained in our psychology and customs. The association is felt by both victims and perpetrators. After suffering an assault, victims often describe themselves as being "dirty." One victim goes further, saying, "Abuse is already in my blood."[1] Some with moral failings regard themselves as stained.

Even the prospect of wrongdoing elicits strong disgust. In 2018, allegations of sexual misconduct emerged against Bollywood director Vikas Bahl. Actor Imran Khan acknowledged that stories of Vikas's conduct had circulated for years. He added, "I cannot be silent about it anymore. My conscience will not allow me to. . . . I do not want them to feel that men in the industry are not standing by them. I have chosen my words and said what I intended to say. I have been silent for long enough and it makes me feel dirty."[2]

Associating with someone regarded as immoral can make us feel unclean. A 2017 rally in Charlottesville, Virginia, turned deadly after a neo-Nazi drove his car into the packed crowd. Afterwards, President Trump refused to condemn the white supremacist protesters. Trump's silence was too much for Leslie Wexner, CEO of L Brands and longtime donor to the Republican Party. In 2018, he announced, "I'm no longer a Republican." The reason? "The CEO recalled a time in the past year when he told his employees that he felt 'dirty' and 'ashamed'

---

[1] Athandile Siyo, "Abuse Is Already in My Blood, Says Teen Repeatedly Raped by Father," *Cape Times*, March 18, 2020, iol.co.za/capetimes/news/abuse-is-already-in-my-blood-says-teen-repeatedly -raped-by-father-45186856.

[2] "Imran Khan Says 3 Actresses Told Him About Vikas Bahl, Feels Dirty About Not Speaking Up Earlier," *Hindustan Times*, October 10, 2018, accessed April 22, 2020, www.hindustantimes.com /bollywood/imran-khan-says-3-actresses-told-him-about-vikas-bahl-feels-dirty-about-not-speaking -up-earlier/story-0yrKBBeJ9IjDClmWKeJIUJ.html.

when Trump found it hard to roundly condemn the white nationalist violence that occurred at a rally in Charlottesville, Virginia, last year."[3] The conscience often speaks in the language of purity and impurity.

What happens when we cannot *or* do not avoid immoral people and behaviors? We take matters into our own hands. For Lady Macbeth, obsessive washing could not scrub away her shame. Pontius Pilate thought a little wiping with water cleansed him from guilt in condemning Jesus.

The biblical writers likewise draw from a fount of images. Purification is a prominent metaphor used to describe atonement.[4] This imagery naturally fits with observations from the previous chapters concerning the basic worldview espoused by Israel's priests. Accordingly, the world is divided into categories like clean and unclean, holy and common. To make atonement, purification is required. For example, Leviticus 14:19-20 says, "The priest shall offer the reconciliation offering, to make atonement for the one to be cleansed from his uncleanness. Afterward he shall slaughter the burnt offering; and the priest shall offer the burnt offering and the grain offering on the altar. Thus the priest shall make atonement on his behalf and he shall be clean" (NRSV, author's adaptation).[5] This chapter examines several passages that speak of atonement in terms of purification. First, we look at the Day of Atonement (or Yom Kipper) in Leviticus 16, when the high priest makes atonement for the Holy Place. We then will turn to Hebrews 9–10 to consider how Christ purifies his people.

THE DAY OF ATONEMENT

In Leviticus 16, Israel collectively seeks to make atonement before God. They engage in a complex, multilayered ritual that scholars find difficult to interpret. We'll consider the live goat (the so-called scapegoat) in the next chapter. The vast number of details can overwhelm readers, so we must first identify the key offerings and sequence of events.

Leviticus 16 mentions five animals and four distinct offerings (see fig. 6.1 below). First, Aaron presents a bull as a reconciliation offering to make atonement

---

[3]Shmuley Boteach, "Should Jews Owe Gratitude to Trump?," *Jerusalem Post*, September 18, 2018, accessed April 22, 2020, www.jpost.com/opinion/should-jews-owe-gratitude-to-trump-567466.

[4]As will be seen, I disagree with Fleming Rutledge's claim that purification "plays little role in the New Testament," in *The Crucifixion: Understanding the Death of Jesus Christ* (Grand Rapids, MI: Eerdmans, 2015), 204.

[5]Cf. Lev 12:6-7; 16:30; Num 8:21.

for himself and his house (Leviticus 16:6, 11). Second, he atones for the congregation, sacrificing one of two goats as a reconciliation offering (Leviticus 16:15). In both cases, the blood of the bull and goat are applied to the Holy Place, tent of meeting, and the altar. The people's iniquities and transgressions are placed on the live goat, which is sent into the wilderness (Leviticus 16:21-22). No blood is shed, nor is it considered a reconciliation offering or burnt offering.[6] Finally, Aaron sacrifices the rams. He offers "his burnt offering and the burnt offering of the people and make[s] atonement for himself and for the people" (Leviticus 16:24 ESV). The fat of the reconciliation offerings is then burned at the altar. The rams' blood is thrown against the side of the altar (Leviticus 1:11; 8:18).

Figure 6.1. Sequence of offerings in Leviticus 16

Sequence of Offerings				
Leviticus		**for the benefit of**	**blood applied to**	**used to make atonement?**
Lev 16:6, 11	bull reconciliation offering	Aaron and his house	Holy Place, tent of meeting, altar	Yes
Lev 16:15	goat reconciliation offering	congregation		Yes
Lev 16:21-22	live goat (sent out)	congregation		
Lev 16:24	ram burnt offering	Aaron and his house	altar	Yes
	ram burnt offering	congregation	altar	Yes

After each bull, goat, and ram are slaughtered, the writer explicitly states that atonement is made. The direct objects receiving atonement include the Holy Place, tent of meeting, and the altar (Leviticus 16:33). However, atonement is made for the benefit of the congregation or Aaron and his house. Leviticus 16:10 is peculiar. It says, "The goat on which the lot fell for Azazel shall be presented alive before the LORD to make atonement over it, that it may be sent away into the wilderness to Azazel."[7] We'll consider this verse in the next chapter.

---

[6]Lev 16:5 seems to suggest that both goats together constitute one reconciliation offering. However, Lev 16:9 indicates that the killed goat is the reconciliation offering. In other words, in Lev 16:5, it is unknown which goat will become the reconciliation offering. From these two goats, one will be chosen. The contrast between the two goats is made explicit in Lev 16:9-10.

[7]The "it" in Lev 16:10 refers to the live goat. Although the NRSV says "over it," the Hebrew phrase consistently means "for" it, him, or her.

UNCLEANNESS AND TRANSGRESSIONS

After the high priest readies himself to serve in the sanctuary, we arrive at Leviticus 16:15-20.

> ### LEVITICUS 16:15-20
>
> He shall slaughter the goat of the reconciliation offering that is for the people and bring its blood inside the curtain, and do with its blood as he did with the blood of the bull, sprinkling it upon the mercy seat and before the mercy seat. Thus he shall make atonement for the sanctuary, *because of the uncleannesses* [*tumoth*] of the people of Israel, and *because of their transgressions* [*pesha*], all their sins; and so he shall do for the tent of meeting, which remains with them in the midst of their uncleannesses. No one shall be in the tent of meeting from the time he enters to make atonement in the sanctuary until he comes out and has made atonement for himself and for his house and for all the assembly of Israel. Then he shall go out to the altar that is before the LORD and make atonement on its behalf, and shall take some of the blood of the bull and of the blood of the goat, and put it on each of the horns of the altar. He shall sprinkle some of the blood on it with his finger seven times, and cleanse it and hallow it from the uncleannesses of the people of Israel. When he has finished atoning for the Holy Place and the tent of meeting and the altar, he shall present the live goat.

In chapter two, we saw that impurity and sin do not pollute the inner sanctuary itself. They do not infect the tabernacle per se. They connect to people, not sacred objects. It is the sinner who defiles what is sacred.

Why then is atonement made for the Holy Place? The writer seems to lump uncleanness and transgressions together under the phrase "all their sins" (Leviticus 16:16).[8] One can understand why transgressions are counted among their sins. The word *pesha* (transgression) routinely refers to deliberate rebellion. By contrast, a person can become unclean for any number of reasons, even childbirth. Also, "In Lev 11-15, *tumoth* 'impurities' always refers to people with bodily impurities and not moral faults."[9]

To complicate things, Leviticus 16:21 reiterates Leviticus 16:16, yet with a significant adjustment. Leviticus 16:21 says, "Then Aaron shall lay both his hands

---

[8] In Hebrew, *lĕkāl-ḥaṭṭō 'tām*.
[9] James Greenberg, *A New Look at the Atonement in Leviticus: The Meaning and Purpose of Kipper Revisited* (University Park: Penn State University Press, 2020), 158.

on the head of the live goat, and confess over it all the *iniquities* of the people of Israel, and all their transgressions, all their sins, putting them on the head of the goat, and sending it away into the wilderness by means of someone designated for the task." Instead of "uncleanness," the writer substitutes "iniquities" (*'āwōn*). The text appears to equate uncleanness with iniquities. While iniquity is described as impurity, uncleanness itself is rarely, if ever, called iniquity.

The equating of uncleanness and iniquity makes sense when we recall that ritual impurity alone does not provoke God's anger; rather, *the danger comes in not rectifying the problem.*[10] In the case of unintentional sin and impurity, *punishment results from rejecting God's remedy*. Thus, the uncleanness in Leviticus 9:16 is not general ritual impurity; it is uncleanness for which people have rejected God's sacrificial remedy.[11] This rejection is iniquity.

Both Leviticus and Numbers underscore the consequence for anyone who rejects God's remedy. In Numbers 19:20, the writer warns, "Any who are unclean but do not purify themselves, those persons shall be cut off from the assembly, for they have defiled the sanctuary of the LORD. Since the water for cleansing has not been dashed on them, they are unclean."[12] The stipulation that one be "cut off" or cast outside the camp certainly resonates with what follows in Leviticus 16. Once the priest confesses Israel's iniquities and transgressions over the live goat, he shall send "it away into the wilderness by means of someone designated for the task. The goat shall bear on itself all their iniquities to a barren region; and the goat shall be set free in the wilderness" (Leviticus 16:21-22).

CLEANSING ATONEMENT

This section considers several key questions. What happens over the course of the Day of Atonement ritual? Why do the offerings make atonement twice for both the people and Aaron? Also, how does Leviticus 16 use purity language to speak of atonement?

Sin and impurity are attached to the people, not the Holy Place. Atonement is needed to bring about their purification.[13] Thus, Leviticus 16:30 summarizes what results from the Day of Atonement: "For on this day shall atonement be made for you *to cleanse* [*ṭhr*] you; from all your sins you *shall be clean* [*ṭhr*] before the LORD."

---

[10]This was discussed in chap. 2.
[11]Cf. Greenberg, *New Look*, 160.
[12]Cf. Lev 7:20-22; 22:3; Num 19:13.
[13]Also see Lev 12:6-8; 14:18-22, 29-31; Num 8:21.

Our discussion in previous chapters equips us to interpret the process through which cleansing occurs. Leviticus 16:32-33 gives an overview of the entire day's ritual: "The priest who is anointed and consecrated as priest in his father's place shall make atonement, wearing the linen vestments, the holy vestments. He shall make atonement for the sanctuary, and he shall make atonement for the tent of meeting and for the altar, and he shall make atonement for the priests and for all the people of the assembly." First, Aaron presents the reconciliation offerings for himself and the people. No absorbing materials are mentioned. Based on our discussion in chapter three, the blood from the first offering binds the priest to the Holy Place and tent of meeting (Leviticus 16:11-14). The blood from the congregation's offering binds them to the Holy Place, tent of meeting, and the altar of the burnt offering (Leviticus 16:15-19).[14] Through the process of atonement, they are cleansed, no longer bound to the uncleanness and sin that obstruct fellowship with God.

Leviticus 16:19 is peculiar in several respects. It says, "And he shall sprinkle some of the blood on it with his finger seven times, and cleanse it and hallow it from the uncleannesses of the people of Israel." Most importantly, while making atonement for the altar, the priest uses blood both to *cleanse* (*ṭhr*) and *consecrate* (*qdš*) the altar. The altar along with the rest of the tabernacle are already consecrated (Exodus 29; Leviticus 8). If the altar needs to be *re*consecrated, why not the tent of meeting and the Holy Place?[15] Greenberg poses the question, "If the sacrificial altar has lost its holiness, why does YHWH continue to reside in the sanctuary?" Drawing from numerous observations in the passage, he concludes,

> Just as the *ḥaṭṭāʾt* [reconciliation offering] rituals in Lev 12-15 make the offerer clean before YHWH, *kipper* in step three makes the sacrificial altar clean before YHWH. YHWH removed from his presence the impurities of rebellious people, and now he connects to the altar. Thus, the altar has the status of clean before YHWH. A natural result of YHWH's connection to the altar is that it is made holy. . . . It is not that the altar was ever desanctified; however, the atmosphere of the people's rebellious acts caused the altar to be in a state of limbo. It had been holy before YHWH (compare Lev 8 / Exod 29) but at the same time not holy, because it was no longer connected to YHWH's presence.[16]

---

[14]For a typical reconciliation offering, the blood would not enter the most Holy Place, where the ark rests.

[15]This and other observations in this paragraph come from Greenberg, *New Look*, 169-71.

[16]Greenberg, *New Look*, 171. He also notes that verse does not mention the pouring out of blood at the altar's base (a typical part of the ritual; Lev 4:7); attention then focuses on the sprinkling of blood seven times. "It seems that a seven-times gesture, at least when performed in the sanctuary (thus

The altar's state of "limbo" reflects its unique position. Unlike the tent of meeting and the Holy Place, the outer altar interacts with common, nonpriestly worshipers.

In summary, Leviticus 16 demonstrates how atonement changes the relationship between worshipers and the tabernacle, the sacred space in which God dwells with his people. God's presence ensures the holiness of his habitation. Yet, his people become unclean and commit unintentional sin. Through atonement, impurities are removed that threaten to break fellowship between God and the people.

On the Day of Atonement, the priest offers reconciliation offerings first for himself, then for the congregation. After symbolically removing iniquity from the camp (via the live goat), the priest offers two burnt offerings, one for himself and the other for the assembly. In this process, the priest binds himself to the Lord; whatever encumbers relationship to God is removed. The priest, as God's holy representative, mediates on behalf of the congregation. In so doing, God reaffirms a positive, connected relationship with his people.

SAME SYMBOLS, DIFFERENT STORIES

At this point, we do well to heed a warning in Matthew Bennett's pioneering work *Narratives in Conflict.* Too much that goes by the name *contextualization* is superficial. In Islam, for example, purification is an important concept. Christians might be tempted to equate purification in Islam with the idea expressed in biblical atonement. Yet, according to Bennett, "Arabic speaking Christians and Muslims use shared language to describe divergent concepts."[17] Furthermore, Islam teaches that purification is not part of the process of atonement, which comes directly from God.[18] He makes a more salient observation when he compares the symbolism within Islam and biblical Christianity: "For the missiologist seeking to communicate the Christian perspective of atonement, however, it is vitally important to consider how Islam's treatment of the concept of atonement does not merely exchange one ritual for another, but rather, using shared vocabulary and history, tells a different story based upon a different worldview."[19]

---

excluding the bird rituals in 14:7, 51), is a gesture to interact with YHWH in some way, either directly or indirectly, to create a positive relationship with him" (17n70).

[17]Matthew A. Bennett, *Narratives in Conflict: Atonement in Hebrews and the Qur'an* (Eugene, OR: Pickwick, 2019), 120.

[18]Bennett, *Narratives in Conflict*, 122-23.

[19]Bennett, *Narratives in Conflict*, 119.

How so? One example comes from Islam's disregard for certain elements in the Hebrew Bible. Islam replaces Judaism's focus on the Day of Atonement, giving greater attention to Ramadan and the annual celebration of *'id al-Adha,* which commemorates Abraham's offering of Isaac (Genesis 22). According to Bennett, blood, sin, and atonement have no inherent relationship within a Muslim worldview. In short, he argues, "The qur'anic worldview diverges substantially from the biblical worldview, and that the concept of atonement is a central point at which this divergence might be recognized."[20]

Still, some aspects within Islam create space for communicating a biblical view of atonement. For instance, "sacrificing an animal is seen in the Qur'an as an outward symbol of gratitude, trust, and worship of God. Further, it is a symbol that is given to each people in order that they might both worship and demonstrate their faithful allegiance to God."[21] On this narrow but critical point, Muslims understand a vital part of the Bible's underlying logic of atonement.

Bennett concludes, "Therefore, when attempting to communicate a complex concept such as biblical atonement, one must first orient the audience to the larger narrative in which doctrines of atonement, sacrificial rituals, blood, and ultimately Christ's cross and resurrection exist in order to avoid importing qur'anic, and thereby divergent, understanding of component parts."[22] Hebrews picks up on the Bible's narrative trajectory. To appreciate the tapestry of atonement presented in Scripture, we need to understand how biblical metaphors weave together.

The Context in Hebrews 9–10

The first summer at the United States Military Academy at West Point is known as "Beast Barracks." Cadets endure a litany of stressors, both physical and psychological. Arguably, it's designed to "strip you of your personality." At least that's what my wife tells me. We met when I transferred from West Point after my freshman year.

Prior to my first room inspection, my roommates and I were nervous. The upperclassman would certainly do their best to find some item out of place. But

---

[20]Bennett, *Narratives in Conflict,* 7.
[21]Bennett, *Narratives in Conflict,* 138.
[22]Bennett, *Narratives in Conflict,* 175–76.

we were hopeful that we'd overcome the odds and our efforts wouldn't be futile. We had heard a story from the Air Force Academy where cadets unscrewed a light switch cover to expose lingering dust. Our leaders did not fail in their mission. After several minutes of perfunctory criticism, one cadre opened our window. He dragged his index finger across the stone ledge before exploding in a tirade of indignation. "How did you not clean all that dirt outside?!" he screamed in exasperation.

A reader of the Old Testament could easily get the impression that ancient Israel felt a similar sense of despair when hearing God's laws. In truth, the saying "Cleanliness is next to godliness" is not an actual verse in the Bible. So, one can hardly be blamed in thinking that ancient purification rituals are archaic and antithetical to Christianity. Turning to Hebrews, however, we find that the author does not dismiss such language; rather, he reappropriates it.

How does the writer use purity language and expand our understanding of atonement? How does the Day of Atonement shape the ideas in Hebrews 9–10? The density of thought in Hebrews is profound. The difficulty of interpreting this book can be intimidating. The following survey explores how the writer of Hebrews interprets Jesus' sacrifice, especially in view of purification. It raises several questions that are answered in later chapters.

First, where are the most obvious links to atonement, such as purification, the reconciliation offering, and the Day of Atonement? In the opening paragraph, Hebrews says, "When he had made purification for sins, he sat down at the right hand of the Majesty on high" (Hebrews 1:3). The most explicit references to cleansing are packed into Hebrews 9–10 (Hebrews 9:13, 14, 22, 23; 10:2, 22). While scholars debate possible allusions to the Day of Atonement, no one contests whether the Day of Atonement shapes texts like Hebrews 9:1-14, 23-28; 10:11-14.

What undergoes purification? Several answers are given, such as "defiled" persons, "the flesh" as well as "the scroll itself and all the people" (Hebrews 9:13, 19). The heart or conscience of worshipers is cleansed in Hebrews 9:14; 10:2, 22. Not only "the tent and all the vessels used in worship," but the "heavenly things" are purified (Hebrews 9:21, 23). With what are these things purified? Blood. In fact, "almost everything is purified with blood" (Hebrews 9:22).

What about the reconciliation offering? People generally recognize the reference in Hebrews 10:6, 8, which draw from the writer's quotation of Psalm 40:6-8.

HEBREWS 10:3-10

But in these sacrifices there is a reminder of sin year after year. For it is impossible for the blood of bulls and goats to take away sins. Consequently, when Christ came into the world, he said,

"Sacrifices [*thysia*] and offerings [*prosphora*] you have not desired,/but a body have you prepared for me;/in burnt offerings and *reconciliation offerings* [*peri hamartias*]/you have taken no pleasure. Then I said, 'See, I have come to do your will, O God/(in the scroll of the book it is written of me).'"

When he said above, "You have neither desired nor taken pleasure in sacrifices and offerings and burnt offerings and *reconciliation offerings* [*peri hamartias*]" (these are offered according to the law), then he added, "See, I have come to do your will." He abolishes the first in order to establish the second. And it is by God's will that we have been sanctified through the offering of the body of Jesus Christ once for all. (NRSV, author's adaptation)

In the Greek Old Testament (LXX), the standard phrase indicating the reconciliation offering is *peri hamartias*. In fact, one is hard pressed to find unambiguous examples in the LXX where *peri hamartias* does *not* refer to the reconciliation offering. So, it is all the more peculiar that translations render the same expression differently just a few sentences later. For example,

Where there is forgiveness of these, there is no longer any *offering for sin* [*prosphora peri hamartias*]. (Hebrews 10:18)[23]

For if we willfully persist in sin after having received the knowledge of the truth, there no longer remains a *sacrifice for sins* [*peri hamartias . . . thysia*]. (Hebrews 10:26)

For the bodies of those animals whose blood is brought into the sanctuary by the high priest as a *sacrifice for sin* [*peri hamartias*] are burned outside the camp. (Hebrews 13:11)

Is it grammatically possible these verses don't refer to the reconciliation offering? Yes, but it's not likely, especially since the writer draws from the precise wording in Psalm 40. It is inconceivable to me that Hebrews 13:11 doesn't mention the reconciliation offering.[24]

---

[23]Lev 16:9 says, "*prosoisei peri hamartias*," clearly referencing the reconciliation offering.

[24]Translations of Heb 5:3 also obscure the allusion to the reconciliation offering. The NRSV states, "Because of this he must offer sacrifice for his own sins as well as for those of the people." In

Hebrews 9 opens by surveying various stipulations concerning the work of a high priest in the Holy Place. Building on Hebrews 8, the writer identifies limitations or inadequacies with the arrangement set up by the covenant. Hebrews 9:11-14 highlights the supremacy of Christ over the high priests of ancient Israel. This leads to Hebrews 9:15-22, a central text for our study.

Key to interpreting the passage is identifying the *emphasis* in each section (not merely true theological statements). A few observations are noteworthy. Hebrews 9:15 explains how a new covenant becomes possible: a death occurs. As a result, people are redeemed from the transgressions under the first covenant. The purpose of Hebrews 9:16-17 is to explain why a death is necessary.[25]

> **HEBREWS 9:11-12, 15-23**
>
> Christ . . . entered once for all into the Holy Place, not with the blood of goats and calves, but with his own blood, thus obtaining eternal redemption.
>
> For *this reason* he is the mediator of a new covenant, so that those who are called may receive the promised eternal inheritance, *because* a death has occurred that redeems them from the transgressions committed under the first covenant. [For] where a will is involved, the death of the one who made it must be established. (For a will takes effect only at death, since it is not in force as long as the one who made it is alive.)
>
> *Hence* not even the first covenant was inaugurated without blood. For when every commandment had been told to all the people by Moses in accordance with the law, he took the blood of calves and goats, with water and scarlet wool and hyssop, and sprinkled both the scroll itself and all the people, saying, "This is the blood of the covenant that God has ordained for you." And in the same way he sprinkled with the blood both the tent and all the vessels used in worship. Indeed, under the law almost everything is purified with blood, and without the shedding of blood there is no forgiveness of sins. Thus it was necessary for the sketches of the heavenly things to be *purified with these rites*, but the heavenly things themselves need better sacrifices than these.

Greek: *kai di' autēn opheilei, kathōs peri tou laou, houtōs kai peri hautou prospherein peri hamartiōn.* However, the phrase *peri hautou* (his own or concerning himself) is clearly distinguished from the standard *peri hamartiōn* (i.e., reconciliation offering). An approximate translation of Heb 5:3 is, "Because of this he is obligated to offer the reconciliation offering for himself just as for the people." The verse could allude to the standard offering or that given on the Day of Atonement (Lev 4:3-12; 16:6, 11; cf. Heb 9:7).

[25]Scott Hahn, "Broken Covenant Curse and the Curse of Death: A Study of Hebrews 9:15-22," *CBQ* 66, no. 3 (July 2004): 431.

LEVITICUS 17 IN HEBREWS 9:22

Having mentioned the reconciliation offering, we now pause to apply insights from chapter four. How might the reference to atonement in Leviticus 17:11 affect our understanding of Hebrews 9:22? We saw two ways that atonement in the Old Testament changes the state of an object or person. Atonement effects the transition

- from unclean to clean
- from clean to holy

How does the writer of Hebrews interpret Leviticus? He seems to have the latter transition in view: atonement in Leviticus 17:11 moves one from being clean to holy.[26] A basic transition in Hebrews 8–10 is from people being unclean transgressors to becoming holy.[27]

God's people attain redemption and freedom through blood (Hebrews 9:12, 22). Yet, the surrounding context seems also to call this a process of purification, even sanctification. The latter is even more plausible in view of Hebrews 13:11-12, "For the bodies of those animals whose blood is brought into the sanctuary by the high priest as *a reconciliation offering* [*peri hamartias*] are burned outside the camp. Therefore Jesus also suffered outside the city gate *in order to sanctify* [*hina hagiasē*] the people by his own blood."[28] The blood of Jesus, who is the final reconciliation offering (Hebrews 10), sanctifies his people. When atonement brings about holiness, not mere purification, it requires bloodshed, such as with a reconciliation offering. In other words, blood is necessary whenever atonement brings about sanctification or consecration.[29] In the Old Testament, the firstborn of Israel are both consecrated *and* redeemed through sacrifice (Exodus 13:1, 13, 15; cf. Numbers 18:15-17). The dual act of consecration and redemption is akin to Exodus 11:7, where the blood of the Passover distinguishes Israel from the Egyptians.

---

[26]In this case, there is no need to form a sharp dichotomy since cleansing preceded sanctification when atonement was made for the priests, the Levites, and the tabernacle. The point here is that the writer seems to have holiness in view, not merely cleansing.

[27]Cf. Heb 9:13, 14, 22, 23; 10:2, 10, 14, 29.

[28]See Heb 9:13-14; 10:10, 14, 29.

[29]For example, Ex 29; Lev 8. Recall that deeming something "holy" can be relative to its context. In the Pentateuch, Israel was holy respective to Egypt. Yet, within Israel, only priests and Levites were considered holy. Nonpriestly Israelites were merely common. When atonement concerned insiders, (i.e., unclean Israelites merely becoming clean Israelites), atonement does not necessarily involve consecration.

COVENANT OR WILL

Most translations of the Bible inexplicably use different English words to explain *diathēkē*. Scholars typically translate this word as "will" in Hebrews 9:16-17. However, Hebrews 9:15, 18 clearly talk about a "covenant" (another translation for *diathēkē*).

This inconsistency is awkward. Since Hebrews 9:16-17 explains Hebrews 9:15, the sequence of thought indicates that *diathēkē* refers to the same concept. It should have the same translation. The writer has not changed the topic. In the New Testament, the original word *diathēkē* appears thirty-three times. Of these, seventeen instances are in Hebrews. In Hebrews 7–10, *diathēkē* appears fifteen times. Hebrews 9 uses *diathēkē* seven times. We have no reason to switch terms to translate this key word. Other clues suggest the writer does not talk about a will.[30] The use of "transgressions" (Hebrews 9:15) makes sense in a covenant context. Transgressions and will are unrelated.

Why then do translators use "will"? Interpreters struggle to understand why someone must die before a covenant is put in effect (Hebrews 9:16-17). Another observation offers a clue. Violating the first covenant leads to death. Hebrews 9:15 seems to imply this consequence as do other texts in the book. Hebrews 3:17 says, "And with whom was he provoked for forty years? Was it not with those who sinned, whose bodies fell in the wilderness?"[31] Also, Hebrews 10:28 adds, "Anyone who has set aside the law of Moses dies without mercy on the evidence of two or three witnesses."[32]

We infer a subtle implication from Hebrews 9:16, which says, "*For where a covenant is involved* [*hopou gar diathēkē*], *the death of the one who made it must be established.*" The opening phrase indicates a cause-effect relationship.[33] The front part of the sentence is a condition; the last part contains the necessary result. Without the latter, no covenant remains in effect.

Hebrews 9:17 explains Hebrews 9:16. Israel committed transgressions under the first covenant (Hebrews 9:15). According to Hebrews 9:16, this circum-stance triggers the covenant's conditions to go into effect. As Scott Hahn puts

---

[30]In Heb 9:16-17, *bebaios* and *ischyō* do not have the meaning of "executed" as in Hellenistic or Roman usage. Rather, it conveys "to be valid" or be "ratified." One writer says the testament or will translation is "impossible." Hahn, "Broken Covenant Curse," 417-18; citing John Hughes, "Hebrews IX 15ff. and Galatians III 15ff: A Study in Covenant Practice and Procedure," *Novum Testamentum* 21 (1979): 60-62.

[31]Cf. "wrath" in Heb 3:11.

[32]Cf. 3:11; perhaps Heb 2:15-18.

[33]Cf. "*hopou*" BDAG, i.e., "whenever there is," as in, "since" or "given that"; cf. 1 Cor 3:3; Heb 10:18; Jas 3:16.

it, "A covenant—or any law, for that matter—is not in force if it is not enforced."[34]
If breaking the covenant has no effect, that covenant is not in effect. In essence,
a key idea in Hebrews 9:16-17 is this: unless someone has died, no one has enforced the covenant.

Hebrews 9:18-21 suggests the logic of Hebrews 9:16-17 stems from the Old
Testament. (Hebrews 9:18 begins with "therefore.") Indeed, several passages
provide relevant covenant symbolism. First, consider the significance of
Genesis 15:8-18 and Jeremiah 34:17-20. In Genesis 15, the Lord confirms his
covenant with Abraham with an ancient ritual known as a self-maledictory
oath. The Lord passes through the dead animal parts. The act testifies to the
consequence should one forsake the covenant. In effect, the party says, "If I
break this covenant, I'll become like these animals." The meaning of the ritual
is plain in Jeremiah 34:17-20. Those who transgress their covenant with God
will become "like the calf when they cut in two and passed between its parts."
Thus, the people suffer death at the hands of their enemies.

JEREMIAH 34:17-20

Therefore, thus says the Lord: You have not obeyed me by granting a release
to your neighbors and friends; I am going to grant a release to you, says the
Lord—a release to the sword, to pestilence, and to famine. I will make you a
horror to all the kingdoms of the earth. *And those who transgressed my
covenant and did not keep the terms of the covenant that they made before me,
I will make like the calf when they cut it in two and passed between its parts*: the
officials of Judah, the officials of Jerusalem, the eunuchs, the priests, and all
the people of the land who passed between the parts of the calf shall be
handed over to their enemies and to those who seek their lives. Their corpses
shall become food for the birds of the air and the wild animals of the earth.

Likewise, in Ezekiel 17:13-19, a covenant is clearly established between the
Lord and the king. Yet, the king spurns his oath and thus will not escape the
consequence. He will die because he broke covenant with the Lord.

In summary, breaking covenant with God leads to death. The ritual that
initiated the covenant set the conditions of that covenant. The one who breaks
it must die. From this Old Testament perspective, Hebrews 9:18 makes sense. It
says, "Not even the first covenant was inaugurated without blood." The Old

---

[34]Hahn, "Broken Covenant Curse," 434.

Testament blood ceremony that inaugurates Israel's covenant with God effectively acts as a self-maledictory oath.[35]

INAUGURATING A BETTER COVENANT

Bruce Thomas shares the following story:

> One day our helper told us that when she was a little girl she had a friend who used to feel her mother's hair in the morning to see if it was damp. Her friend did this so that she could tell if her mother, who was divorced, had been messing around. According to Islam, you are unclean after you have had sex and must take a complete bath, to include washing your hair, in order to be clean again.
>
> When asked why her friend's mother would bother to take the bath if she was already committing adultery, our helper responded that no one would dare think of not taking the ritual bath after having had sex. Such a person would be a curse and the ground they walked on would be cursed. In other words, a prolonged state of ritual uncleanness following sexual intercourse was more unthinkable than adultery.[36]

Many people are primarily concerned with outward or ritual purity. Yet, Christ's atoning work goes much deeper.

In Hebrews, Jesus' death has "both retrospective and prospective effects."[37] Besides dealing with the law's punitive sanctions, Christ secures the new covenant's promised salvation. Hebrews 8 contains a lengthy citation of Jeremiah 31:31-34, which foretells of a better covenant. Hebrews 9–10 emphasize two parts of Jeremiah 31 that stand in contrast to the first covenant.[38]

First, the writer highlights a glaring weakness of the old covenant: "Gifts and sacrifices are offered that cannot perfect the *conscience* [*syneidēsis*] of the worshiper" (Hebrews 9:9). Hebrews 10:1-2 expands on this idea. It says,

> Since the law has only a shadow of the good things to come and not the true form of these realities, it can never, by the same sacrifices that are continually offered

---

[35]In agreement, R. B. Jamieson, "Not Without Blood: Jesus' Death and Heavenly Offering in Hebrews" (PhD diss., Selwyn College, 2017), 123. Also, see Hahn, "Broken Covenant Curse," 434-35; Gareth Lee Crockerill, *The Epistle to the Hebrews*, NICNT (Grand Rapids, MI: Eerdmans, 2012), 407. Heb 9:19-21 recalls Israel's making covenant with God. In fact, Heb 9:20 explicitly quotes Ex 24:8, where Israel establishes covenant with God at Mount Sinai.

[36]Bruce Thomas, "The Gospel for Shame Cultures," *EMQ* 30, no. 3 (July 1994): 284.

[37]Jamieson, "Not Without Blood," 115.

[38]This chapter only addresses the first part of the Jeremiah quotation. The next chapter will look at the second promise from Jer 31:34, quoted in Heb 8:12; 10:17.

year after year, make perfect those who approach. Otherwise, would they not have ceased being offered, since the worshipers, cleansed once for all, would no longer have any *conscience [syneidēsis]* for sins?[39]

In light of the new covenant, Hebrews 9:14 proclaims, "How much more will the blood of Christ . . . purify our *conscience* from dead works to worship the living God." Therefore, "let us draw near with a true heart in full assurance of faith, with our hearts sprinkled clean from an evil *conscience*" (Hebrews 10:22).

Conscience refers the heart's capacity to discern good from evil.[40] The heart is a reccurring theme in Hebrews. The writer warns against a hardened heart that goes astray from the Lord (Hebrews 3:8, 10, 12, 15; 4:7). Recall that "the word of God is living and active . . . able to judge the thoughts and intentions of the heart" (Hebrews 4:12).

The writer's emphasis is unmistakable. Hebrews 8:10, 10:16 repeat the promise from Jeremiah 31:33, where the Lord says, "This is the covenant that I will make with the house of Israel after those days, says the LORD: I will put my law within them, and I will write it on their hearts." When Christ "purifies our conscience," he cleanses our hearts (Hebrews 10:22). In effect, this is the fulfillment of the new covenant promise foretold in Jeremiah.

Why is this so important? This new heart brings a transformation of identity. For some people, they need to know that impurity does not fundamentally determine their identity. Consider the remarks of Joshua Harris, whose book *I Kissed Dating Goodbye* reinforced a "purity culture" among churches in the 1990s. He says,

> There are all kinds of categories of sin where we sin and we don't change our status, like you know, if you lie, you don't say, "Oh well, I'm no longer, you know, a lying virgin or something. . . ." [laughter] We just don't think that way. We just say, "You know what? I sinned. I want to repent of that. I want to move forward."

> But with this issue, it's like, if you have sex, you're no longer a virgin, you know, *it's like your status has somehow changed.* And I think that's an emphasis on one particular sin out of the millions of ways that we can sin that I think is actually not healthy. It makes the focus not so much "Who am I in relationship to God, who loves and relates to sinners and shows grace to sinners." *It becomes this "Do I have this badge and this identity of being a virgin?"*

---

[39]The NRSV uses "any consciousness of sins" rather than "a conscience for sins" in Heb 10:2, despite *syneidēsis* having a consistent meaning throughout the surrounding context; cf. Heb 9:14; 10:22.
[40]See "*syneidēsis*," BDAG.

And if I don't have that, then I feel like I've lost something and *I'm no longer as valuable*. . . . I think that led a lot of us astray.[41]

In effect, purity culture conveyed the idea that one particular sin—sex outside of marriage—led one to perpetually being stained. This link between one sin and an altered identity led to decades of turmoil for many who have struggled to untangle sex and shame.

Finally, Richard Beck notes a practical implication of framing the atonement in terms of impurity. He says, "Some sins are unique loci of shame as they are almost universally regulated by purity metaphors."[42] This point is significant as we think about how the atonement alleviates shame. He explains,

> Most sin categories are structured by metaphors that entail rehabilitation. But purity metaphors have no such entailments. Recall that contamination judgments are governed by the attribution of permanence. Once a foodstuff is judged to be polluted or contaminated nothing can be done to rehabilitate the situation. The fly in the soup ruins it. Consequently, when sins are structured by purity metaphors there is no obvious route to repentance. The metaphor only entails permanent defilement and ruin.[43]

An advantage of purity metaphors is that they "erect strong emotional and behavioral taboos that can be harnessed by moral communities"; however, they also "trigger disgust."[44] These observations underscore the value of purity metaphors when speaking to a variety of sins that make one feel permanently stained. Accordingly, contextualizing the atonement via purity language can help to solve a seemingly intractable problem. In short, "All *sins* might be equal, but all *metaphors* are not."[45]

CONCLUSION

It is the richness of Hebrews 9–10 that makes interpreting it so difficult. In appendix D, I explain in more detail how the writer weaves several key metaphors to develop his argument. The writer embeds a theology of atonement within

---

[41]From the documentary "I Survived I Kissed Dating Goodbye," August 30, 2019, youtu.be /ybYTkkQJw_M.

[42]Richard Beck, *Unclean: Meditations on Purity, Hospitality, and Mortality* (Eugene, OR: Cascade, 2011), 48.

[43]Beck, *Unclean*, 49.

[44]Beck, *Unclean*, 49.

[45]Beck, *Unclean*, 50.

layers of Old Testament allusions. Furthermore, the text portrays Christ as both high priest and sacrifice. His death has multiple functions somewhat analogous to the sacrifices offered under the Mosaic law. The reconciliation offering of ancient Israel purified the sanctuary. The first covenant was inaugurated through sacrifice. The inauguration rite was both a self-maledictory ritual and a consecration ceremony. Similarly, Christ purifies the conscience of his people. He inaugurates the new covenant, takes away sin, and sanctifies his people (Hebrews 9:13; 10:10, 14). At the same time, his death redeems people from under the first covenant.

7

WHO BEARS THE BURDEN OF SIN?

BIBLICAL WRITERS DEPICT SIN AS A BURDEN TO BE BORNE. This imagery is familiar to anyone who reads the Bible. Books like Leviticus and Numbers have a common refrain—"He shall bear his iniquity"—applied to those who disobey the Lord. Echoing Isaiah, 1 Peter 2:24 says of Christ, "He himself bore our sins in his body on the tree, that we might die to sin and live to righteousness." Texts that concern atonement commonly use this burden metaphor. This chapter considers what it means to "bear sin."[1]

SIN-BEARING ATONEMENT

What is the connection between atonement and sin-bearing? In a word, offerings or sacrifices that make atonement are frequently said to bear sin or iniquity. Speaking to Aaron's sons in Leviticus 10:17, Moses asks, "Why have you not eaten the reconciliation offering in the place of the sanctuary, since it is a thing most holy and has been given to you that you *may bear* [*nāśāʾ*] the iniquity of the congregation, *to make atonement* for them before the LORD?" (ESV, author's adaptation).

Similarly, in Exodus 32:30-32, the correlation between making atonement and bearing sin is direct, although most translations mask the Hebrew metaphor. The text says,

---

[1]For simplicity, I interchange phrases like bear sin, bear guilt, or bear iniquity.

On the next day Moses said to the people, "You have sinned a great sin. But now
I will go up to the LORD; perhaps I can *make atonement* for your sin." So Moses
returned to the LORD and said, "Alas, this people has sinned a great sin; they have
made for themselves gods of gold. But now, if you will only *forgive* [*nāśā'*] their
sin—but if not, blot me out of the book that you have written."

In Exodus 32:32, Moses literally petitions the Lord to "*bear* their sin." Why do
translators use "forgive"? As we'll see, bearing sin (or iniquity) is a common
expression that can have opposite connotations in the Bible. It routinely
conveys the notion of saving people from sin. For now, the above examples are
sufficient to show that making atonement can be portrayed as bearing sin.

WHAT DOES IT MEAN TO "BEAR SIN"?

Interpreters typically assume that bearing sin essentially means "to endure
punishment" for one's sin. However, this is not necessarily true. In fact, in
Leviticus 5:17-18, a man bears his own sin but does not receive punishment.
It says,

> If anyone sins, doing any of the things that by the LORD's commandments ought
> not to be done, though he did not know it, then realizes his guilt, he *shall bear*
> [*nāśā'*] *his iniquity*. He shall bring to the priest a ram without blemish out of the
> flock, or its equivalent for a reparation offering, and the priest *shall make*
> *atonement* [*kpr*] for him for the mistake that he made unintentionally, and *he*
> *shall be forgiven* [*sĕlaḥ*]. (ESV)

Many readers understand "bearing his iniquity" to indicate the man will be
punished. By this logic, a person who is forgiven does not "bear his sin." Yet,
the man in this passage both bears his sin *and* is forgiven.

Leviticus 5:18 clarifies the way this person bears his iniquity. The phrase
suggests that he bears responsibility for sin. It does not necessarily imply his
being punished. It can indicate his dealing with the problem. "Taking responsibility for sin" is a general gloss that helps to elucidate the meaning of this
important phrase. In specific contexts, however, this broad sense conveys two
seemingly contradictory meanings.

On the one hand, this phraseology could imply "suffering punishment." On
the other hand, it can mean "to forgive sin." For example, Exodus 28 suggests
the idea of bearing punishment. Exodus 28:43 says, "They shall be on Aaron
and on his sons when they go into the tent of meeting or when they come near

the altar to minister in the Holy Place, lest they *bear* [*nāśā'*] guilt and die. This shall be a statute forever for him and for his offspring after him" (ESV).

By contrast, in Exodus 34:6-7, God proclaims, "The LORD, the LORD, a God merciful and gracious, slow to anger, and abounding in steadfast love and faithfulness, keeping steadfast love for thousands, *forgiving* [*nāśā'*] iniquity and transgression and sin, but who will by no means clear the guilty" (ESV). In Hebrew, "forgiving iniquity" more literally is "bearing iniquity" in Exodus 34:7 (cf. Numbers 14:19; Job 7:21). Also, Saul says to Samuel, "Now therefore, please *pardon* [*nāśā'*] my sin and return with me that I may bow before the LORD" (1 Samuel 15:25 ESV; cf. Genesis 50:17).

Throughout the Bible, this same phrasing has directly opposite meanings in different passages.[2] How is this possible? The solution "is as brilliant as it is ordinary."[3] We must keep in mind this key verb *nāśā'*, translated "bearing" above, employs metaphorical language. Metaphors draw meaning from one sphere of life and map it onto another domain. They routinely appeal to concrete objects or situations in order to help make sense of abstract ideas.

From one perspective, a person may bear or carry a burden, weight, or obligation. In this case, such a burden can be painful. In another situation, to say someone "bears" a burden could underscore a new circumstance. In that case, a second party assumes the first person's load, thus relieving or rescuing the latter from the wearisome affliction.[4] Both perspectives are not only legitimate ways of using the same metaphor; they are pervasive throughout the Bible. Each usage has a different emphasis.

This verb *nāśā'* appears over 600 times throughout the Old Testament. Its most basic meaning is "to lift, raise, bear, or carry."[5] Recounting God's guiding Israel through the wilderness, Deuteronomy 1:31 says, "You have seen how the LORD your God *carried* you, as a man *carries* his son, all the way that you went until you came to this place" (ESV). Likewise, the Lord commands Joshua, "Command the priests *bearing* the ark of the testimony to come up out of the Jordan" (Joshua 4:15-16 ESV).

---

[2]See appendix C for an extensive list of examples categorized by meaning.
[3]Gary Anderson, *Sin: A History* (New Haven, CT: Yale University Press, 2009), 18. He draws from Baruch Schwartz, "The Bearing of Sin in Priestly Literature," in *Pomegranates and Golden Bells*, ed. D. Wright, D. N. Freedman, and A. Hurwitz (Winona Lake, IN: Eisenbrauns, 1995), 3-21.
[4]Anderson's emphasis is slightly different from mine. He contrasts the act of bearing a burden (case 1) in contrast to assuming the burden (case 2). I focus more on what results—suffering the burden oneself (case 1) versus removing another's burden (case 2).
[5]See Gen 27:3; Ex 37:5; Is 40:11. See "*nsa*," HALOT.

DISCERNING THE DIFFERENCE

How do we distinguish texts—where bearing sin entails punishment—from passages that connote salvation or forgiveness? In the Bible, we see a consistent pattern that should govern our interpretation of the metaphor. Whenever someone bears their own sin, iniquity, transgression, guilt, shame, and so on, the connotation is typically punitive. The verbiage implies that people will suffer some pain or punishment due to their sin.

However, whenever the Bible introduces an innocent second party, who bears a burden on behalf of a guilty person, the emphasis changes entirely. The language carries a positive connotation. It concerns salvation, that the guilty person is relieved from the burden. Furthermore, there is *no unambiguous example* where bearing language indicates that the innocent second party is *punished in place of or instead of* the offender. This is a point that we mustn't ignore.

Of course, some people will object to this claim, citing the suffering servant in Isaiah 53 or texts like 1 Peter 2:24. "Don't these texts suggest that Christ was punished in our place instead of us?" they ask. And what about reconciliation offerings and other sacrifices? In response, we must be careful not to beg the question. We must not yet assume or assert what the New Testament means when it says Christ "bore" sin. Unless we consider how biblical writers use their words, we ought not presume to explain the logic that governs the sacrificial system. In other words, we need first to understand how the Old Testament, especially the Pentateuch, uses this loadbearing imagery. Only then can one discern how New Testament authors apply such language to Christ. Otherwise, our interpretation becomes a mere assertion of a theological assumption.

In light of the above discussion, we instead need to consider which meaning of *nāśā'* is implied when the Bible describes the work of Christ and the sacrificial system. As we've seen, the phrase "Person X bears sin" *by itself* is ambiguous. It could even have opposite connotations depending on the context. Because of tradition and customary ways of speaking today, many people assume bearing sin necessitates the meaning "to endure punishment." Bearing language itself does not necessitate having that inference. In fact, we find that innocent parties who bear the sin or transgression of a guilty person often live. We must let the Bible define its own terms. Words have meaning based on how they are used, not based on what we think they should mean.

So, what are our main options? Whenever someone or something in the Bible "bears" (*nāśā '*) sin, iniquity, transgression, and the like, what specific connotations might such phrases have? We've discussed two primary options.

1. Person A bears his sin	*implies*	Person A suffers punishment for his sin.
2. Person B bears Person A's sin	*implies*	Person B forgives Person A's sin (i.e., removes the burden caused by sin).

Notably, each is a different way that someone "takes responsibility" for Person A's sin (cf. Leviticus 5:17-18).[6]

Since theologians traditionally emphasize the first option, a modern analogy may help explain the second meaning. Suppose a criminal is sentenced to endure forced labor. His work includes carrying an agonizing load of stone out from a mine. His foreman wants to show compassion to the criminal. So, the foreman uses a wheelbarrow cart to bear away or remove the criminal's burden. In this example, there is nothing inherent to the metaphor that requires us to say the second party (the foreman bearing the load) suffers the punishment as a substitute in the criminal's stead.

Several biblical texts illustrate the point. In the Old Testament, priests bear Israel's iniquity or guilt; yet they are not punished in place of the guilty. In Numbers 18:1, God explains to Aaron the priesthood's function. He says, "So the LORD said to Aaron, 'You and your sons and your father's house with you shall *bear* iniquity connected with the sanctuary, and you and your sons with you shall *bear* iniquity connected with your priesthood'" (ESV). The responsibility of the priesthood is not to receive punishment *instead of* the people. As standard practice, priests remain alive after offering sacrifices.

Therefore, in Exodus 28:36-39, we read,

> You shall make a plate of pure gold and engrave on it, like the engraving of a signet, "Holy to the LORD." And you shall fasten it on the turban by a cord of blue.

---

[6]In one instance, Jeremiah uses the metaphor but with a different verb. In Lam 5:7, he writes, "Our fathers sinned, and are no more; and we *bear* [*sbl*] their iniquities." This usage is more generalized, fitting neither of the meanings above. In effect, this meaning of *bear* in this verse conforms to the following pattern: the statement "Person X bears Person A's sin" implies "Person X suffers as an effect of Person A's sin." The meaning here is broad, even mundane, in the sense that countless people suffer as an effect of any number of other people. Children suffer for their parents' bad decisions. Countries suffer the effects of their leaders' foolishness. Bearing, in this sense, does not necessarily convey punishment or rescue as implied by the options above.

It shall be on the front of the turban. It shall be on Aaron's forehead, and Aaron *shall bear* any guilt from the holy things that the people of Israel consecrate as their holy gifts. It shall regularly be on his forehead, that they may be accepted before the LORD. (ESV)[7]

Aaron often offers sacrifice but does not for this reason die. The priests bear iniquity in that they symbolically remove the other's guilt.

BIBLICAL EXAMPLES

Several other passages cannot indicate that the innocent sin-bearer dies in place of the guilty. After the golden calf rebellion, Moses, in Exodus 32:32, pleads to God, "But now, if you will only *forgive* [*nāśā'*] their sin—but if not, blot me out of the book that you have written."

The verse sets up a contrast ("but if not"). The second part makes a negative request ("blot me out of the book"). Therefore, the first part of the verse carries a positive connotation (hence the translation "forgive their sin"). However, we normally think bearing another's sin has a negative meaning. The contrast creates a logical pivot. It makes clear that bearing their sin cannot mean *God* receives their deserved punishment. Likewise, we cannot imagine Moses asking God to die instead of Israel for their sin.

This second meaning of *bear sin* routinely goes unnoticed by readers. Why? Most translations render such phrases only to express the idea of bearing punishment. However, when the same phrase has positive connotations, they leave out references to "bearing" and simply use "pardon" or "forgive." While the latter translation is understandable, it leads to a natural consequence. Readers will not see how common the second use of "to bear" is.

Compare Numbers 14:18-19, which says,

"The LORD is slow to anger
and abounding in steadfast love,
forgiving [*nāśā'*] iniquity and transgression,
but by no means clearing the guilty,
visiting the iniquity of the parents
upon the children,
to the third and the fourth generation."

---

[7]On the significance of Aaron's bearing, see Carmen Imes, *Bearing God's Name: Why Sinai Still Matters* (Downers Grove, IL: IVP Academic, 2019).

> *Forgive* [*sĕlaḥ*] the iniquity of this people, according to the greatness of your steadfast love, just as you have *pardoned* [*nāśā*ʾ] this people, from Egypt even until now.

Two times, translators use "forgive, pardon" to translate *bearing* of sin. Once again, Moses wants God to take away their sin-burden. He does not ask God to die.

Ezekiel 18:19-20 is interesting. God explicitly rejects an often-heard notion, namely, that an innocent person can be punished in place of the guilty:

> Yet you say, "Why should not the son *suffer for* [*nāśā*ʾ] the *iniquity* of the father?" When the son has done what is lawful and right, and has been careful to observe all my statutes, he shall surely live. The person who sins shall die. The son shall not *suffer for* [*nāśā*ʾ] the iniquity of a parent, nor a parent *suffer for* [*nāśā*ʾ] the iniquity of a child. The righteousness of the righteous shall be his own, and the wickedness of the wicked shall be his own.

This key text confirms what is said above. These verses momentarily pose a hypothetical scenario—that an innocent man bears another person's sin such that he suffers their punishment. However, *the entire point of the supposition is to reject it.* If *bear* here means "being punished" for someone else's sin, Ezekiel 18 flatly rejects the idea as unjust. Ezekiel denies the substitutionary *punishment*, rather than proving the possibility.[8]

We must not forget a critical point, one that frequently gets overlooked. Being punished for someone and dying for that person are not equivalent actions. Jesus' death saves people from their death, but this fact alone does not make death and punishment synonymous.

Why? Because Jesus' death removes the cause (i.e., burden of debt) for which people otherwise stand condemned. Just because Jesus dies instead of us does not imply that the nature of our deserved death functions the same way as Christ's death. We'll return to this important point later.

THE LIVING GOAT BEARS SIN

The Day of Atonement is central to any discussion about atonement. In Leviticus 16, both cleansing and carrying are critical metaphors. Theologians often use this

---

[8] As we'll show, atonement involves substitution. One might affirm a form of penal substitution. Nevertheless, this text does not support substitutionary punishment.

passage to support penal substitutionary atonement (PSA). Does the text endorse this theory? It depends on what one means by *penal substitution*.

In different ways, both ideas—penalty and substitution—are present in the text. We'll look at the idea of penalty later. However, the manner of substitution is not as many think. Leviticus 16:21-22 mentions a second, living goat (sometimes called the "scapegoat").

> Then Aaron shall lay both his hands on the head of the live goat, and confess over it all the iniquities of the people of Israel, and all their transgressions, all their sins, putting them on the head of the goat, and sending it away into the wilderness by means of someone designated for the task. The goat shall *bear on itself all their iniquities to a barren region*; and the goat shall be set free in the wilderness.

The goat takes away the people's sin. The priest symbolically lays sin on the goat's head. This is substitution. Leviticus 16:22 clearly indicates that sin's location changes. This verse does not say the goat dies. The goat takes away the people's guilt.

However, if we say more than this, we beg the question. We assume more than the text states. Although the goat will one day die in the wilderness, this is certainly not what the chapter explicitly says.[9] The chapter explicitly contrasts the dead goat and the living goat (Leviticus 16:10, 15-22). We must not confuse what the passage explicitly says with possible, but unstated speculation. Regardless of what happens to the live goat, the Bible's focus is that sin moves places. The dead goat does not bear the people's sin.

What does Leviticus 16:10 tell us about the purpose of the living goat? It's notoriously difficult to interpret. It says, "The goat on which the lot fell for Azazel shall be presented alive before the LORD to make atonement *over/for* [*'al*] it, that it may be sent away into the wilderness" (NRSV, author's adaptation).[10] The word *'al* could mean "over," "on," or "for." There is little consensus among scholars about its meaning here.[11] Is atonement made for the benefit of the living goat?[12] Is

---

[9] After all, the goat's expected lifespan within the camp would not be long, given the prospect of becoming a meal or sacrifice.

[10] I do not here speculate about the meaning of *Azazel* in Lev 16. To do so would take us far adrift from the main ideas in this book.

[11] The Lexham English Septuagint (LES) even translates the LXX as "in order to make atonement through it" (*exilasasthai ep' autou*). When added to *kpr*, *'al* typically indicates "for."

[12] One possible interpretation is not explored in the literature I've seen. Within the context of Israel's sacrificial worship, we note a pattern. The instrument used by God to bear sin and bring atonement is considered holy (e.g., priests). Perhaps, the living goat effectively is consecrated and thus qualified to bear Israel's sin.

atonement made through it or on it? How does this peculiar verse help us understand atonement and the function of the living goat?

ATONEMENT IN LEVITICUS 14

Leviticus 14 prepares us to interpret Leviticus 16. The former explains the process for cleansing a leprous person and house.

> ### LEVITICUS 14:1-7
>
> The LORD spoke to Moses, saying: This shall be the ritual for the leprous person at the time of his cleansing: He shall be brought to the priest; the priest shall go out of the camp, and the priest shall make an examination. If the disease is healed in the leprous person, the priest shall command that two living clean birds and cedarwood and crimson yarn and hyssop be brought for the one who is to be cleansed. The priest shall command that one of the birds be slaughtered over fresh water in an earthen vessel. He shall take the living bird with the cedarwood and the crimson yarn and the hyssop, and dip them and the living bird in the blood of the bird that was slaughtered over the fresh water. He shall sprinkle it seven times upon the one who is to be cleansed of the leprous disease; *then he shall pronounce him clean, and he shall let the living bird go into the open field.*

Several elements are common to both chapters. The rituals in Leviticus 14 and 16 narrow their focus on two animals. Leviticus 14 has two birds. The first is killed; the second is released. Both the living bird and living goat *go* [*šlḥ*] out into an open space. The result is purification and, eventually, atonement.[13] The parallel ritual in Leviticus 16 leads to atonement and people being cleansed.[14]

> ### LEVITICUS 14:48-53
>
> If the priest comes and makes an inspection, and the disease has not spread in the house after the house was plastered, the priest shall pronounce the house clean; the disease is healed. For the cleansing of the house he shall take two birds, with cedarwood and crimson yarn and hyssop, and shall slaughter one of the birds over fresh water in an earthen vessel, and shall take the cedarwood and the hyssop and the crimson yarn, along with the living bird, and dip them in the blood of the slaughtered bird and the fresh water, and sprinkle the house seven times. *Thus he shall* cleanse the house with the blood of the bird,

---

[13]See Lev 14:7-9, 18-21, 29, 31, 53.
[14]See Lev 16:10, 21, 22, 26.

and with the fresh water, and with the living bird, and with the cedarwood and hyssop and scarlet yarn; and he shall let the living bird go out of the city *into the open field. So he shall make atonement for the house, and it shall be clean.*

In each instance, atonement requires the living animal to remove either leprosy, uncleanness, or sin. We've seen that atonement "is a process that is dependent on its ritual variables and objective."[15] The live bird with the cedarwood and the scarlet yarn and the hyssop are used to cleanse the leprous person. For the house, the priest cleanses the house "*with* the blood of the bird, and *with* the fresh water, and *with* the living bird, and *with* the cedarwood and hyssop and scarlet yarn." The live bird is an implement used ultimately to effect atonement. In the same way, the living goat in Leviticus 16 seems to act as an instrument used to cleanse Israel.[16]

What then is the significance of the living animal? Its purpose is to carry away impurity, not suffer punishment. By any construal, the bird in Leviticus 14 does not suffer punishment. Neither the leprous person nor house deserves punishment. Having a disease is not a sin and does not evoke God's anger.

The goat in Leviticus 16 also does not suffer punishment. Like the bird, it carries away uncleanness and sin. Someone might object that we should not conflate the two chapters since the bird deals with leprosy whereas the goat bears sin. I offer two responses. First, we find elsewhere that Israel uses the same process when atoning for both uncleanness and sin. Second, Leviticus 14 and 16 are in close proximity to one another and share several common features. This fact inclines us to read the Day of Atonement ritual in light of Leviticus 14. The burden of proof falls heavily on those who argue otherwise.

Leviticus 14 also resolves a long-debated question. Some scholars speculate that the second goat's significance consists in the fact that it dies in the wilderness. However, in Leviticus 14, we cannot say that people eventually kill the freed bird. The point is not punishment (i.e., symbolic exile). Rather, it takes away defilement. In Leviticus 16:22, "The goat shall bear on itself all their iniquities to a barren region; and the goat shall be set free in the wilderness." What is indicated? Sin is removed to a remote area. Its location changes. If one insists

---

[15] James Greenberg, *A New Look at the Atonement in Leviticus: The Meaning and Purpose of Kipper Revisited* (University Park: Penn State University Press, 2020), 176.

[16] Contrary to many scholars, the living goat is not the reconciliation offering itself, just as the living bird is not a reconciliation offering. Yet, both play key roles in the process.

on arguing that the living goat suffers punishment, it is a complete supposition. It comes from our assumptions.

AN APPLICATION TO HEBREWS 9

In the last chapter, we observed that Hebrews 9–10 underscore Christ's work to inaugurate the new covenant. The writer first considers the promise of a new heart. We observed how the Day of Atonement shapes the presentation of Christ and his sacrifice in Hebrews 9–10. Christ is compared to the living goat who brings "release" to his people (Hebrews 9:22).

Our study of Leviticus 16 reinforces our interpretation of Hebrews 9–10. After Hebrews 9:22, the writer gives prolonged attention to a second new covenant blessing. Hebrews 8:12, 10:17 both quote Jeremiah 31:34, where the Lord promises, "I will remember their sins and their lawless deeds no more." The writer's language shifts slightly. The writer speaks of forgiveness secured through an offering (Hebrews 9:22; 10:18). Christ has "been offered once *to bear* the sins of many" (Hebrews 9:28). The context clarifies the meaning of "bear." Hebrews 9:26 says, Christ "has appeared once for all at the end of the ages to *put away* [*athetēsis*] sin by the sacrifice of himself" (ESV). The law serves as a foil to magnify Christ's sacrifice in Hebrews 10:4, which says, "it is impossible for the blood of bulls and goats *to take away* [*aphaireō*] sins." In context, to speak of Christ bearing sin is to say Christ *removes* sin. Bearing is explained by "put away" and "take away."

THE SERVANT IN ISAIAH 53

The above discussion raises questions about the servant of Isaiah 52:13–53:12. New Testament writers apply this famous passage to Christ. Our study helps us to interpret several key verses spanning Isaiah 53:4-12 that speak of bearing.

> **ISAIAH 52:13–53:12**
>
> See, my servant shall prosper; / he shall be exalted and lifted up, / and shall be very high. / Just as there were many who were astonished at him / —so marred was his appearance, beyond human semblance, / and his form beyond that of mortals / —so he shall startle many nations; / kings shall shut their mouths because of him; / for that which had not been told them they shall see, / and that which they had not heard they shall contemplate.
>
> Who has believed what we have heard? / And to whom has the arm of the LORD been revealed? / For he grew up before him like a young plant, / and like a root out

of dry ground;/he had no form or majesty that we should look at him,/nothing in his appearance that we should desire him./He was despised and rejected by others;/a man of suffering and acquainted with infirmity;/and as one from whom others hide their faces/he was despised, and we held him of no account.

Surely he has *borne* [nāśāʾ] our infirmities/and *carried* [sbl] our diseases;/yet we accounted him stricken,/struck down by God, and afflicted./But he was wounded for our transgressions,/crushed for our iniquities;/upon him was the *punishment* [mûsar] that made us whole,/and by his bruises we are healed./All we like sheep have gone astray;/we have all turned to our own way,/and the LORD has laid on him/the iniquity of us all./He was oppressed, and he was afflicted,/yet he did not open his mouth;/like a lamb that is led to the slaughter,/and like a sheep that before its shearers is silent,/so he did not open his mouth./By a perversion of justice he was taken away./Who could have imagined his future?/For he was cut off from the land of the living,/stricken for the transgression of my people./They made his grave with the wicked/and his tomb with the rich,/although he had done no violence,/and there was no deceit in his mouth.

Yet it was the will of the LORD to crush him with pain./When you make his life an offering for sin,/he shall see his offspring, and shall prolong his days;/through him the will of the LORD shall prosper./Out of his anguish he shall see light;/he shall find satisfaction through his knowledge./The righteous one, my servant, shall make many righteous,/and he shall *bear* [sbl] their iniquities./Therefore I will allot him a portion with the great,/and he shall divide the spoil with the strong;/because he poured out himself to death,/and was numbered with the transgressors;/yet he *bore* [nāśāʾ] the sin of many,/and made intercession for the transgressors.

We begin with Isaiah 53:4, 11, 12. The NRSV translates *nāśāʾ* as "borne" in Isaiah 53:4. It parallels the verb *sbl*, meaning to "support," "lift up," or "carry."[17] What does the servant bear? In Isaiah 53:4, he bears our "infirmities" and carries our "diseases." These same two verbs, *sbl* and *nāśāʾ*, are in Isaiah 53:11-12 respectively. This time, however, the NRSV renders *sbl* as "bear" in Isaiah 53:11. In these verses, the servant bears iniquities and sin.

These observations pose a difficulty for certain popular readings of Isaiah. Although Isaiah 53:4, 12 both use *nāśāʾ*, many interpreters treat the two objects

---

[17]See "*sbl*" in *HALOT*. Verse 11 uses this same verb.

in Isaiah 53:4 differently than "sin" in Isaiah 53:12. For some theorists, "bearing sin" in Isaiah 53:12 means that the servant (and therefore Jesus) "suffers our punishment due to sin." They suggest that bearing sin means suffering the punishment of sin. If so, how would we understand the parallel language found in Isaiah 53:4? It would seem to say the servant suffers the punishment for our infirmities and diseases. Isaiah 53:4 is in the same context and uses the same verb *nāśā'*. The only difference is what's being borne—infirmities and diseases. If we translate Isaiah 53:4 consistently with Isaiah 53:12, it would convey this idea: Because we have infirmities and diseases, we suffer punishment. Obviously, Isaiah 53:4 does not have this meaning. As that reading makes no sense, we have cause to doubt the conventional view of Isaiah 53:12 above.

Isaiah 53:4 has a positive, nonpunitive tone. The servant takes away our infirmities and diseases ("grief and sorrows" ESV). Therefore, we have reason to say Isaiah 53:12 has a similar meaning. The Lord's servant takes away the sin of many. The last clause of Isaiah 53:12 elaborates on the phrase "bear sin." The servant makes intercession for transgressors.

What about Isaiah 53:5, which says, "But he was wounded for our transgressions, crushed for our iniquities; upon him was the *punishment* [*mûsar*] that made us whole, and by his bruises we are healed." The key word here, *mûsar*, is translated "punishment" by the NRSV. But this rendering is unnecessary. In fact, the word commonly carries more positive, constructive connotations. It indicates instruction, training, discipline, and correction. For example, Proverbs 15:33 says, "The fear of the LORD is *instruction* [*mûsar*] in wisdom, and humility comes before honor."[18] The person receiving *mûsar* can gain some sort of benefit, even if the process temporarily causes pain. Perhaps, we could translate *mûsar* as "affliction" if understood in a neutral sense, not necessarily conveying punishment.

In addition, the LXX uses *paidia* in place of *mûsar*. This word also carries positive connotations. In the New Testament, Hebrews 12 sheds light on the meaning of *paidia*.[19] Hebrews 12:2 tells readers to look to Jesus "who for the joy that was set before him endured the cross, despising the shame, and is seated at the right hand of the throne of God" (ESV). The entire chapter reminds us that God uses *paidia* in order to love his children. Hebrews 12:5-8 says,

---

[18] Also see Job 20:3; Jer 2:30.

[19] As we've seen, multiple chapters before Heb 12 depict Christ as a sacrificial offering.

And have you forgotten the exhortation that addresses you as children? "My child, do not regard lightly the discipline of the Lord, / or lose heart when you are punished by him; / for the Lord *disciplines* [*paideuō*] those whom he loves, / and chastises every son whom he accepts." Endure trials for the sake of discipline. God is treating you as children; for what child is there whom a parent does not *discipline* [*paideuō*]? If you do not have that discipline in which all children share, then you are illegitimate and not his children.[20]

Hebrews 12:6 quotes Proverbs 3:11, which uses *mûsar*, which the NRSV translates as "punishment" in Isaiah 53:5. However, both Hebrews 12:5 and Proverbs 3:11 indicate that *mûsar* and *paidia* can have the meaning "discipline." We are not to despise *mûsar*. In view of Hebrews 12:1-3, even Jesus receives this kind of training.[21] Apparently, Hebrews 12 applies Jesus' experience to us.

In short, "punishment" in Isaiah 53:5 could mislead readers. The word may well have positive connotations, indicating suffering that brings benefit. Even if *mûsar* implies punishment in Isaiah 53:5, the text does not say this "punishment" is the punishment that is due to us as sinners. Moreover, Isaiah never says this is God's punishment. The punishment suffered comes from the servant's enemies. The suffering of Isaiah 53:3-4, 7-8 is unjust. Nevertheless, this injustice brings us peace.[22] The entire passage highlights how people misunderstand and mistreat the servant. But God will vindicate him.

Isaiah 53:6 says, "All we like sheep have gone astray; / we have all turned to our own way, / and the LORD *has laid* [*pg ʿ*] on him / the iniquity of us all."[23] Again, the NRSV translates the same word differently in Isaiah 53:6, 12 despite it sharing the same context. Isaiah 53:6 renders *pg ʿ* as "laid." Isaiah 53:12 translates *pg ʿ* as "made intercession." The word typically means "to intercede for" or "look after someone."[24]

---

[20]Heb 12:9-11 again use the verb *paideuō* and noun *paidia* four more times. We must be careful not to read English connotations into the text. For example, the word *mastigoō* (chastises) in Heb 12:6 can indicate flogging, scourging, or whipping—hardly words that people today associate with loving parental behavior.

[21]See "*mûsar*" in *HALOT*; cf. Heb 5:8-9, "Although he was a Son, he learned obedience through what he suffered; and having been made perfect, he became the source of eternal salvation for all who obey him."

[22]Cf. Allen P. Ross, *A Commentary on the Psalms* (Grand Rapids, MI: Kregel, 2011), 262-63n14. Note Acts 3:13, "The God of Abraham, the God of Isaac, and the God of Jacob, the God of our ancestors has glorified his servant Jesus, whom you handed over and rejected in the presence of Pilate, though he had decided to release him." Also, Acts 2:23-24; 3:26.

[23]For more on this verse, see chap. 10.

[24]See "*pg ʿ*" in *HALOT*. Other usages of the hiphil for *pg ʿ* include Is 59:16; Jer 15:11; 36:25; Job 36:32. See chap. 10 for an explanation as to why translators use "laid" in Is 53:6 and an analysis of the surrounding syntax.

A more natural rendering of Isaiah 53:6 is "the LORD *made intercession* through him for the iniquity of us all." Isaiah 53:12 reinforces this reading while also using *pg'*. The one making intercession in Isaiah 53:12 is the servant through whom the Lord makes intercession in Isaiah 53:6. In what way is intercession made for "the iniquity of us all"? According to Isaiah 53:11, he takes away iniquity.[25]

These observations raise questions or even challenge some evangelical readings of Isaiah 53. For example, proponents of penal substitutionary atonement widely cite this text in teaching that Christ suffered the punishment we deserve for our sin. Was it not the will of the Lord to crush him? (Isaiah 53:10). We will return to Isaiah 53:10 and potential objections in the following chapters.

CHANGING THE TONE

Much of this chapter has studied the meaning of *bearing sin* and its theological implications. We will look at some practical applications later in the book. For now, I want us to reflect on the subtle change of tone that occurs when we discern the biblical concept of bearing.

For many, bearing sin refers only to a person enduring punishment for their wrongdoing. Yet, we've seen how much more the Bible includes when speaking of bearing sin and iniquity. Such language vividly captures the sense of relief that we should feel when we hear the message of atonement. It hints at a trial put on the one who bears the weight of our sin. There are certainly two sides to the Bible's use of bearing imagery. However, for many people, they have only seen the punitive side of that picture. The day will certainly come when God calls the world to account. But until then, he bears with our failures and weakness.

In this way, the biblical story of atonement calls us to repair past wrongs through restoration rather than retribution. Perhaps this is also a better way of seeing the death of Christ. We have long focused on punishment as the dominating theme of atonement, drowning out other biblical themes. Perhaps this is where we have gone wrong when talking about atonement. Might we do better to magnify how Christ sets the world right by becoming a holy reparation, restoring to God what is his? This will be a question for us to consider in the next chapter.

---

[25]What if Is 53:6 means "the LORD *has laid* on him the iniquity of us all"? Even granting this unlikely translation, the verse does not indicate that the servant receives punishment or endures wrath. For example, priests bore Israel's sin. The living goat of Leviticus 16 bore iniquity. Yet, they did not die.

CONCLUSION

This chapter examined several biblical passages that use bearing language when speaking of the atonement. We first considered what it means to "bear sin." Notably, the phrase conveys opposite meanings depending on the context. When the Bible describes a person bearing his own sin, it generally refers to that person enduring the punitive consequences of their sin. However, when God or some other party bears the sin of another, the text consistently conveys salvation, forgiveness, and the removing of sin. We find no examples of the latter usage where "bearing sin" unambiguously connotes God punishing the loadbearer in place of the sinner.

We then turned to several important passages that concern atonement. Leviticus 14 shed light on Leviticus 16. The priest uses two birds to cleanse leprosy in Leviticus 14. One is killed; the other carries away leprosy. Likewise, it is the living goat, not the sacrificed goat, that bears Israel's sin. The text underscores a change in the location of sin. This reading further corroborated our earlier interpretation of Hebrews 9–10. Finally, we looked at Isaiah 53. The servant not only bears the sins of many; he bears our infirmities and diseases. By interpreting the meaning of *bear* consistently, we understand the text to say the servant *takes away* the sins of many.

8

DOES GOD WANT RECOMPENSE OR RETRIBUTION?

COMPENSATION OR PAYMENT is another basic metaphor that describes atonement. This imagery is used whenever people say that Christ paid our debt on the cross. Such language is so commonplace, however, that we could easily miss the way biblical writers use the metaphor. In fact, some readers will find the link between atonement and payment scandalous.

ATONEMENT AS RESTITUTION

Various sacrifices or offerings serve as restitution or ransom payments. As we'll see, they fulfill an obligation and thus pay a debt. The word *asham*, sometimes rendered "guilt offering" or "reparation offering," can also be translated as "restitution." It points to people's obligation to bring about restoration. This obligation is tantamount to a debt. Accordingly, we see how biblical writers use economic terms to describe how an offering effects atonement.

Consider Numbers 5:5-10, which says,

> The LORD spoke to Moses, saying: Speak to the Israelites: When a man or a woman wrongs another, breaking faith with the LORD, that person incurs guilt and shall confess the sin that has been committed. The person shall make *restitution* [*asham*] for the wrong, adding one-fifth to it, and giving it to the one who was wronged. If the injured party has no next of kin to whom *restitution* [*asham*] may be made for the wrong, the *restitution* [*asham*] for wrong shall go to the LORD for the priest, in addition to the ram of atonement

with which atonement is made for the guilty party. Among all the sacred donations of the Israelites, every gift that they bring to the priest shall be his. The sacred donations of all are their own; whatever anyone gives to the priest shall be his.

This *asham* is clearly a type of payment that is even given to the Lord in the case when the man (against whom he wronged) has no next of kin. This compensatory gift is able to atone for sin.

In Leviticus 5:6, the reconciliation offering is regarded as an *asham* payment: "He shall bring to the LORD as his *compensation* for the sin that he has committed, a female from the flock, a lamb or a goat, for a reconciliation offering. And the priest shall make atonement for him for his sin" (ESV, author's adaptation).[1] Not until Leviticus 5:14-16 does the author talk about the reparation offering.

> The LORD spoke to Moses, saying, "If anyone commits a breach of faith and sins unintentionally in any of the holy things of the LORD, he shall bring to the LORD as his *compensation* [*asham*], a ram without blemish out of the flock, valued in silver shekels, according to the shekel of the sanctuary, for a *reparation offering* [*asham*]. He shall also *make restitution* [*shlm*] for what he has done amiss in the holy thing and shall add a fifth to it and give it to the priest. And the priest shall *make atonement* [*kpr*] for him with the ram of the *reparation offering* [*asham*], and he shall be forgiven." (ESV, author's adaptation)

Asham appears three times in Leviticus 5:15-16. In Leviticus 5:15, it is a ram that must have a certain monetary value.

Notice the first verb in Leviticus 15:16 is *shlm*, which can be translated "make restitution" or "repay." Not only does this word reinforce the meaning of *asham*, *shlm* further clarifies what it means to atone for sin. Its economic overtones are evident in other passages.

> But if it was known that the ox was accustomed to gore in the past, and its owner has not restrained it, the owner shall *restore* [*shlm*] ox for ox, but keep the dead animal. (Exodus 21:36)

> She came and told the man of God [Elisha], and he said, "Go, sell the oil and *pay* [*shlm*] your debts, and you and your children can live on the rest." (2 Kings 4:7; cf. Psalm 37:21)

---

[1] Interestingly, the NRSV renders *asham* as "penalty," which echoes the distinction between penalty and punishment that I make below.

Leviticus 6:5-7 and 2 Samuel 12:6 are both noteworthy because the economic value to be repaid is explicitly calculable. Again, I reference these passages to reinforce the point that *asham*, as reparation, carries economic connotations.

COMPENSATION APPEASES GOD'S WRATH

When atonement is portrayed as reparation, what does it achieve? Sacrificial compensation appeases God's anger against sin. I'll first summarize the biblical logic that leads to this connection, then examine several passages that confirm the point. In short,

- (a) compensation brings atonement
- (b) atonement appeases God's wrath[2]
  - therefore
- (c) compensation appeases God's wrath

The following texts use *kofer*, translated "atonement" or "ransom," the noun form of the verb meaning "to atone." Observe the effects of atonement or ransom. We begin with Exodus 21:29-30, "If the ox has been accustomed to gore in the past, and its owner has been warned but has not restrained it, and it kills a man or a woman, the ox shall be stoned, and its owner also shall be put to death. If a *ransom* [*kofer*] is imposed on the owner, then the owner shall pay whatever is imposed for the redemption of the victim's life." Notice this man deserves death, but people can give payment (i.e., compensation). This ransom is a monetary payment, *not* another person's death. To the chagrin to some readers, the Mosaic law did not regard this ransom payment as unjust compensation in this case, despite the owner's warranting the death penalty. The Mosaic law and the idea of a compensatory atonement have no inherent contradiction.

Exodus 30:11-16 also depicts atonement in economic or financial terms.

The LORD spoke to Moses: When you take a census of the Israelites to register them, at registration all of them shall give a *ransom* [*kofer*] for their lives to the LORD, *so that no plague may come upon them for being registered.* This is what each one who is registered shall give: half a *shekel* according to the shekel of the sanctuary (the shekel is twenty gerahs), *half a shekel as an offering to the LORD.* Each one who is registered, from twenty years old and upward, shall give the LORD's

---

[2]Recall from chap. 4 that atonement primarily refers to entreating or seeking favor. In circumstances where wrongdoing or offense is involved, atonement can connote appeasement.

offering. The rich shall not give more, and the poor shall not give less, than the *half shekel*, when you bring this offering to the Lord to make atonement for your lives. You shall take the *atonement money [kippurim kesef]* from the Israelites and shall designate it for the service of the tent of meeting; before the Lord it will be a reminder to the Israelites of the *ransom given [kpr*, "make atonement," ESV] for your lives.

According to Exodus 30:12, people's lives are at stake. Because of their sin, God threatens a plague. With respect to the atonement, all the typical components are present; namely, sin and a threat. In addition, we see a ransom or atonement price. In this passage, paying money is the means of atonement. This payment atones for their lives. Intriguingly, God allows the people to use money to take away his wrath. After all, if they don't pay the required amount, they'll suffer a plague.

It appears that Numbers applies Exodus 30:15-16. Numbers 31:50 says, "And we have brought the LORD's offering, what each of us found, articles of gold, armlets and bracelets, signet rings, earrings, and pendants, to *make atonement* for ourselves before the LORD." What brings atonement? Jewelry.

After Saul unjustly struck down the Gibeonites, David seeks to make atonement for the bloodguilt that remained on Saul and his house. In 2 Samuel 21:3-4, we read, "And David said to the Gibeonites, 'What shall I do for you? And how shall I *make atonement*, that you may bless the heritage of the LORD?' The Gibeonites said to him, 'It is not a matter of silver or gold between us and Saul or his house; neither is it for us to put any man to death in Israel.' And he said, 'What do you say that I shall do for you?'" (ESV). Their answer implicitly indicates that people commonly used money or some economic means to atone for sin.

Conceptually, the connection between a payment or gift and appeasing wrath is found in several other passages. Proverbs 21:14 says, "A gift in secret *averts [kph]* anger, and a concealed bribe in the bosom, strong wrath." In principle, a gift is able to atone or appease anger. Also, "Wealth is a *ransom [kofer]* but the poor get no threats" (Proverbs 13:8). Again, we see a conceptual link. This person's ransom is able to atone for his life. In this situation, his ransom is a payment.

One might argue that Proverbs 6:34-35 contradicts the above argument that a ransom alleviates wrath. The writer says, "For jealousy arouses a husband's fury, and he shows no restraint when he takes revenge. He will accept no *compensation* [*kofer*], and refuses a bribe no matter how great." To this point, the verses we've studied speak of people who use gifts as a means of appeasement or apology. The basic assumption presented here is that a ransom or payment can appease anger. A gift is a *possible* means of atonement. This was a normal custom. However, Proverbs 6 identifies an exception. We mustn't forget that Proverbs wants to teach wisdom to readers. These verses do not directly talk about Christ's atonement and so should not shape our atonement theology as though they do. The purpose of our present study is merely to learn how people used words. We want to know the relationship between concepts.

Whereas ancient readers normally expected a gift to appease another's anger, in the context of Proverbs 6, the writer's point is simply this: in normal life, an offended husband will not accept a gift. In order for the writer to state this exception, society must have a custom. Otherwise, the exception makes no sense. The exception proves the rule.

What about Psalm 49:7-9? Notice how the key concepts interrelate: "Truly no *ransom* [*pdh*] avails for one's life, / there is no *price* [*kofer*] one can give for it. / For the *ransom* [*pidyon*] of life is costly, / and can never suffice, / that one should live forever / and never see the grave." On the surface, it appears that a ransom cannot pay the debt. However, the writer does not say that. Rather, people *themselves* cannot pay the debt. Why? This sort of ransom is costly. (With respect to Christ's atonement, Christians can agree. We cannot pay our debt.) My point here is simply to highlight key conceptual connections. In particular, a ransom theoretically can save people's life. But we ourselves can't afford it.

Do we see anything similar in the New Testament? Yes. For example, Matthew 18:34-35 says, "And in anger his lord handed him over to be tortured until he would pay his entire debt. So my heavenly Father will also do to every one of you, if you do not forgive your brother or sister from your heart." Observe the key idea: paying the debt theoretically would appease the master's anger and release the person from punishment.

As we'll soon see, biblical interpreters often confuse debt and punishment.[3] People say Jesus paid our debt; yet, their meaning is that Jesus paid our death, that is, our punishment. This way of speaking mixes metaphors. Jesus

---

[3]For example, William Lane Craig says we owe a "debt of punishment" in his *Atonement and the Death of Christ: An Exegetical, Historical, and Philosophical Exploration* (Waco, TX: Baylor University Press, 2020), 261. Craig affirms the idea that payment occurs through God's "punishing Christ" (260).

distinguishes three ideas: anger, debt, and punishment. In Jesus' parable, paying a debt removes punishment. Debt is distinguished from punishment.

This metaphorical way of speaking is not true merely for human relationships. Even in the relationship between God and humans, debt leads to punishment. Therefore, paying the debt appeases wrath. As a result, we no longer receive punishment.[4]

In summary, we have traced the biblical logic. First, we see that making compensation or restitution is a way of effecting atonement. Second, we note that atonement appeases God's wrath, removing punishment that would otherwise result. Thus, we find that such reparation payments were a means for appeasing God's anger.

We previously noted that the Bible uses economic language to describe sin. It should not surprise us then that a solution to a problem couched in economic imagery would itself use a monetary metaphor. Elsewhere, the Bible uses other economic-oriented verbiage (i.e., ransom, redemption) to describe the means of salvation from death. Hosea 13:14 says, "Shall I *ransom* them from the power of Sheol? / Shall I *redeem* them from Death? / O Death, where are your plagues? / O Sheol, where is your destruction? / Compassion is hidden from my eyes." "Death" is presented as a personified slave owner. Metaphorically speaking, a ransom can free people from death (cf. Job 5:20). As one can imagine, this observation has important implications when we consider Christ's atoning work.[5]

PAYMENT, PENALTY, OR PUNISHMENT?

My friend Greg worked in a church for multiple decades, eventually becoming one of its most senior leaders. His tenure and position afforded him many opportunities, including the chance to steal hundreds of thousands of dollars from the church. Before his case went to court, he worked tirelessly, but we couldn't gather enough money to repay what he owed. Finally, a judge gave him a long prison sentence with few chances of parole. Greg was separated from his wife and kids. He lost countless friends. But he had gained an orange prison

---

[4]Cf. Phil 1:18-19, where Paul says he will repay the "wrong" or debt "owed," which should be charged to Paul's account. Of course, Onesimus's debt deserves punishment. Yet, taking on this debt does not imply that Paul expects he'll be punished.

[5]Interestingly, 1 Cor 15:55 (quoting Hos 13:14) and Rom 6 have an overlapping resurrection theme. The problem of slavery in Rom 6 is represented in Rom 7:14 as being "sold under sin." The solution is found in Rom 8:23, which refers to the "redemption of our bodies."

suit and massive debt. As an inmate, he earned less than a dollar per hour at his prison job.

The church insisted on full repayment. Until they received every dime, they would not advocate on his behalf to the judge. A few weeks before Greg's first parole hearing, a family friend offered to pay the balance that Greg still owed his former church. With his debt paid, the church agreed not to stand in Greg's way. He was released from prison and reunited with his family. His family friend generously relieved Greg of a heavy burden, a consequence of several years of sin. How did this burden get lifted? Greg's friend did not take his place in prison. A felony charge was not placed on the friend's permanent record rather than on Greg's. This friend simply paid the debt that had led to punishment. When that was paid, Greg was freed.

In my retelling of Greg's story, anyone can understand the metaphorical distinctions I draw. His debt is a burden, but his time in prison is a punishment. Unfortunately, popular theology frequently confuses concepts like payment, penalty, and punishment. For instance, one hears, "Christ paid our debt," which is then explained as Christ being punished in our place. This way of speaking scrambles the biblical imagery. The figure below depicts the relationship between three key terms. The word *penalty* is ambiguous. It can be understood either as a payment or punishment.

Figure 8.1. The relationship between payment, penalty, and punishment

The Bible routinely distinguishes payment from punishment. People who cannot pay their debt to God suffer punishment, such as slavery, shame, or death. This basic connection is found throughout the canon. The distinction between payment and punishment is fundamental to Jesus' comment in Matthew 18:25, where he says, "And, as he could not pay, his lord ordered him to be sold, together with his wife and children and all his possessions, and payment to be made."

Biblical writers readily make use of these metaphors. In the Old Testament, God's people are sold into slavery due to sin. Isaiah 50:1 says, "Because of your sins you were sold, and for your transgressions your mother was put away." Paul uses a similar word picture. He portrays people as slaves to sin and says, "I am of the flesh, sold into slavery under sin" (Romans 7:14; cf. 6:16-19). No wonder we find that God's people make "payments" (i.e., make reparation, fulfilling their debt) in order to avoid a plague. For example, in Exodus 30:12, "When you take the census of the Israelites to register them, at registration all of them shall *give a ransom for their lives* to the LORD, *so that no plague may come upon them* for being registered."[6]

The way biblical writers speak of ransom or restitution payments suggests the need for rethinking our own manner of speaking. Perhaps an additional distinction is needed. If these payments are not punishments, as we've seen, what are they? *It seems these payments serve more like penalties than punishment.* To use a modern analogy, they appear more akin to fines and restitution payments in contrast to imprisonment or corporal punishment. In this sense, the requisite offerings are penalties, which people are obligated to pay as a result of impurity or sin. If one does not pay the penalty (i.e., payment), they will incur punishment.

When we distinguish penalty from punishment in this way, one begins to see how Christ acts as a penal substitute yet without necessarily implying that God the Father punishes Christ the Son. He is a penal substitute at least in this sense: Christ pays the penalty (i.e., restitution) required as a consequence of sin. In making this payment, he acts as a substitute in our place. As penal substitute, he appeases God's wrath. Thus, the repentant Christ-follower no longer warrants punishment. *Penal* here need not imply that God punishes Christ rather than sinners.[7]

———

The day finally came for my two friends to get married. Decorations welcomed guests, who were arriving early at the wedding venue. To the surprise of the groom, the hour had also come to pay the rest of the rental fee to the facility manager. My friend thought that he already paid the money; instead, he had only given a down payment. Now, the manager threatened to shut down the wedding. My friend went into full panic mode, knowing he didn't have that money readily available. He insisted that he already paid the full amount due, but he didn't have a receipt to prove it. Now he would pay the penalty either for not paying the bill previously or for losing the receipt.

While he scrambled to come up with a solution, several groomsmen met with the manager. They pitched in to pay the bill, putting the charge on one of

---

[6]We saw the same connection above when discussing Hos 13:14. Cf. Num 8:19; 16:46-47.
[7]More on this in chap. 9 and appendix B.

their credit cards. The wedding was saved. My friend had a financial obligation. The consequence (punishment) for not paying his debt was significant—no wedding, public shame, and the loss of funds already spent. However, because the required payment was made, he did not incur the painful consequence that would otherwise follow. This story from my friends' wedding day is an imperfect analogy. Still, it can help readers begin to discern how one might distinguish payment, penalty, and punishment in the context of atonement.

How Is Forgiveness Possible?

Does all this talk of compensation undermine the idea that God forgives? After all, can we say a person forgives if the offender makes restitution? Furthermore, is such compensation actually possible in light of our sin?

Why can God embrace us despite our hate, deceit, arrogance, and countless other plagues that mark human society? In 1963, George Wallace in his inaugural address as governor of Alabama declared his opposition to school integration of Black and White students. He bellowed, "Segregation now! Segregation tomorrow! And segregation forever!" Martin Luther King Jr. even called him the "most dangerous racist in America."[8]

What many people don't realize is that he later renounced his racist politics, eventually winning 90 percent of the Black vote in his 1982 gubernatorial run.[9] But how do a series of meetings and public apologies compensate for the terror he unleashed on Black protesters throughout the 1960s? Many died while Wallace turned a blind eye. John Lewis was fortunate to keep his life after being gassed and beaten, suffering a skull fracture at the hands of Alabama state troopers. So, what happened in 1979, when George Wallace called Lewis to ask for forgiveness? John Lewis's response gives a glimpse into the heart of God. In an article published after Wallace's death, Lewis wrote, "When I met George Wallace, I had to forgive him, because to do otherwise—to hate him—would only perpetuate the evil system we sought to destroy."[10]

---

[8]"Wallace, George Corley, Jr," Standford University, The Martin Luther King, Jr. Research and Education Institute, accessed July 18, 2022 https://kinginstitute.stanford.edu/encyclopedia/wallace-george -corley-jr

[9]Jonathon Capehart, "How Segregationist George Wallace Became a Model for Racial Reconciliation: 'Voices of the Movement' Episode 6," *Washington Post*, May 16, 2019, washingtonpost.com/opinions /2019/05/16/changed-minds-reconciliation-voices-movement-episode/.

[10]John Lewis, "Forgiving George Wallace," *New York Times*, September 16, 1998, www.nytimes.com /1998/09/16/opinion/forgiving-george-wallace.html.

Nothing can entirely make up for the evil deeds we commit. If that were necessary, atonement would be impossible. Yet, reconciliation is possible. Forgiveness is more than an idealistic dream. What does the Bible mean then when it speaks of compensation being paid to secure atonement? Such recompense, whether money or an animal, does not alleviate the impact of hateful actions or lives that dishonor God. But let's not forget that "restitution authenticates our repentance for theft."[11] Such gifts not only manifest our contrition; they serve as our confession that God is worthy of supreme glory.

Precisely because mere repentance does not undo the reality and consequences of our sin, God can forgive us. Forgiveness is possible because God receives us although nothing can be done to erase the fact that we have sinned against him. Certainly, our response is a prerequisite of atonement, but it is not sufficient. Rather, atonement is possible because to do otherwise—to hate sinners—would only perpetuate the evil system Christ sought to destroy.

CONNECTING PURITY AND THE BURDEN OF PAYMENT

How do we connect payment and purity? In short, God's people are called holy. God does not dwell with defiled or impure people. Defilement or pollution endangers his people. God cannot tolerate impurity. Defilement threatens the relationship between God and his people.

Figure 8.2. Impurity and obligation

Therefore, God's people have an obligation. They must seek cleansing. Pollution creates debt such that purification in effect is a repayment of debt. Sacrificial offerings are an obligation of God's people to bring about restoration. This explains why the Bible can say that a ransom payment satisfies God's demands. Thus, atonement removes the threat of danger.

Another significant metaphor sheds light on this payment or restitution language. Since biblical writers portray sin as a burden and debt, we might expect to see these metaphors linked when we speak of salvation. Indeed, we

---

[11]Duke L. Kwon and Gregory Thompson, *Reparations: A Christian Call for Repentance and Repair* (Grand Rapids, MI: Brazos, 2021), 150.

do. In Hosea 14:2, the prophet says, "Take with you words / and return to the LORD; / say to him, / '*Take away all iniquity*; / accept what is good, / and *we will pay* with bulls / the vows of our lips'" (ESV). More literally, they should ask the Lord to "bear" away their iniquity. Offering the bull effectively pays their debt by fulfilling their vow. In response, God bears or removes the burden that is their iniquity.

Leviticus 5:17-18 applies both metaphors to the worshiper.

> If anyone sins, doing any of the things that by the LORD's commandments ought not to be done, though he did not know it, then realizes his guilt, *he shall bear his iniquity*. He shall bring to the priest a ram without blemish out of the flock, or its equivalent, for *a reparation offering* [= compensation; *asham*], and the priest shall *make atonement* for him for the mistake that he made unintentionally, and he shall be forgiven. (ESV, author adaptation)

How does the offender "bear his iniquity"? It is not by his receiving punishment. Rather, he pays restitution to the Lord.

IS PASSOVER A "PENAL" SACRIFICE?

For ancient Israel, the exodus is the quintessential act of redemption. Redemption and ransom are frequently associated. Does that mean the Passover lamb is a type of ransom? Theologians have long used the Passover to explain the significance of Christ's death. We now turn to consider the relationship between atonement and the Passover.

Many writers are prone not only to mix metaphors but also assume their meanings. This habit leads to confusion.[12] When speaking of the Passover lamb in Exodus 12, Mark Dever and Michael Lawrence write,

> While there may not be explicit mention of the lamb bearing the sins of many, that is implicit in the lamb bearing the punishment for Israel's sins, and in those who are marked by the lamb's blood being delivered from the penalty they justly deserved. . . . My friend, if you're not a Christian, God is calling you to trust him, to believe that One has been sacrificed to pay your penalty, to bear your burden, to save you from God's judgment for your sins. That's the message that this Passover account has for us.[13]

---

[12]Cf. Darrin Snyder Belousek's critique in *Atonement, Justice, and Peace: The Message of the Cross and the Mission of the Church* (Grand Rapids, MI: Eerdmans, 2012), 156-64.

[13]Mark Dever and Michael Lawrence, *It Is Well* (Wheaton, IL: Crossway, 2010), 21, 23.

The lamb (and ultimately Christ) is said to bear the sins of many, Israel's punishment, and our burden. A sacrifice pays the penalty such that people are delivered from the penalty they deserve.

The excerpt above has several problems. First, the authors merely assert that bearing sin is equivalent to bearing punishment. We've already seen the flaw in this assumption. Second, they conflate payment and penalty language. Exodus 12 gives no warrant for that idea. Dever and Lawrence do not defend what they presume to be "implicit."

Third, nothing in the context of the Passover suggests that the lamb is a penal substitute. Many theologians use the Passover to affirm penal substitutionary atonement (PSA). Here are a few quotes from supporters of PSA.[14]

> The substitutionary element in the Passover is therefore beyond dispute. Moreover, given that the plagues function unambiguously as instruments of divine judgment, *penal* substitution is plainly taught here.[15]

> I can find numerous places in Scripture where we are taught, explicitly or implicitly, that the wrath of God was directed on Jesus at the cross. One thinks of the Passover in Exodus 12. Penal substitution lies at the heart of the Passover— God poured out His wrath on the slain lamb instead of His people.[16]

> This reference to the Jewish Passover indicates that Christ's blood shed on the cross propitiates the divine wrath, delivers from the guilt of sin, and secures exemption from divine judgment.[17]

> Passover presented the first clear picture of penal substitution attesting to death as the penalty as well as the death of the sacrifice.[18]

The link between the Passover lamb and PSA is rarely defended. One exception is Kenneth Reid, who says, "The Passover was penal because the Israelites were

---

[14]See John MacArthur and Richard Mayhue, *Biblical Doctrine: A Systematic Summary of Bible Truth* (Wheaton, IL: Crossway, 2017), 303, 522; Royce Gordon Gruenler, "Atonement in the Synoptic Gospels and Acts," in *The Glory of the Atonement: Biblical, Theological & Practical Perspectives*, ed. Charles E. Hill and Frank A. James III (Downers Grove, IL: IVP Academic, 2004), 103.

[15]Steve Jeffery, Michael Ovey, and Andrew Sach, *Pierced for Our Transgressions: Rediscovering the Glory of Penal Substitution* (Wheaton, IL: Crossway, 2007), 38. They add, "The Passover lamb functioned as a penal substitute, dying in the place of the firstborn sons of the Israelites, in order that they might escape the wrath of God" (p. 34).

[16]Kevin DeYoung and Jerry Bridges, *The Good News We Almost Forgot Rediscovering the Gospel in a 16th Century Catechism* (Chicago, IL: Moody, 2010), 42.

[17]Demarest refers to 1 Cor 5:7. Bruce Demarest, *The Cross and Salvation* (Wheaton, IL: Crossway, 2017), 174.

[18]William Barrick, "Penal Substitution in the Old Testament," *TMSJ* 20, no. 2 (Fall 2009): 169, 158.

not exempt from God's judgment because they worshiped the Egyptian idols. The Israelites did not bear the penalty of death, but the lamb died so that they would not bear God's judgment."[19] However, he attempts to tie the Passover to later texts that never mention any element of the Passover. This connection is more convenient than coherent. By this reasoning, nearly any offering could be called a "penal" sacrifice because the worshipers sin at some point in life. Neither Exodus 12 nor other texts attach the Passover sacrifice to Israel's sin prior to the exodus.

This common reading of the Passover illustrates the piecemeal reasoning of many proponents of PSA. They see a phenomenon that draws to mind the concept of substitution, such as the giving of the Passover lamb. People then look for possible links to death, punishment, or sin. Although such elements might be in the text for other reasons, interpreters assume a connection between them and substitution. All the while, the reader affirms a series of biblical ideas. However, the logic that directly associates them does not come from Scripture itself.

THE PASSOVER LAMB

Exodus 12 explains why the Israelites sacrificed the Passover lamb. We should observe that the writer never says the sacrifice is designed to absorb a punishment deserved by Israel. Instead, God uses the lamb as a "sign" (*oth*). This sign distinguishes his people from those who reject him.[20] Multiple times, the Lord expressly states this goal—to make a distinction between Israel and Egypt.[21] Those who offer the sacrifice set themselves apart as the Lord's people. They are then spared of the coming judgment. According to Exodus 12:12, this judgment particularly targets "the firstborn in the land of Egypt, both man and beast; and on all the gods of Egypt."

In this way, the Lamb brings redemption to God's people (Exodus 13:13; cf. 34:20; Revelation 14:4). Exodus 13 interprets the Passover and then Moses makes a conclusion.

When in the future your child asks you, "What does this mean?" you shall answer, "By strength of hand the LORD brought us out of Egypt, from the house of slavery.

---

[19] Kenneth James Reid, "Penal Substitutionary Atonement as the Basis for New Covenant and New Creation" (PhD diss., Southern Baptist Theological Seminary, 2015), 93. On pp. 28-31, he appeals to Josh 24:14; Ezek 20:4-10.

[20] Cf. Ex 12:13, 23, 27, 31; 13:11-16.

[21] See Ex 8:22; 9:4; 11:7.

"When Pharaoh stubbornly refused to let us go, the LORD killed all the firstborn in the land of Egypt, from human firstborn to the firstborn of animals. Therefore I sacrifice to the LORD every male that first opens the womb, but every firstborn of my sons I redeem." It shall serve as a *sign* on your hand and as an emblem on your forehead that by strength of hand the LORD brought us out of Egypt. (Exodus 13:14-16)

Exodus 13:15 is significant because it shows that the ongoing sacrifice is *not* due to Israel's sin; rather, it represents God distinguishing the firstborn as belonging to God.[22] The sacrifice glorifies the Lord. The blood is a "mark" to commemorate Israel's redemption.

One can reckon the Passover lamb to be a substitute for Israel. If any Israelites do not sacrifice the Passover lamb, God would deem them as enemies. In essence, such rebels align with Pharaoh. They choose Pharaoh as king, not the Lord. They want Pharaoh to remain their slave master. In that case, God would judge them. The punishment for such rebellion is death.[23]

The death of the Passover lamb has a different meaning than would the death of the rebels. The lamb dies instead of the Israelites; yet the text never indicates that the lamb receives the punishment already deserved by Israel. Quite the opposite— the lamb takes away any potential, pending judgment. The Passover story includes the concept of substitution. It foreshadows Jesus' death and our redemption. But Scripture never says that the Lamb's blood was due to Israel's sin.[24] A substitute does not necessarily receive the *punishment* of the one for whom it is a substitute. In Numbers 18, the Levites substitute for Israel's firstborn. However, Scripture never says the Levites substitute for the firstborn because of sin.

Furthermore, the verb *pasach* is typically translated as "pass over."[25] This rendering masks another piece of evidence. Exodus 12:13 says, "And when I see the blood, I will *pass over* [*pasach*] you, and no plague shall destroy you when I strike the land of Egypt." Scholars have long noted that *pasach* in Exodus 12:13 means "to protect" or "to spare."[26] This is precisely the meaning

---

[22] A coherent explanation for the death of the firstborn may come from the concept of a devoted thing (discussed in chaps. 3–4). God demands that the firstborn be offered to him. Only those firstborn who are not offered to God will suffer death. God sees them as devoted to him.

[23] This entire paragraph intends to echo Paul's clear application of the exodus in Rom 6; see N. T. Wright, "The Letter to the Romans," in *The New Interpreter's Bible* (Nashville: Abingdon, 2002), 533-48.

[24] Also note that the animals' firstborn died, but they have no sin.

[25] This is influenced by the Vulgate, Jerome's Latin translation of the Bible.

[26] T. Francis Glasson, "The 'Passover,' a Misnomer: The Meaning of the Verb 'Pasach,'" *JTS* 10, no. 1 (April 1959): 79-84.

conveyed in Isaiah 31:5, which says, "Like birds hovering, so the LORD of hosts / will protect Jerusalem; / he will protect and deliver it; / he *will spare* [*pasach*] and rescue it." Likewise, the LXX uses *skepazō* (Exodus 12:13, 27) and *peripoieō* (Isaiah 31:5). Both *skepazō* and *peripoieō* indicate ideas such as protecting, saving, preserving, and so on.[27] In short, the Lord does not merely pass over in the sense of *not* punishing Israel. Instead, the blood was "a signal to the Lord: 'Protect this house.'"[28] Returning to Exodus 12:13, the Lord says, "When I see the blood, I will *protect* [*pasach*] you." Such wording hardly suits the claim that God sought to vent his wrath on Israel at the Passover. He wanted to protect, not punish Israel.

JESUS, LAMB OF GOD

Paul expressly calls Christ "our Passover Lamb" in 1 Corinthians 5:7. In what sense is this so? John's Gospel offers clues, although its answers are not as explicit as some readers might prefer. John does present Jesus as a Passover sacrifice.[29] How then should we interpret John the Baptist's statement that Jesus is "the Lamb of God who takes away the sin of the world!" (John 1:29; cf. 1:36)? The Gospel's use of imagery is rich and robust, so we need to carefully examine its meaning.

John's meaning is far from obvious.[30] Even his term for "lamb" (*amnos*) in John 1:29 differs from the word found in Exodus 12.[31] Leon Morris notes that, in the LXX, *amnos* overwhelmingly refers to lambs used in sacrifice (mostly as burnt offerings).[32] Furthermore, the "Passover victim was not always a lamb, and therefore an explicit identification with the Passover sacrifice would not necessarily have followed."[33] The reference to Jesus as "lamb of God" is more complex and integrated with various images used throughout the book. In effect, the title functions as a composite description of what Jesus will

---

[27]Cf. "*peripoieō*," *GELS*; "*skepazō*," *GELS*.

[28]Glasson, "'Passover,' a Misnomer," 80.

[29]For example, see Jn 19:36, echoing Ex 12:46; Num 9:12.

[30]As many show, such as George Carey, "The Lamb of God and Atonement Theories," *Tyndale Bulletin* 32 (1981): 97-122; Christopher Skinner, "Another Look at 'the Lamb of God,'" *Bibliotheca Sacra* 161 (Jan–March 2004): 89-104.

[31]Ex 12 repeatedly uses *probaton*. Gen 22 (the offering of Isaac) also uses *probaton*.

[32]Leon Morris, *Apostolic Preaching* (Grand Rapids, MI: Eerdmans, 1965), 142-43. Both Morris and George Carey ("Lamb of God") also identify problems with attributing John's language to Is 53:7.

[33]Skinner, "Another Look at 'the Lamb of God,'" 97-98. He notes Ex 12:5 ("You may take it from the sheep or from the goats") and John's familiarity with Passover terminology.

accomplish throughout John's Gospel. In this way, "lamb of God" can have connotations of the exodus.[34]

Because of the Passover lamb's clear connection to redemption, we discern its subtler association with atonement. John portrays Jesus as the one who brings about Israel's redemption, a new exodus. Hoskins highlights several links between the Passover and John 8, which contains contrasts between slavery and freedom, and life and death. He says,

> In light of John 8, Jesus as Passover lamb is the suitable sacrifice given the overall picture that John is painting. The transfer from the kingdom of the world/devil to the kingdom of God requires redemption from that kingdom. The Passover lamb is the preeminent sacrifice associated with the redemption of the people of God in the OT. God's plan of redemption from bondage requires the sacrifice of the Passover lamb (Exodus 12). . . . Without it, they would die in Egypt, the kingdom of bondage, and never see freedom. Similarly, according to John's Passover typology, the Lamb of God is necessary in order to take away one's sins so that one will not die due to sin and never see life and freedom from bondage to sin and the devil.[35]

In short, God redeemed Israel from Egypt through a Passover lamb that rescues them from death.

From this perspective, "one might look for Jesus to deliver from a plague from God, namely, death."[36] Why are God's people threatened by death? Sin. Jesus even likens his listeners to those enslaved by Pharaoh. In John 8:34-36, he says, "Everyone who commits sin is a *slave to sin*. The slave does not have a permanent place in the household; the son has a place there forever. So if the Son makes you free, you will be free indeed." Sin is a personified Pharaoh. Following or practicing sin leads to death. In taking away sin, Jesus takes away the plague of death.[37]

---

[34]For extensive scholarly studies, see Paul Hoskins, "Deliverance from Death by the True Passover Lamb: A Significant Aspect of the Fulfillment of the Passover in the Gospel of John," *JETS* 52 (2009): 285-99; Christiane Shaker, "The 'Lamb of God' Title in John's Gospel: Background, Exegesis, and Major Themes" (PhD diss., Setan Hall, 2016).

[35]Hoskins, "Deliverance from Death," 293.

[36]Hoskins, "Deliverance from Death," 289.

[37]A possible verbal link is found in the Septuagint's use of *periaireō* (Ex 8:8, 31), referring to the "taking away" of the frog and flies plagues. This word is closely related to *airō*, found in Jn 1:29.

ATONEMENT IN THE PASSOVER?

What is the relationship between this redemption and atonement? I suggest three possible connections. First, Hoskins identifies several instances where "making atonement delivers God's people from a deadly plague that displays God's wrath on his people due to their sin."[38] We studied some of these passages in chapter four. On those occasions, atonement was not used to address past sins. Atonement was not punitive; rather, it was protective and preventative. Such circumstances resemble that found at the Passover in Exodus 12. The blood marked people as the Lord's. The lamb thus served to protect them against God's wrath poured out against those who sided with Pharaoh.

Second, recall an underlying meaning of *kpr* (atonement)—namely, seeking or entreating favor from someone. This includes removing whatever obstructs one's relationship with another. In the Passover, the lamb accomplishes this purpose. The blood expresses the people's desire to bind themselves to the Lord. Not to sacrifice the lamb would have signified a separation in their relationship with God.

Finally, Jesus' words during his final Passover meal offer a third connection. Luke 22:20 says, "And he did the same with the cup after supper, saying, 'This cup that is poured out for you is the new covenant in my blood.'"[39] While the Gospel writers portray Christ as a Passover sacrifice, Jesus gives an interpretation. His blood inaugurates the new covenant "which is poured out for many for the forgiveness of sins" (Matthew 26:28). The fulfillment of God's new covenant promises signals Israel's redemption and the end of exile.[40] In this way, Christ, the Passover lamb, achieves atonement for his people.

EXODUS 30:11-12, 16

The LORD said to Moses, "When you take the census of the people of Israel, then each shall give a ransom for his life to the LORD when you number them, *that there be no plague* among them when you number them. . . . You shall take the atonement money from the people of Israel and shall give it for the service of the tent of meeting, that it may bring the people of Israel to remembrance before the LORD, so as to make atonement for your lives." (ESV; cf. Numbers 8:19)

---

[38]Hoskins, "Deliverance from Death," 293. He cites Ex 30:11-16; cf. 2 Sam 24, especially 2 Sam 24:21; 1 Chron 21:22-27; Num 16:41-50; 25:7-13. Also, see Num 8:19.

[39]Cf. Mt 26:27-28; Mk 14:24.

[40]See Ezek 36–37; Jer 31; Is 52. In Is 49–53, the servant is instrumental in bringing about redemption. For a discussion about Israel's ongoing exile, see James Scott, *Exile: A Conversation with N. T. Wright* (Downers Grove, IL: IVP Academic, 2017).

If Christ brings redemption, does this imply that he is a ransom? Jesus even says, "For the Son of Man came not to be served but to serve, and to give his life a ransom for many" (Mark 10:45). We should consider this question in light of the Passover. After all, the exodus is the archetype of redemption in the Old Testament. In a sense, the Passover lamb serves as a type of ransom, securing the freedom of God's enslaved people. However, God does not compensate Pharaoh for his lost slaves. Israel does not pay a ransom to Pharaoh. If anything, we might say Israel pays a ransom to God. What sort of ransom? This is the same kind of ransom we just saw in Exodus 30:12. Likewise, in Numbers 3:48-49, the Lord says, "Give the money to Aaron and his sons as the *redemption price* [*peduyim*] for those who are over. So Moses took the redemption money from those who were over and above those redeemed by the Levites" (ESV). In neither case is the ransom paid to the devil or an evil ruler. Rather, the ransom is an offering wherein they commit themselves to God and so preserve their lives.

CONCLUSION

This chapter surveyed various ways the Bible speaks of atonement using compensation or payment language. Restitution is needed to restore relationship. Worshipers make compensation and so appease God's wrath. Unfortunately, some people confuse payment with punishment. Comments like "Christ paid our debt by receiving our punishment" are not helpful. A payment is required to prevent punishment. Without a payment, one receives punishment. Conflating these metaphors sows confusion.

When we consider the primary metaphors linked with atonement, we discern an underlying logic. Because of impurity and sin, people have an obligation or debt to fix the problem. The solution is a type of compensation or restitution. That obligation is a kind of burden to bear. If recompense is not made, one becomes worthy of punishment. A question for people to debate concerns the concept of a penalty. Does *penalty* refer to the payment of restitution *or* the punishment that would follow for not making compensation? I suggest that distinguishing penalty from punishment might be helpful when discussing atonement.

Our study of Passover illustrated various ways that interpreters tend to use these metaphors. People make certain assumptions about their meaning and significance. We saw that the Passover lamb is not punished for Israel's sins. Rather, the lamb's blood serves as a mark identifying those in the house as belonging to the Lord. It was an act of allegiance, which all God's people were obliged to do. Not to do so would hasten God's wrath.

The observations in this chapter might startle some readers. They seem to raise more questions than answers. People will fear possible misreadings of the biblical text. Potential misinterpretations, however, do not negate the consistent way the Bible uses key metaphors to explain the atonement. Might we underestimate the significance of the payment language because of our relative wealth? If biblical authors did intend to use restitution and other monetary metaphors, we might predict that people would trivialize the sacrificial system, eventually seeking to exploit it. In fact, this distorted abuse of biblical teaching pervades the Prophets.[41] In the next chapter, we'll consider several debated passages in order to answer objections to the views shared in this book.

---

[41]Cf. Mal 1:7-13; Ps 50.

9

DOES THE FATHER
PUNISH THE SON?

OBSERVATIONS FROM THE PREVIOUS chapters challenge certain popular versions of penal substitutionary atonement (PSA). Specifically, many evangelicals assert that God the Father punishes Christ the Son for our sin. This, they say, is how atonement is accomplished. This view is entrenched within Protestant thinking.[1] Here are just a few examples:

Charles Wesley: "For what you have done, his blood must atone; The Father hath punished for you his dear Son."[2]

Martin Luther: "God himself struck and punished Christ."[3]

Herman Bavinck: "God condemned sin in the flesh (Romans 8:3) and punished him with the accursed death on the cross."[4]

---

[1]Howard Marshall contests this claim asking, "Where are these evangelicals who say that God punished Christ? Name them!" See his "The Theology of Atonement," in *The Atonement Debate: Papers from the London Symposium on the Theology of Atonement*, ed. Derek Tidball (Grand Rapids, MI: Zondervan, 2008), 63. In response, writers offer extensive lists of names. See Daniel J. Hill and Joseph Jedwab, "Atonement and the Concept of Punishment," in *Locating the Atonement*, ed. Oliver Crisp and Fred Sanders, Los Angeles Theology Conference Series (Grand Rapids, MI: Zondervan, 2015), 150-53.

[2]Charles Wesley, "All Ye That Pass By, Hymn 707," in *A Collection of Hymns*, ed. John Wesley London (1779; repr. Wesleyan-Methodist-Book-Room, 1889), www.hymntime.com/tch/htm/a/y/e/ayetpaby.htm.

[3]Martin Luther, "Ipse Deus percussit et punivet Christum," in *Werke: Kritische Gesamtausgabe*, vol. 40, part 3, ed. J. F. K. Knaake (Weimar: Bohlaus, 1930).

[4]Herman Bavinck, *Reformed Dogmatics*, vol. 3, ed. John Bolt, trans. John Vriend (Grand Rapids, MI: Baker Academic, 2006).

More recent examples include the following.[5]

> Robert Peterson: "How is that possible if God has not spent his holy hatred against sin? The answer is that God punished Christ with the wrath we sinners all deserve."[6]

> Stephen Nichols: "He perfectly kept the law. Yet, on the cross, God poured out His wrath on Christ."[7]

> Dan B. Allender and Tremper Longman III: "God chose to violate His Son in our place. The Son stared into the mocking eyes of God; He heard the laugher of the Father's derision and felt Him depart in disgust. . . . In a mysterious instant, the Father who loved the Son from all eternity turned from Him in hatred. The Son became odious to the Father."[8]

> Jack Arnold: "God took out his wrath on Christ instead of on sinners."[9]

> Abner Chou: "In that death the wrath of God was poured out on Christ, and the darkness exploded. In that instant God cursed Jesus, putting Him in a position of absolute, perfect hatred. God hated Him and desired to make Him nothing (Matthew 27)."[10]

> Sam Storms: "Why is it so difficult to envision a scenario in which by voluntary agreement the Father 'punishes' the Son in the place of those for whom he dies?"[11]

Often, this sentiment is hidden by sentences that use the passive voice. Teachers and doctrinal statements speak of Christ's "punishment being counted as ours" or his "being punished instead of us." Such phraseology obscures the implied punisher—God the Father. Others, like John Stott, seem at first to affirm PSA

---

[5]We can add John Piper, who answers the question "Why Is God Just to Punish Jesus for Our Sins When Doing a Similar Thing Would Be So Unjust for a Human Judge to Do?," September 4, 2020, www.desiringgod.org/interviews/why-is-god-just-to-punish-jesus-for-our-sins-when-doing -a-similar-thing-would-be-so-unjust-for-a-human-judge-to-do.

[6]Robert Peterson, *Salvation Accomplished by the Son: The Work of Christ* (Wheaton, IL: Crossway, 2012), 86.

[7]Stephen Nichols, "The Doctrine of Imputation: The Ligonier Statement on Christology," *Ligonier.org* (blog), April 16, 2016, www.ligonier.org/blog/doctrine-imputation-ligonier-statement-christology/.

[8]Dan Allender and Tremper Longman, *In the Cry of the Soul: How Our Emotions Reveal Our Deepest Questions About God*, 2nd ed. (Colorado Springs, CO: NavPress, 2015), 184-85 (emphasis added).

[9]Jack Arnold, "Propitiation: A Study on Romans 3:24-26," *IIIM Magazine Online* 1, no. 22 (1999), reformedperspectives.org/newfiles/jac_arnold/NT.Arnold.Rom.19.html.

[10]Abner Chou, "'The Big Picture of God's Mission': A Concise Overview of the Entire Bible" (blog), July 25, 2015, https://adam-setser-hlrz.squarespace.com/blog/2015/7/25/the-big-picture-of-gods -mission-a-concise-overview-of-the-entire-bible-by-dr-abner-chou.

[11]Sam Storms, "10 Things You Should Know About Penal Substitution," accessed April 13, 2020, www .samstorms.org/all-articles/post/article-10-things-you-should-know-about-penal-substitution.

while rejecting the claim that Christ is "the object of God's punishment."[12] On closer reflection, Stott agrees that Christ is "the victim of God's harsh justice" but that Christ endured the cross willingly.

This chapter answers two primary questions. First, does God the Father punish Christ the Son? Second, how do the insights from previous chapters help us to interpret several passages used to support certain versions of PSA? We begin by looking at two Old Testament texts cited by the Gospel writers. Then, we'll turn to a few key passages in Paul's letters.

DOES THE FATHER FORSAKE THE SON?

Psalm 22:1 is central to our discussion. The psalmist cries out, "My God, my God, why have you forsaken me? Why are you so far from saving me, from the words of my groaning?" As much as any other passage, theologians use this text to develop their view of PSA. J. I. Packer even writes,

> Jesus endured the true taste of hell for us on Calvary's cross. The essence of hell is God-forsakenness. The experience of hell was testified to when Jesus said, "My God, my God why have you forsaken me?" Jesus knew perfectly well why he was forsaken, but he asks this question to quote Psalm 22:1. He did this to reveal to his hearers that he was *tasting hell for them* and let them know that Scripture was being fulfilled.[13]

What does the psalmist mean by "forsaken"? Does Packer properly interpret the psalm in relation to Christ? Inexplicably, interpreters rarely (if ever) claim that God *completely* rejects the psalmist, even though he is the original author of these words.

MARK 15:21-34

They compelled a passer-by, who was coming in from the country, to carry his cross; it was Simon of Cyrene, the father of Alexander and Rufus. Then they brought Jesus to the place called Golgotha (which means the place of a skull). And they offered him wine mixed with myrrh; but he did not take it. And they crucified him, and divided his clothes among them, casting lots to decide what each should take. It was nine o'clock in the morning when they crucified him. The inscription of the charge against him read, "The King of the Jews."

---

[12]John Stott, *The Cross of Christ* (Downers Grove, IL: IVP Academic, 2012), 151.
[13]J. I. Packer, "The Necessity of Atonement," in *Atonement*, ed. Gabriel N. E. Fluhrer (Phillipsburg, PA: P&R Publishing, 2010), 15 (emphasis mine).

> And with him they crucified two bandits, one on his right and one on his left. Those who passed by derided him, shaking their heads and saying, "Aha! You who would destroy the temple and build it in three days, save yourself, and come down from the cross!" In the same way the chief priests, along with the scribes, were also mocking him among themselves and saying, "He saved others; he cannot save himself. Let the Messiah, the King of Israel, come down from the cross now, so that we may see and believe." Those who were crucified with him also taunted him.
>
> When it was noon, darkness came over the whole land until three in the afternoon. At three o'clock Jesus cried out with a loud voice, "Eloi, Eloi, lema sabachthani?" which means, "My God, my God, why have you forsaken me?"

Jesus quotes Psalm 22:1 while hanging on the cross.[14] The context of Jesus' crucifixion is important for determining the writer's intention for reporting these words. Notably, the influence of Psalm 22 in Mark is pervasive. In addition to thematic connections, Mark has several verbal links to Psalm 22.[15]

Mark	Psalm
15:24	22:18
15:29	22:7
15:30-31	22:8 (?)
15:32	22:6
15:34	22:1

In their accounts of Jesus' trial, Matthew and Mark underscore Christ's kingship. Their method is patently ironic. They recount the soldiers' mocking of Jesus ("Hail, King of the Jews") as he wore a purple cloak and crown of thorns. When Christ is lifted up, an inscription is set above him, "The King of the Jews." The criminals to his left and right give conflicting assessments about who Jesus is. Even the centurion overseeing the execution pronounces, "Truly this man was God's Son," a title with well-known royal connotations (Matthew 27:54; Mark 15:39).[16]

---

[14]Mt 27:46; Mk 15:34. The Gospel writers also draw from Ps 22:6 (Mt 27:39, 44; Mk 15:29, 32); Ps 22:7 (Mt 27:39; Mk 15:29); Ps 22:8 (Mt 27:43); Ps 22:16 (cf. Jn 20:24-27); Ps 22:17 (cf. Jn 19:32, 33, 36); Ps 22:18 (Mt 27:35; Mk 15:24; Jn 19:23-24); Ps 22:22 (Heb 2:12). Bauckham suggests Jn 19:30 might also allude to Ps 22:31. "Richard Bauckham Interview," *London Christian Thinkers*, January 29, 2015, accessed Jan 8, 2016, www.youtube.com/watch?v=oHSoovmy4cw.

[15]Thematically, Rikki Watts connects Mk 15:39/Ps 22:27; Mk 15:43/Ps 22:28; Mk 16:6/Ps 22:29; Mk 16:7 /Ps 22:30-31. See Rikki Watts, "Mark 15," *CNTOT*, loc. 8994-96, Kindle.

[16]Cf. Jn 1:49; 2 Sam 7:14; Ps 89. Also see Gerald Cooke, "The Israelite King as Son of God," *ZAW* 73 (1961): 202-25; F. J. Matera, "The Kingship of Jesus: Composition and Theology in Mark 15," SBL Dissertation Series 66 (Atlanta: SBL, 1982).

THE CONTEXT OF PSALM 22

What does "forsaken" (*'zb*) entail in Psalm 22? In Psalm 22:1-2, the psalmist says, "My God, my God, why have you forsaken me? / Why are you so far from helping me, from the words of my groaning? / O my God, I cry by day, but you do not answer; / and by night, but find no rest." As we've seen, many theologians assume that "forsaken" implies punishment or utter rejection by God.[17] Is this correct? We gain a better sense for the meaning of *'zb* by looking at the surrounding context.

The psalmist says God is "so far from helping me," does "not answer" him, and so "I find no rest" (Psalm 22:1-2). His repetition of the word *far* gives structure to the psalm (Psalm 22:1, 11, 19). Psalm 22:11 prays, "Be not *far* from me, for trouble is near and there is none to help." Likewise, he asks, "But you, O LORD, do not be far away!" (Psalm 22:19). Other texts also link distance and forsakenness. Psalm 38:21 says, "Do not forsake [*'zb*] me, O LORD; O my God, do not be far from me." At this point, we should make explicit a simple observation. God's being "far" away is not the same as being rejected or spurned by God. The former is not as strong an assertion as the latter.

> **PSALM 22:19-31**
>
> But you, O LORD, do not be far away! / O my help, come quickly to my aid! / Deliver my soul from the sword, / my life from the power of the dog! / Save me from the mouth of the lion! / From the horns of the wild oxen you have rescued me.
>
> I will tell of your name to my brothers and sisters; / in the midst of the congregation I will praise you: / You who fear the LORD, praise him! / All you offspring of Jacob, glorify him; / stand in awe of him, all you offspring of Israel!
>
> For he did not despise or abhor / the affliction of the afflicted, / and he did not hide his face from me, / but heard when I cried to him. / From you comes my praise in the great congregation; / my vows I will pay before those who fear him. / The poor shall eat and be satisfied; / those who seek him shall praise the LORD. / May your hearts live forever!
>
> All the ends of the earth shall remember / and turn to the LORD; / and all the families of the nations shall worship before him. / For dominion belongs to the LORD, / and he rules over the nations. To him, indeed, shall all who sleep in the earth bow down; / before him shall bow all who go down to the dust, / and

---

[17]While *'zb* can convey one's complete rejection of an enemy (e.g., Ps 71:11), the word has a wider range of meaning.

> I shall live for him. / Posterity shall serve him; / future generations will be told about the Lord; / and proclaim his deliverance to a people yet unborn, / saying that he has done it.

Theologians too often minimize or overlook the second half of the psalm when interpreting Jesus' words. Psalm 22:22-31 sharply contrasts popular views of Psalm 22:1. The psalmist expresses an expectation that God will save him. He fully expects to proclaim God's righteousness amid the congregation (Psalm 22:22, 31). In Psalm 22:19-21, his prayer suggests he does not think that "forsaking" is an absolute rejection (as implied by the notion that God forsook Christ in the way he condemns sinners). Furthermore, the psalmist is confident he will praise God for his coming deliverance in Psalm 22:22-23. This is proof that the writer does not think that God forsakes him in the sense of utter rejection or condemnation. Psalm 22:24 reinforces the point since God "did not despise or abhor the affliction of the afflicted, and he did not hide his face from me, but heard when I cried to him."

The psalmist does more than express wishful thinking; his expectations well exceed the plight of his circumstances. Psalm 22:27-28 recall God's covenants with Abraham and David. God will fulfill the covenant promises because he is king. For this reason, Mark 15:39 is noteworthy: "Now when the centurion, who stood facing him, saw that in this way he breathed his last, he said, 'Truly this man was God's Son!'" In effect, a Gentile (unknowingly) announces Jesus's kingship. Psalm 22:29 seems to point to a future resurrection. God will deliver David, his chosen king. He will keep his promises and establish righteousness in all the earth (Psalm 22:31).

The context of the psalm raises doubts about the conventional reading of Psalm 22:1. Forsaken (*'zb*) does not mean "rejected" as if God spurned the psalmist in the same way theologians say God must condemn sinners.[18] Instead, God's forsaking the psalmist merely conveys God's seeming absence from a situation. God's apparent absence leads to the psalmist's suffering, whereas his presence could bring salvation. God was "far" when he could have chosen to be near and present.

In different languages, words have varied connotations. Readers today can easily suppose that *forsaken* entails rejection. After all, the consequence of

---

[18]This point is sufficiently clear by the first appearance of the *'zb* in the Bible. Gen 2:24 says, "Therefore a man shall *leave* [*'zb*] his father and his mother and hold fast to his wife, and they shall become one flesh."

being forsaken includes suffering; yet that assumption misses a consistent, underlying aspect of the term. The psalmist complains of God's *inaction*.[19]

GOD VINDICATES THE FORSAKEN

Throughout the Old Testament, we see a similar understanding of being forsaken. In Lamentations 5:20-22, Jeremiah draws an important contrast. He says, "Why have you forgotten us completely? / Why have you *forsaken* ['zb] us these many days? / Restore us to yourself, O LORD, that we may be restored; / renew our days as of old— / unless you have *utterly rejected us,* / and are angry with us beyond measure." Although claiming God has forsaken them, he still prays for God's restoration. Jeremiah contrasts "utter rejection" with restoration, implicitly distinguishing it from their current forsakenness. His language clearly shows that *forsaken* does not mean the utter rejection that would be due sinners as punishment. Isaiah highlights the temporary nature of God-forsakenness. In Isaiah 54:7-8, the Lord says, "'For a brief moment I *abandoned* ['zb] you, / but with great compassion I will gather you. / In overflowing wrath for a moment / I hid my face from you, / but with everlasting love I will have compassion on you,' / says the LORD, your Redeemer." What is everlasting will overshadow that which is momentary, that is, God's forsaking his people.

In fact, several passages take pains to emphasize that God will not forsake his people.[20] In Psalm 37:28-29, the psalmist says, "For the LORD loves justice; / he will not *forsake* ['zb] his faithful ones. / The righteous shall be kept safe forever, / but the children of the wicked shall be cut off. / The righteous shall inherit the land, / and live in it forever." Furthermore, he adds, "The wicked watch for the righteous, / and seek to kill them. / The LORD will not *abandon* ['zb] them to their power, / or let them be condemned when they are brought to trial" (Psalm 37:32-33). Apparently, God's temporary absence or inaction does not express his utter rejection.[21] The common assumption that *forsaken* implies punishment or utter rejection by God is based on theological speculation at best.

---

[19]Other texts use 'zb to convey a passivity, ceasing to act, or leaving alone. The result could be positive, negative, or neutral; cf. Lev 19:10; 23:22; Judg 2:21; Ruth 2:16; 1 Chron 16:37; 2 Chron 32:31; Neh 5:10; Mal 4:1.

[20]See Ps 9:10; 27:9-10; 94:14; Is 40:27-29; 41:17; 42:14-16; 49:14-15. Each passage uses 'zb.

[21]In fact, biblical writers often use hyperbole and anthropologic language for effect. For example, the Lord says in Ezek 8:12, "Mortal, have you seen what the elders of the house of Israel are doing in the dark, each in his room of images? For they say, 'The LORD does not see us, the LORD has

How then should we understand Psalm 22:1? In essence, the writer says, "God, why have you not intervened but have instead left me to suffer in this way?" Richard Bauckham captures the meaning of forsaken in Psalm 22 saying, "To be forsaken by God means that he has allowed this to happen and does nothing to help."[22]

Psalmists routinely pose questions quite similar to that found in Psalm 22:1.[23] In fact, scholars have long observed a pattern that spans the psalter. Many psalms focus on an innocent or righteous person suffering unjustly. In the face of injustice, Psalm 71 says, "You who have made me see many troubles and calamities" (Psalm 71:20). Still, the writer prays, "Do not cast me off in the time of old age; / do not forsake me when my strength is spent. / For my enemies speak concerning me, / those who watch for my life consult together. / They say, 'Pursue and seize that person / whom God has forsaken, / for there is no one to deliver.' O God, do not be far from me; / O my God, make haste to help me!" (Psalm 71:9-12). One of most important passages that highlights the "righteous sufferer" is Psalm 69. Like Psalm 22, this passage significantly influences how the Gospel writers present their accounts of Jesus' trial and death.[24] In alluding to Psalm 69, Mark applies its expectation of vindication to Christ, the righteous sufferer.[25]

WHAT DID JESUS MEAN?

When we consider Christ's words in the context of the Gospels and Psalm 22, a consistent picture emerges.[26] The Gospel writers prepare readers to understand the significance of his words. He is the righteous sufferer whom God will vindicate. Rikki Watts says, "Psalm 22 likewise assumes Yahweh's able protection of his own. Consequently, while not detracting from Jesus' suffering, it is hard to understand why Mark would work so hard at evoking Ps. 22 if he did not also expect his informed readers to know exactly what was coming next: a

---

forsaken the land.'" We can hardly imagine the elders claiming that God is actually "blind" or unable to see them. However, it aptly expresses what it meant to say the land is forsaken.

[22] Richard Bauckham, *Jesus and the God of Israel* (Grand Rapids, MI: Eerdmans, 2008), loc. 3191-92, Kindle.

[23] Cf. Ps 10:1; 43:2; 44:22-23; 74:1, 11; 88:14.

[24] Among others, see Holly J. Carey, *Jesus' Cry from the Cross: Towards a First-Century Understanding of the Intertextual Relationship Between Psalm 22 and the Narrative of Mark's Gospel* (New York: T&T Clark, 2009), 89.

[25] Cf. Mk 14:57 (Ps 69:4); Mk 15:32 (Ps 69:9); Mk 15:36 (Ps 69:21). Similarly, Lk 23:45-47 draws from Ps 31:5. Ps 31 points to God's vindication. In these contexts, God will save his people, not condemn them.

[26] For an exceptional and extensive study, see Carey, *Jesus' Cry from the Cross*.

startling reversal and deliverance."[27] Jesus' cry must be understood in light of the entire psalm. Psalm 22 ultimately points to the hope that God will rescue David. In the same way, Jesus' call points to his hope of vindication. Christ knows that the Father is "my God." In a single line, he recalls the rest of the psalm and its expectation that God will be faithful. He knows what the psalmist knows. "Beyond the forsakenness, God intervened to deliver."[28]

Jesus' quote from Psalm 22:1 indicates the opposite of what is supposed by many popular readings. God does not condemn Jesus; instead, God will condemn his enemies. Christ's words foretell God's verdict on humanity. Contemporary readers should be reminded of the famous movie line from *Terminator*, where Arnold Schwarzenegger's character says, "I'll be back." In essence, this is the intended effect of Christ's words. While his followers grieve, Jesus assures them of victory.[29]

In summary, we have two major options when interpreting Jesus when he quotes Psalm 22:1. What does he mean by "Why have you forsaken me?" Many theologians assert that God treats Jesus with the contempt deserved by sinful humanity. On the cross, Christ is utterly rejected by God the Father. For some reason, these same scholars do not argue that God fully rejects the psalmist, despite being the original speaker of these words.

I've suggested that this is an overreading of the text. In fact, looking at the biblical context, a second interpretation is more likely. For the psalmist, God's forsaking him merely implies that God has not (yet) chosen to deliver him from his trial. In fact, the psalm resembles many other passages where the writer shows confidence that God will vindicate the righteous sufferer. Christ does not lament the fact that God punishes him or deems him "odious." Instead, he anticipates the day when the Father will vindicate him and his people.

Does the Father Strike the Son?

As Jesus eats his last meal with his disciples, he tells them, "You will all become deserters; for it is written, 'I will strike the shepherd, and the sheep will be scattered'" (Mark 14:27; cf. Matthew 26:31).[30] This quotation from Zechariah 13:7

---

[27] Watts, "Mark," loc. 8994-96, Kindle.

[28] Bauckham, *Jesus and the God of Israel*, loc. 3223-24, Kindle.

[29] Cf. L. Paul Trudinger, "Eli, Eli, Lama Sabachthani? A Cry of Dereliction or Victory?," *JETS* 17, no. 4 (Fall 1974): 235-38.

[30] Notably, the Gospels adapt the quote from Zech 13:7. In Hebrew, the verb "(You) strike" uses the second-person singular. The Greek LXX uses the second-person plural "(You all) strike." The

appears to support the claim that God the Father strikes Jesus. We again should look at the biblical context to understand the point of the passage.

MARK 14:27-29

And Jesus said to them, "You will all be deserters, for it is written, 'I will strike the shepherd, / and the sheep will be scattered.' But after I am raised up, I will go before you to Galilee." Peter said to him, "Even though they all become deserters, I will not."

ZECHARIAH 13:7

"Awake, O sword, against my shepherd, / against the man who is my associate," says the LORD of hosts. "Strike the shepherd, / that the sheep may be scattered; / I will turn my hand against the little ones."

We first look at the context around Mark 14:27. In Mark 14:18-21, Jesus predicts someone will betray him. Peter denies Christ in Mark 14:29-31. Mark 14:32-52 show how the disciples scatter in the face of danger. One man even "left the linen cloth and ran off naked" (Mark 14:52). Finally, Mark reports Peter's additional denials of Jesus in Mark 14:66-72.

Keep in mind that Mark 14:27 begins with a prediction, "You will all be deserters." Jesus only then introduces Zechariah's text ("for"). The quotation serves merely to support the main assertion that his disciples will fall away. The surrounding context further underscores the disciples' negative reaction to Christ's arrest.

Why does this matter? The purpose of citing Zechariah is not to highlight or develop an atonement theology. Jesus simply emphasizes the point that the sheep will scatter when the shepherd is struck. We immediately witness the fulfillment of Jesus' prophecy in the ensuing paragraphs (e.g., Peter's denial; one runs away naked).

What about the context of Zechariah 13:7? Who are the shepherds? They are Israel's leaders (including prophets), who mislead the people. The shepherd of Zechariah 10 is corrupt (Zechariah 10:2, 3; 11:3-6). In other words, the shepherd in Zechariah 13 is not the shepherd of Mark 14. Then in Zechariah 13:8-9, we read, "In the whole land, says the LORD, / two thirds shall be cut off and perish, / and one third shall be left alive. / And I will put this third into the fire, / refine them

---

Gospels use the first-person singular, "I will strike." We can only speculate why Mark and Matthew modify the wording.

as one refines silver, / and test them as gold is tested. / They will call on my name, / and I will answer them. / I will say, 'They are my people'; / and they will say, 'The LORD is our God.'"[31] Once again, the focus of the text is this: God's people will be scattered, but he will bring them back.[32]

What do Mark 14 and Zechariah 13 have in common? Both contexts highlight the misfortune faced by God's people and the future hope that will follow. Likewise, the reason Jesus appeals to Zechariah is to stress the *scattering* of the sheep. This emphasis is made explicit by the "for." Whereas theologians typically focus on the shepherd, Christ and the prophet focus on the sheep.[33]

CONDEMNING SIN (ROMANS 8:3)

Advocates of PSA frequently appeal to Romans 8:3. How does God condemn sin in Christ? Romans 8:1-4 says,

> There is therefore now no condemnation for those who are in Christ Jesus. For the law of the Spirit of life in Christ Jesus has set you free from the law of sin and of death. For God has done what the law, weakened by the flesh, could not do: *by sending his own Son in the likeness of sinful flesh*, and to deal with sin, he condemned sin in the flesh, so that the just requirement of the law might be fulfilled in us, who walk not according to the flesh but according to the Spirit.

According to conventional readings, Romans 8:3 says that sin is condemned by Jesus enduring our punishment. However, this view misunderstands the context and imagery of Romans 8:3, which belongs to a larger unit of thought. Romans 5:12 to Romans 8 form a unit of thought. In Romans 5, Paul introduces "sin" into his argument. Throughout Romans 5–7, sin is personified as a king or slavemaster.[34] In Romans 5:17, Paul says, "As sin reigned in death, grace also might reign through righteousness."

Romans 6–7 continues this royal imagery. He contrasts sin and righteousness, presenting them as royal slavemasters. This explains why the *wages* of sin is death in Romans 6:23. Death is sin's "salary" to us. Paul does not only talk about people's actions. He uses a metaphor whereby sin is like Pharaoh. Sin enslaves God's people.

---

[31]Cf. Ps 66:10, 12; Is 48:10; Mal 3:2-3.

[32]In this respect, Mk 14:28 may hint at the disciples' restoration.

[33]Even if one still wants to focus on God's action, this is not a problem. In Zech 13, what is God's purpose? To purify his people. The very people God will save are those he decides to put into the fire. God's striking is an expression of his grace. The thrust of attention is still given to the sheep. I am not saying that Jesus takes Zechariah out of context.

[34]For example, Rom 5:21; 6:12, 14, 20. Death reigns in Rom 5:17.

In Romans 7:8-14, sin is an active adversary. For example, "sin, seizing an opportunity through the commandment, deceived me and through it killed me" (Romans 7:11). Also "we know that the law is spiritual; but I am of the flesh, sold into slavery under sin" (Romans 7:14). The sharp contrast that pervades Romans 7 is between "sin" and "me." Accordingly, Paul concludes, "But in fact it is no longer I that do it, but sin that dwells within me. . . . Now if I do what I do not want, it is no longer I that do it, but sin that dwells in me" (Romans 7:17, 20). In Romans 8, sin stands in contrast to the Holy Spirit, who dwells within believers.

Therefore, when we arrive at Romans 8, a natural response is to regard sin as a personification. Observe the contrast in Romans 8:1, 3. Paul first says, "There is therefore now no condemnation for those who are in Christ Jesus." Then he adds, "By sending his own Son in the likeness of sinful flesh and to deal with sin, he condemned sin in the flesh" (Romans 8:3). Both verses use the same root word. Verse 1 uses the noun *katakrima*. Romans 8:3 uses the verb *katakrinō*. Their objects are different. Through Jesus, God condemns sin rather than those who are in Christ Jesus. Just as Romans 8:1 refers to a person, in the same way, Romans 8:3 refers to a person, namely, "sin," the royal master from Romans 5–7.

God conducts a trial where sin is the defendant. In Romans 7:13, the law exposes sin's true face. In Romans 6, God already changes his people's hearts; they now have new desires. If I "do the very thing I hate," Paul concludes, "it is no longer I who do it, but sin that dwells within me" (Romans 7:15, 17). In Romans 7, Paul goes to great lengths to distinguish "sin" from "me." "Sin" and "I" have very different fates. God declares "me" righteous, but he condemns "sin." (Notice that Paul never says that God punishes or condemns Jesus. Nor does Paul teach that God condemns us.)

How does he do this? The answer is found in Romans 8:3, though obscured by some translations. By God sending his son "for sin, he condemned sin in the flesh" (ESV).[35] However, *peri hamartias* is the standard phrase referring to the reconciliation offering.[36] The "condemning" of sin is the conquering of sin, just as he defeated Pharoah and the Egyptian gods during the exodus. In Romans 8, Paul explains that the reconciliation offering is the means by which Jesus secured ultimate victory.

---

[35]Greek: *peri hamartias katekrine tēn hamartian en tē sarki.*

[36]The ESV acknowledges this option in a footnote. Also see N. T. Wright, "On Becoming the Righteousness of God," in *Pauline Theology*, ed. D. M. Hay, vol. 2 (Minneapolis: Augsburg Fortress, 1993), 208n14; Wright, *The Climax of the Covenant* (Minneapolis: Fortress, 1993), 221n10. Wright lists examples like Ex 29:14, 36; Lev 4:8, 20, 24, 25, 29, 32, 33, 34; 5:12; 6:17 (LXX/MT 6:10); 6:25; Num 6:14.

How do we put it all together? How does God atone for sin? God sends Jesus to become a reconciliation offering. This offering pays our debt to entreat God's favor. It frees people from the law. The law cannot accuse us and so we are not punished. As a result, sin has no power and death no longer reigns over our lives. Because we are free from the law, we are able to obey God's words from the heart.[37] The reconciliation offering is God's means of overcoming sin.

DID CHRIST BECOME SIN? (2 CORINTHIANS 5:21)

What about 2 Corinthians 5:21? According to the NRSV, Paul says, "For our sake [God] made him [Christ] to be *sin [hamartian epoiēsen]* who knew no sin, so that in him we might become the righteousness of God." Biblical scholars have long debated how to translate this verse. A key phrase is "to be sin." Several interpreters suggest the phrase means that Christ became a reconciliation offering.[38]

Many people assert the traditional translation without defense.[39] Wright and others note, "*hamartian* is of course a regular LXX way of rendering the various phrases for 'sin-offering' [reconciliation offering]."[40] This observation fits a major motif of the context of 2 Corinthians—reconciliation (2 Corinthians 5:18-20). Because Christ became a reconciliation offering, we can be reconciled to God.

> ## 2 CORINTHIANS 5:14-21
>
> For the love of Christ urges us on, because we are convinced that one has died for all; therefore all have died. And he died for all, so that those who live might live no longer for themselves, but for him who died and was raised for them.
>
> From now on, therefore, we regard no one from a human point of view; even though we once knew Christ from a human point of view, we know him no longer in that way. So if anyone is in Christ, there is a new creation:

---

[37]By "we," I don't imply that anyone today has ever been "under the Mosaic law."

[38]For example, J. D. G. Dunn, "Paul's Understanding of the Death of Jesus as Sacrifice," in *Sacrifice and Redemption: Durham Essays in Theology*, ed. S. W. Sykes (Cambridge: Cambridge University Press, 2007), 42-43; Wright, "On Becoming the Righteousness of God."

[39]For examples, see David L. Turner, "Paul and the Ministry of Reconciliation in 2 Cor 5:11-6:2," *Criswell Theological Review* 4, no. 1 (1989): 87; John Piper, *The Future of Justification: A Response to N. T. Wright* (Wheaton, IL: Crossway, 2007). Although dealing with the phrase "righteousness of God," he simply assumes the traditional translation "sin" rather than "sin offering"; Adrian Warnock, "2 Corinthians 5 and Romans 5—Two Critical Passages on Justification," *Adrian Warnock* (blog), November 14, 2007, www.patheos.com/blogs/adrianwarnock/2007/11/2-corinthians-5-and-romans-5-two.

[40]Wright, "On Becoming the Righteousness of God," 208n14.

everything old has passed away; see, everything has become new! All this is from God, who reconciled us to himself through Christ, and has given us the ministry of reconciliation; that is, in Christ God was reconciling the world to himself, not counting their trespasses against them, and entrusting the message of reconciliation to us. So we are ambassadors for Christ, since God is making his appeal through us; we entreat you on behalf of Christ, be reconciled to God. For our sake he made him to be *sin* [= reconciliation offering] who knew no sin, so that in him we might become the righteousness of God.

Notice the parallel phrasing in 2 Corinthians 5:15 (*hyper autōn*, "for their sake") and 2 Corinthians 5:21 (*hyper hēmōn*, "for our sake").[41] Paul in 2 Corinthians 5:21 elaborates on the significance of Christ's death (mentioned in 2 Corinthians 5:15). Paul changes his way of speaking in 2 Corinthians 5:21. Rather than saying "Jesus died," he says, "Jesus became a reconciliation offering." "Reconciliation offering" expresses the significance of Jesus' death. In short, 2 Corinthians 5:21 explains 2 Corinthians 5:15. Jesus' death "for their sake" is a reconciliation offering "for our sake." This is why Christ brings reconciliation.

A few observations not only support this conclusion; they also answer possible objections. First, someone might say that the word for "sin" appears twice in the same verse and so should not have two translations (i.e., "sin" and "sin offering").[42] However, this dual translation is typical in the context of the sanctuary and sacrifice.[43] In fact, 2 Corinthians 5:21 is squeezed between paragraphs that evoke tabernacle and temple imagery (2 Corinthians 5:1-4; 6:14-18). So, in the case of 2 Corinthians 5, using two translations for *hamartia* in the same verse is not at all surprising. Rather, it is almost expected.

Second, some people might object that the translation "to be a sin offering [reconciliation offering]" disrupts the verse's symmetry. They say that "become sin" parallels "become God's righteousness." In response, observe that the two phrases use different Greek verbs (*poieō, ginomai*). Thus, the sentence's so-called symmetry does not necessarily exist.

In addition, the combination of words that form the phrase "to be sin" are often together in the Old Testament. The verb *poieō* normally indicates the doing

---

[41]In 2 Corinthians 5:15, Paul says of Christ: "he died for all, that those who live might no longer live for themselves but for him who *for their sake* [*hyper autōn*] died and was raised." Then, in 2 Cor 5:16, the *Hōste* (thus, therefore) indicates that the verses following 2 Cor 5:15 are logical implications of 2 Cor 5:15.
[42]Again, I suggest "reconciliation offering" better translates the term for sin offering.
[43]For example, Lev 4:20-21; 5:6.

of an action. Interestingly, this phrase *hamartian epoiēsen* (do/be sin) is able to have two contrary meanings: "to do sin" and "be a reconciliation offering."[44]

So, how do we translate 2 Corinthians 5:21? We'll consider three possible translations of this key sentence.

God "made the one who knew no sin to do sin."

God "made him to be sin who knew no sin."

God "made the one who knew no sin to become a reconciliation offering."

The first option is obviously wrong. Of the two remaining possibilities, the second translation is traditional but unlikely. It is not a natural rendering. Not only this, but traditional explanations given by theologians neither fit the original Greek nor the traditional translation. Why? Such theologians often say that "becoming sin" means that Jesus receives or bears our sin. Conflating these two actions leads to confusion and relies entirely on speculation. Receiving something (like sin) does not mean one becomes that thing! I can accept a person's apology, but that doesn't mean I become the apology. Therefore, the final translation is the best choice. It is a natural rendering of the verse and suits the surrounding context.

WHEN DID JESUS BECOME A CURSE? (GALATIANS 3)

In this section, we examine how Galatians might contribute to our view of Christ's atoning work. Interpreters often assume that Galatians 3:13, quoting Deuteronomy 21:23, refers to the mechanism by which Christ secures atonement from the law's curse. As Daniel Streett notes, this reading has significant obstacles. For starters, he says,

> Deut 21:23 does not, in context, pronounce a curse on all victims of crucifixion (or hanging) *ipso facto*. . . . Rather, the law explicitly refers only to those who commit a sin punishable by death—most likely blasphemy or apostasy—and who are subsequently executed and displayed. . . . In fact, numerous faithful Jews were crucified under various regimes, but no one believed that those martyrs had therefore fallen under the curse of God simply by virtue of their means of execution. In the OT, the corpses of Saul and Jonathan had been displayed publicly

---

[44]For example, Lev 4:20; 9:7, 22; 14:19; 15:15, 30; 23:19; Num 6:11, 16; 8:12; 28:15; Ezek 43:25; 45:17, 22, 25. In the LXX, the Bible uses such wording when referencing other sacrifices. Essentially, it often communicates the idea "to offer sacrifice."

by the Philistines (2 Sam 21:12), but no one took that to mean that Saul and
Jonathan were cursed by the law.[45]

Moreover, *being a curse* is not equivalent to *be accursed by God*. Concerning
the former, he states, "to become a curse is to become the object of society's
ridicule (*gelōs*) or reproach."[46] After surveying an array of evidence, Streett
concludes, "To become a curse, it seems, is to be thought by others (whether
rightly or wrongly) to be under a curse. It is most important to note that one
who becomes a curse is not necessarily cursed by God."[47]

Supposing, however, that Galatians 3:13 does refer to the mechanism of
atonement, how might we understand Christ becoming a curse? We turn to
consider that possibility. Galatians 3:10-14 says,

> For all who rely on the works of the law are under a curse; for it is written,
> "Cursed is everyone who does not observe and obey all the things written in the
> book of the law." Now it is evident that no one is justified before God by the law;
> for "The one who is righteous will live by faith." But the law does not rest on faith;
> on the contrary, "Whoever does the works of the law will live by them." Christ
> redeemed us from the curse of the law by becoming a curse for us—for it is
> written, "Cursed is everyone who hangs on a tree" in order that in Christ Jesus
> the blessing of Abraham might come to the Gentiles, so that we might receive
> the promise of the Spirit through faith.

Conventionally, Protestants argue that humanity's sin was placed on Jesus.[48]
Consequently, Christ became a curse and thus had to die to bear the punishment of our sin.[49] I argue this sequence is backward: Christ *first* died *then*
became a curse.

---

[45]Daniel Streett, "Cursed by God? Galatians 3:13, Social Status, and Atonement Theory in the Context of Early Jewish Readings of Deuteronomy 21:23," *JSPL* 5, no. 2 (2015): 194-95. Numerous other scholars make similar observations.

[46]Streett, "Cursed by God?," 202. Not only does Paul omit "by God" (*hypo theou*) from the LXX's rendering of Deut 21:23, the church fathers also resoundingly reject the claim that God cursed Jesus. Augustine even suggests that Gal 3:13 fulfills Ps 109:25 ("I am an *object of scorn* to my accusers") (Streett, "Cursed by God?," 206-9). The psalmist then adds, "*Let* them curse [*kataraomai*, LXX], but you will bless" (Ps 109:28).

[47]Streett, "Cursed by God?," 203.

[48]More nuanced is N. T. Wright's view that Christ takes on Israel's "curse of exile" pronounced in Deuteronomy. See Wright, *Climax of the Covenant*, 141; cf. Wright, *Paul and the Faithfulness of God*, vol. 2 (Minneapolis: Fortress, 2013), 865.

[49]For example, see Martin Luther, *Luther's Works: Lectures on Galatians*, vol. 26 (Saint Louis: Concordia, 1963), 277, 280. Cited in Timothy George, "The Atonement in Martin Luther's Theology," in *The Glory of the Atonement: Biblical, Theological & Practical Perspectives*, ed. Charles E. Hill and Frank A. James III

Paul in Galatians 3:13 quotes Deuteronomy 21:23.

> Then all the men of the city shall stone him to death with stones. So you shall purge
> the evil from your midst, and all Israel shall hear, and fear. And if a man has com-
> mitted a crime punishable by death and he is put to death, and you hang him on
> a tree, his body shall not remain all night on the tree, but you shall bury him the
> same day, for a hanged man is cursed by God. You shall not defile your land that
> the LORD your God is giving you for an inheritance. (Deuteronomy 21:21-23)

In Deuteronomy 21:18-21, Moses describes a case where someone should receive capital punishment. If this punishment also includes the offender's body
being hanged from a tree, Moses says what people should do (Deuteronomy 21:22).[50] It must be taken down lest the land be defiled.

CURSING IN CONTEXT

"Hanged from a tree" has what meaning? Ryken, Wilhoit, and Longman explain
"hanging (by a noose) was rarely a means of execution until Roman times." By
contrast, impaling was more common.[51] They add,

> Previously killed bodies were hung up on trees or stakes (usually by their hands,
> Lam 5:12). Such hangings were to expose the body to public scorn; they were
> symbols of the person's total disgrace and rejection by God. They were to be
> limited to one day (Deut 21:23). Examples include Joshua stringing up five
> Amorite kings (Josh 10:26) and the Philistines' triumphant display of Saul and
> Jonathan (2 Sam 21:12).[52]

In ancient Mediterranean culture, doing this exposed and humiliated the dead
person. Symbolically, they are completely shamed and rejected by God.

(Downers Grove, IL: IVP Academic, 2004), 271-75; Richard Gaffin, "Atonement in the Pauline Cor-
pus," in *The Glory of the* Atonement, 159; Bruce Demarest, *The Cross and Salvation: The Doctrine of God*
(Wheaton, IL: Crossway, 2006), 171, 174; Frank Thielmann, "The Atonement," in *Central Themes in
Biblical Theology*, ed. Scott Hafemann and Paul House (Nottingham: Apollos, 2007), 111; William
D. Barrick, "Penal Substitution in the Old Testament," *TMSJ* 20, no. 2 (Fall 2009): 153; J. I. Packer,
"What Did the Cross Achieve? The Logic of Penal Substitution," *TynBul* 25 (1973): 45. Packer says,
"The curse is the divine condemnation of sin which leads to death." Ernest D. Burton, "Redemption
from the Curse of the Law: An Exposition of Gal. 3:13, 14," *AJT* 11, no. 4 (1907): 641-45.

[50]From context, there is no immediate reason to assume the cause of death itself is hanging from a
tree. First, the prior context speaks of one who is stoned to death. In addition, the *waw* most naturally means "and" ("And if a man has committed a crime punishable by death *and* [*waw*] he is put
to death, and you hang him on a tree"). In agreement, Max Wilcox, "'Upon the Tree': Deut 21:22-23
in the New Testament," *JBL* 96, no. 1 (1977): 87.

[51]Ryken, Wilhoit, and Longman, "Hanging," *DBI*, 363.

[52]Ryken, Wilhoit, and Longman, "Hanging," 363.

Hanging a person's body on a tree was not the usual form of burial; rather, this burial method mistreats the corpse.

Joshua 10:26-27 shows how Israel applied Deuteronomy 21: "Afterward Joshua struck them down and put them to death, and he hung them on five trees. And they hung on the trees until evening. At sunset Joshua commanded, and they took them down from the trees and threw them into the cave where they had hidden themselves." Joshua 8:29 reinforces this point: *the cursed hanging is postmortem*. Wilcox and others likewise concur about the standard Jewish reading of Deuteronomy 21: "'Hanging (up) on the tree' is not the execution; it is the corpse that is so treated after execution."[53]

There is a natural reason why people confuse the two contexts. Anyone crucified on a cross will also have their corpse hanged on a tree. Yet, we should note that the opposite order is not true. Having one's body exposed on a tree does not imply crucifixion. The clearest allusions to Deuteronomy 21 in Scripture do not refer to the means of death.[54]

We should not deduce too much. Logically speaking, it is much safer to claim less than more. We certainly have warrant to say Deuteronomy 21 refers to a postmortem cursing. For careful exegesis, we must resist the temptation to press our theological traditions into texts.

For example, people like to say things like "This is obvious," and "This is simple," but these claims and reality are two different things. Although the possibility of the traditional reading exists, the interpretation itself lacks definite scriptural support. The burden of proof is on the traditional view (hanging as a means of death), which claims more but with less evidence.

Jesus perfectly honored the Father. As a sinless man, he himself could not be cursed. Yet, in accordance with Deuteronomy 21:23, Jesus was cursed. That is,

---

[53]Wilcox, "Upon the Tree," 87. Likewise, Ardel Caneday, "'Redeemed from the Curse of the Law': The Use of Deut 21:22-23 in Gal 3:13," *TrinJ* 10 (1989): 198-201. David Fiensy's comments underscore the point that Deut 21:23 refers to a person whose corpse is hanged from a tree: "The Dead Sea document from Qumran, the Temple Scroll, had changed this curse to include those hanged on a tree while still living (thus crucified; 11QT 64:7-13)" (emphasis mine). In the case of the Qumran document, the exception proves the rule. Wilcox ("Upon the Tree," 88) goes further to say that the language of 11QT 64, 7-13 is ambiguous; thus, this potential exception itself cannot be used to overturn the meaning of Deut 21 within its own canonical and historical context. David Fiensy, "Crucifixion," in *The Lexham Bible Dictionary*, ed. John D. Barry and Lazarus Wentz (Bellingham, WA: Logos Bible Software, 2012); cf. JPS's English translation of Deut 21:23, "For an impaled body is an affront to God."

[54]To state it more sharply, Jewish mothers were not concerned that their children not climb trees in case they "hung on a tree." The entire point of the phraseology is to point to a person's having died then hung on the tree. Death is the decisive point between being cursed and not being cursed.

he suffered the public shame of having his body exposed on the cross, being cast away by his people.[55] His people spurn him. In this way, Jesus was perfectly cursed. As Israel's true king, Jesus represents his people. He takes on the curse promised to Israel if she broke covenant with God (Deuteronomy 28–30).

In history, God promised to bless and curse Israel. For example, in Deuteronomy 28–29, God says he will curse unfaithful, covenant-breaking Israel. In Jesus, God is able both to bless and curse Israel. In this way, God shows himself righteous. As a result, the blessing of Abraham comes to the Gentiles (Galatians 3:14). He is able to keep his promises. As a result, Christ unties a proverbial Gordian knot.

Slowly look at the logic. Israel's being cursed leads to death. Supposing Christ wants to bear Israel's curse, making Israel free from the law's curse, what can he do? How can he represent Israel and become a curse? He does not want to sin. Normally, only sinners can suffer a curse. How can an innocent person become a curse? Deuteronomy 21:23 provides a solution. Christ (receiving a curse) is not God's punishment. One's corpse hanging on a tree, itself, signifies a state of cursing. Christ is able to be a curse without sinning. Christ in life was perfect. Christ in death becomes a curse. Christ became a perfect sacrifice.[56]

CONCLUSION

The Bible clearly portrays God's wrath against sin. In many cases, God does not execute the offender. Nor does he execute priests merely because they bear the sin of God's people. Additionally, no text explicitly states that the deaths of the sacrificed animals have the same function or significance as would the death of the sinner. The one who bears his own sin dies as just punishment.

By contrast, we've seen that the slaughtered animals, as sacrificial offerings, serve as compensation that remove the burden of sin, thus the sentence of condemnation. The simple fact that God shows wrath against sin does not necessarily imply he *must* punish sinners for every one of their sins. More is said on this point in appendix B.

---

[55]Being cursed in the Bible carries multiple connotations. For example, besides death, cursing could allude to being slandered, exiled, and cut off from one's people. For discussion on the meaning of being a curse, see Ryken, Wilhoit, and Longman, "Curse," *DBI*; J. A. Motyer, "Curse," *NBD*; Mary J. Evans, "Blessing/Curse," *NDBT*, 397-401; "qĕlālâ," *HALOT*.

[56]For further elaboration on the logic of Gal 3:10-13, see Jeffrey Wisdom, "Blessing for the Nations and the Curse of the Law: Paul's Citation of Genesis and Deuteronomy in Gal 3.8–10" (PhD diss., Durham University, 1998).

Until now, I've not highlighted one of the most striking observations. In the Bible, we cannot find any verse that explicitly states that God's wrath is poured out on the Christ. We also cannot find any verse that explicitly states that God's wrath is poured out on a reconciliation offering. Therefore, *we have no reason to say that a substitute vicariously receives the punishment otherwise due to the guilty party.* The wording in this claim is important. Although Jesus is innocent, he does die for sinners such that they do not have to die. Jesus appeases God's wrath, securing his favor on our behalf.[57] Forgiven sinners do not receive punishment, but this is not because God's wrath punishes Jesus.

In this section, we examined several passages that people commonly use to explain the significance of Christ's death. None of these texts suggest the traditional formulation of penal substitution. My interpretation and traditional ideas reach similar conclusions; yet our paths are very different. At times, these passages even argue against some traditional interpretations. In the next chapter, I will address numerous questions that have yet to be answered.

---

[57]Recall from our discussion of *kpr* and *exilaskomai* (chap. 4) that appeasement entails entreating favor, but it does not necessarily imply wrath or punishment.

SECTION THREE

IMPLICATIONS

and APPLICATIONS

10

ANSWERS TO
LINGERING QUESTIONS

THE PRECEDING CHAPTERS RAISE several questions and objections. However, there is not always a fitting place to answer them. I did not want to break the flow of the main arguments presented in the previous chapters. Inserting discussions about related issues might distract from the main ideas of each chapter.

Accordingly, this chapter addresses an array of lingering questions. In the first part, I reflect on broader concerns that tie everything together. Part two looks at many of the most pressing questions I anticipate readers will ask. The final section offers a few brief comments to help readers interpret important texts concerning the atonement. I assume readers have studied the previous chapters. So, in the attempt to be succinct here, I will assume the conclusions reached in earlier chapters.

BIG PICTURE QUESTIONS

Are you overcomplicating the atonement? Why does it have to be complex? No, I am not making the atonement more complicated than it is in Scripture. The doctrine has always been a rich tapestry of teachings and text. It is only "simple" when we reduce it to something far narrower than what is presented in the Bible. While certain broad contours may be obvious, we shouldn't confuse parts for the whole.

Several factors contribute to the doctrine's inherent complexity, if that's how we choose to frame it. Biblical writers employ various metaphors across an array of contexts. The effects of Christ's atoning work are manifold and diverse.

In addition, there is no single explanation in Scripture concerning *how* Christ achieves atonement on our behalf.

Consider just a few matters that any comprehensive theory of atonement must address. First, one must speak to the relationship between the cross and the law, the old covenant. It should explain the meaning in Galatians of Christ becoming a "curse" for the sake of blessing the Gentiles. How does Christ effect atonement for *both* Israel and Gentiles? Furthermore, a biblical view of the atonement will account for the way in which Christ's death inaugurates the new covenant. He does not merely complete the old covenant. The atonement creates new hearts within God's people. Of course, our interpretation must reflect the sacrificial system found in the Pentateuch. Our doctrine should also incorporate the exodus story, which forms the background for many New Testament texts that look at Christ's atoning work. Finally, a comprehensive theory will reflect those key metaphors used in the Bible to explain the atonement.

None of the most popular theories of atonement are so wide-ranging. They succeed in some areas, but not others. This book has not offered a simplistic, systematized theory. It merely seeks to help us regain the biblical ingredients that form a biblical doctrine of atonement. The previous chapters remind us that this teaching is a signpost to a much larger story. In this way, we do better to describe a biblical doctrine of atonement as *rich*, not merely complex.

What is the interrelationship between the three main metaphors? Impurity prevents a person from approaching a holy God. In this way, impurity endangers people. It also creates an obligation. When they are impure or profane God, his people are required to set right their relationship to God. Another name for this obligation is "debt," something a person must do. Naturally, debts often feel like a burden.

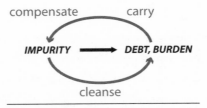

Figure 10.1. Interrelationship between the three main metaphors

The diagram above illustrates the problem and solution. The middle arrow depicts the fact that impurity produces a debt and burden. The top and bottom curved arrows highlight the function of the sacrifices in terms of the three main metaphors, that is, compensation, carrying a burden, and cleansing. Sacrifices (e.g., reconciliation offering, reparation offering) bring purification, cleansing impurity (the bottom, leftward arrow). In this way, they pay one's debt and remove the person's burden (the top, rightward arrow).

Can you give a big picture, simplified summary of the Bible's atonement theology? Sin and impurity create distance in our relationship with God. He is dishonored by sin or uncleanness that has not been addressed. The consequence is alienation or separation in our relationship both with God and others. Fundamentally, sin entails not glorifying God. God is holy and thus worthy of unique honor.

Biblical writers explain the solution using several metaphors or images. At one level, we need cleansing, some way to make compensation and have our sin-impurity carried away. At a deeper level, humans must give God the honor he demands and deserves. We desire reconciliation so that we might come near to him. A person must be wholly given or dedicated to God.

What is the context in which this restoration happens? The Bible routinely portrays the sacrifices as meals of worship. The offerings serve as symbolic food and drink given up to God. These gifts are enjoyed by his representatives or carried up to God through fire. The smoke rises up with a pleasing aroma. In this way, the sacrifices effect reconciliation. God is honored and fellowship is restored.

Perhaps, this grossly simplified summary is captured in four words:

1. Honor[1]

2. Presence

3. Devotion (or Gift)

4. Meal

Honor represents the core problem and solution. Humanity dishonors God and so must turn to glorify him. In this way, honor alludes both to the purpose and the mechanism for atonement. Presence signifies a fundamental purpose for seeking atonement. We desire God's presence. We could debate whether the third word is most apt, yet devotion (or gift) captures an essential aspect that runs throughout the sacrificial system. This is a devoted gift that gives

---

[1]We include glory, respect, esteem, and so on in this category.

honor to God and removes the barriers that obstruct relationship with his people. The fourth word (meal) points to the reconciliation that results. The offerings often symbolize food. The gift or meal functions as a mechanism that effects atonement.[2]

Scholars quickly learn to avoid oversimplification and claiming too much. This is why they hedge their claims with words like "perhaps" and "likely." As an academic, why then do I risk the inevitable criticism that will come by offering this overtly generalized and reductionistic summary of the atonement? Because it's useful. The mind can retain only a limited amount of information. Readers will forget most of the details in this book unless they read it more than once. These four words can at least serve as hangers or boxes to organize our ideas. They can act like a mental map directing our conversation and reflections. They should *not* be used to assess the whole of this book's arguments.[3]

Can you summarize how sacrifices bring about atonement? The following diagram provides a pictorial overview of entire atonement process. Again, it is highly simplistic but helpful for aiding readers to recall the information in this book.

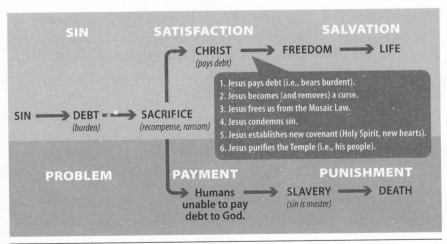

Figure 10.2. How sacrifices bring about atonement

---

[2]Why do I speak about purpose and mechanism? Recall from chap. 1 that atonement theories tend to emphasize either how atonement is achieved (mechanism) or what atonement accomplishes (purpose).

[3]For example, this big picture overview says nothing about covenants, which is a critical aspect of the Bible's atonement theology.

The problem of sin is depicted to the left. As a result, sacrifice is required. This offering functions as satisfaction for the debt owed. This payment can be called a ransom or recompense. Sinful humans are unable to pay this debt. Left alone, we are given over to slavery. In Romans 5–6, we are reckoned slaves to sin. The wages from this slavemaster is death. Slavery unto death is the punishment for sin. However, Christ pays our debt in our stead. Therefore, we have freedom unto life. The box lists six things that Christ achieves through his atoning work.[4]

Why do you emphasize metaphors so much? People cannot help but speak in metaphors. All human cultures use metaphors to convey an array of ideas. Morality, values, and various other abstract notions rely on our borrowing language from the concrete world. So, when someone shows us love, we sometimes say, "They *touched* our heart." To live morally is to live "upright."

Metaphors play an indispensable role in contextualization. They serve as imperfect bridges between cultures, both past and present. By observing how people use metaphors, we get a look at how they view the world. We can discern values, assumptions, and perspectives.

What advantages does this perspective provide us? The view of atonement presented in this book has several significant advantages. First, it integrates rather than separates numerous biblical themes and images. Second, this perspective is more comprehensive than many theories. It draws from the entire biblical canon and interprets the New Testament in light of its Old Testament background. Third, this interpretation makes better sense of several important and difficult passages that puzzle readers of the Bible. Fourth, it provides a paradigm to communicate the message of atonement more effectively, creatively, and faithfully across diverse cultural contexts.

How does this interpretation relate to other traditional theories? This book does not give a theory centered on a single metaphor or benefit of atonement. It intends to map the literary terrain so that we grasp our theological boundaries. The interpretations offered thus far help us to appreciate what traditional theories of atonement get right. At the same time, we have better guardrails to guide our inquiry.

For example, we discern how the Bible uses ransom and redemption language within its proper context. Such imagery is well established in Leviticus

---

[4]This list is not exhaustive.

and elsewhere. In the exodus narrative, God redeems Israel but in no way pays Pharaoh a ransom payment. Likewise, we find no need to surmise some way that Christ acts as a ransom payment to Satan.

Christus Victor highlights a legitimate and glorious implication of the cross and resurrection. This theory coheres with the royal dimension of the sacrificial system (chap. 2). Still, it does not tap into the most common ways the Bible speak of atonement itself. If the atonement becomes shorthand for any and all things related to Christ's saving work, then, yes, Christus Victor is an atonement theory that should be celebrated. An aim of this book, however, is to help the church gain more precision in its language and interpretation of texts. Something similar could be said about recapitulation theory.

What about other theories? I have addressed penal substitutionary atonement (PSA) in myriad ways throughout this book. Our discussion of the Christ's inaugurating the new covenant touches on the root concerns of moral influence theory. The focus on honor and ransom also reflects the major themes found within Anselm's satisfaction theory.

CRITICAL ISSUE QUESTIONS

What about God's wrath? God loves people and therefore is angered by sin (John 3:36; Romans 1:18). All sinners deserve punishment. However, Christ lovingly saves us from the wrath of God. The day will come when God fully inflicts his wrath on those who dishonor him yet never repent (Matthew 3:7; Romans 2:5; Ephesians 5:6; Revelation 14:10; 19:15). The New Testament generally describes God's wrath as being in the future. As 1 Thessalonians 1:10 explains, it is "Jesus who delivers us from the wrath to come."[5] God is glorified in showing wrath against his enemies. When God judges evil, he vindicates his name.[6] Because God is righteous, he sets the world right. To make a righteous world, the Creator God must cleanse the world of rebellion. In short, Christ's death appeases God's wrath. Through his atoning work, we can gain God's favor.

---

[5]See also Rom 5:9; Col 3:6; 1 Thess 2:16; 5:9.

[6]God vindicates the worth of his honor via retribution. This is David deSilva's point regarding Heb 10:26-31 in "Despising Shame: A Cultural-Anthropological Investigation of the Epistle to the Hebrews," *JBL* 113 (1994): 454-55. Also, see deSilva, *Honor, Patronage, Kinship and Purity* (Downers Grove, IL: IVP Academic, 2000), 161n60; cf. Deut 32:35-36; Job 40:10-11; Ps 149:5-19; Is 59:9-19 (especially Is 59:18-19); 66:5-6; Jer 5:9, 29; 9:9; Ezek 38:16-18; Rom 9:22-23; Rev 15:1-8; 19:1-2; cf. Rom 12:19, 1 Thess 4:6. In Ex 34:5-7, God's glory and name is found in his punishing iniquity (Ex 34:7).

How does a sacrificial offering (e.g., Christ's death) appease God's wrath? I'll begin with a few positive answers. First, these offerings vindicate God. Although God deserves honor, people dishonor him. Malachi 2:2 states why people suffer God's curse, "If you will not listen, if you will not lay it to heart to give glory to my name, says the LORD of hosts, then I will send the curse on you and I will curse your blessings." Second, sacrifices essentially act as public confessions of need and sin. Thus, the giver admits his offense, expresses repentance, and acknowledges that he needs forgiveness. Third, when people offer a sacrifice, they express allegiance to God. As with Israel during the exodus (Passover), worshipers publicly distinguish themselves from others. They identify the Lord as their God.

On the other hand, Galatians 3:10-13 may suggest another aspect of Christ's work. As Israel's King, he represents Israel, who was sent into exile and punished for sin. In death, he enters their cursed state. In this way, Christ fulfills the obligation incurred by the Mosaic covenant's self-maledictory oath, in which each party accepts death if they do not satisfy the terms of the covenant. In his resurrection, he frees those who identify with Jesus as the Christ.

The bald fact that all interpreters must acknowledge is this: Galatians 3:13 is ambiguous. I summarize one reading of Galatians 3:13 in this way. By the time of Jesus, Israel has been punished, suffering exile. It was already cursed. God punishes Israel via death and exile; yet Christ's own death is not God's punishment. For Christ to redeem Israel, he does not have to be punished by God himself. He merely needs to enter their cursed state so that, as Israel's king, he might overcome the curse through his resurrection.

In what way is Jesus a substitute? Christ is a substitute. Sinners deserve death. Instead, he dies. Jesus became a curse in place of his people.[7] God's people do not need to suffer the condemnation due to sin. It is not necessary. This is because they are "in Christ." Christ perfectly honors the Father, who has no need to punish his Son. Jesus received an unjust condemnation at the cross. In fact, God overturns the verdict through the resurrection. Therefore, those who belong to Christ will not endure future wrath.

As one "devoted" to God, he is a substitute that redeems our lives in much the same way that sacrifices redeemed Levites who were substitutes for Israel's firstborn. Christ is a substitute in the sense that he makes the payment we

---

[7]In Gal 3, Christ removes the curse from "us," meaning Jewish believers. Because Israel is thus freed, the blessing of Abraham extends to Gentiles.

cannot afford. No sacrifice on our part could suffice (Hebrews 9:12-13). Animal sacrifices were mere shadows of the compensation God requires. We not only have robbed God of his honor; we also cannot pay an offering that truly atones for our offense. He perfectly displays God's glory. His life, death, and resurrection substitute for ours.

To use a modern analogy, Jesus' sacrifice is a substitute in the same way that a payment is given in exchange for a set of goods (e.g., food, paper, books) or state of affairs (e.g., membership in a club, a slave's freedom, entrance into a theater). To state this negatively, his payment substitutes for (i.e., takes the place of) the punishment otherwise due. In this way, economic metaphors and substitution do not conflict. Just as Christ is the priest *and* the sacrifice in Hebrews 8–10, so also he is the substitute payer and payment.

Furthermore, Christ is a substitute in the same way that the death of the high priest substitutes for the death of the one confined to the city of refuge (Numbers 35:25). He dies instead of us. He is a substitute in the sense that he ultimately takes responsibility for our sin as we could not.

If Jesus already pays our debt, why does Jesus need to receive our punishment for us? He doesn't. Jesus does not need to receive our punishment because he already paid our debt. We must not confuse our debt and our punishment (i.e., God's wrath, death). Our debt leads to death. Sinners suffer this punishment because we cannot pay our debt. However, if that debt could be paid, God would not need to punish us. Our death itself cannot exhaust our debt. Jesus pays the debt that resulted in our enslavement to sin. Therefore, Christ's payment redeems us from our deserved punishment.

If we say Christ pays our debt by enduring our punishment, then we confuse concepts. If Jesus already settled our debt, God no longer should punish us. Accordingly, there is no need for Jesus to endure God's punishment for us. If Jesus already paid our debt, legally, we should not receive punishment. Otherwise, God would accept our payment yet still punish us. This is unjust.

How do Jesus' death and the death of sinners differ? The *function* of our deserved death is not equivalent to that of Christ's death. For us, our death is a just consequence for our sin debt. Death is a penalty of sin. Ultimately, only unrepentant sinners suffer the punishment of death in the most ultimate sense. In contrast, Christ's death is a sacrifice of compensation, that is, a payment. This ransom pays the debt we cannot pay. Therefore, it satisfies the demands of

God's law. Christ's sacrifice perfectly glorifies God. As a result, God through Christ puts his enemies to public shame (Romans 8:2-3; Colossians 2:13-15). At the cross, God condemns two enemies—sin and death.

Is traditional penal substitutionary atonement an example of poor contextualization? Yes. Although popular versions of PSA affirm much biblical truth, they misunderstand several key metaphors and texts. Also, the underlying logic of traditional PSA is flawed. See appendix B. At a basic level, these systemic problems with interpretation compromise PSA as good contextualization.

Also, proponents of PSA tend to lay much stress on a narrow set of metaphors. By presenting the atonement only or even primarily in legal terms, we create problems for ourselves. On the one hand, people limit themselves to a single biblical image at the expense of others. On the other hand, one makes the questionable assumption that others share our conception of justice, the function of law, judges, and courts. In many places across the world and in history, one does not find justice in laws and courts.

Finally, I share an email from a person who helps lead an urban ministry that reaches out to the homeless, poor, refugees, and those coming out of prison. He wrote, "And we've found that the penal substitution atonement model, with its attendant image of a wrathful father whose righteous anger can only be assuaged by the death of his own son, is not the best way to present the Gospel to a community that has a large percentage of abusive and absentee fathers." Similarly, untold numbers of people (including myself) have, at one time or another, harbored a secret and dreadful thought: "God loves me because he *has* to, but he doesn't like it. Christ forces the Father to tolerate me." While advocates of PSA rightly reject caricatures of the theory as "divine child abuse," we must understand that many hear this sort of message when told that God the Father poured out his wrath on his beloved and innocent Son.

What if this all makes me a little uneasy? You are in good company. However, everything in this book has been documented by biblical text and scholarship. Nothing in this book is radical. What might be disconcerting is how I bring it all together. We are quite accustomed to theories that act as convenient, short-form answers. There's an appealing comfort in them.

I suggest that most readers can affirm the major ideas in this book, despite disagreeing on certain details. Even if I misunderstand this or that text, readers should reflect on the big picture. There is no single passage that serves as the linchpin to make everything else invalid if I've misread it. In other words, people will disagree on details. Nevertheless, the overall argument is coherent and can help interpreters better connect a number of biblical themes.

How should we understand the Eucharist (i.e., communion the Lord's Supper)? The Eucharist does what the Old Testament, cultic sacrifices did prior to Christ. Just as the offerings point forward to Christ, so the Eucharist looks back on his sacrifice.

Figure 10.3. Eucharist and sacrifice

Neither is efficacious in itself. Rather, both point to Christ's sacrifice, which is effective. And both represent meals that honor God in worship. The Eucharist replaces the Old Testament sacrifices *inasmuch as* it points to the fulfillment of those sacrifices (i.e., Christ).

QUESTIONS ABOUT SPECIFIC PASSAGES

What about Romans 3:24-26? Many people appeal to Romans 3:24-26 to explain the significance of Christ's atonement. There is not enough room in this book to provide a robust exposition of this text. Much of what's been said in previous chapters applies to this passage.[8] I'll mention just a few select points of discussion to limit repetition.

> **ROMANS 3:21-26**
>
> But now, apart from law, the righteousness of God has been manifest, and is attested by the law and the prophets, the righteousness of God through the faith of Jesus Christ for all who believe. For there is no distinction, since all have sinned and lack the glory of God; they are now justified by his grace as a gift, through the redemption that is in Christ Jesus, whom God put forward as the mercy seat, by his blood, through faith. He did this to show his righteousness, because in his divine forbearance he had passed over the sins previously committed; it was to show at the present time that he himself is righteous and that he justifies the one who has faith in Jesus. (NRSV, author's adaptation)

---

[8]Also, I elaborate on Rom 3:24-26 in *Saving God's Face: A Chinese Contextualization of Salvation Through Honor and Shame*, EMS Dissertation Series (Pasadena, CA: WCIUP, 2012), 261-63; *Reading Romans with Eastern Eyes* (Downers Grove, IL: IVP Academic, 2019), 72-75.

The New Testament never uses the most common Greek word for atonement in the LXX (*exilaskomai*). Its stem appears ten times in the New Testament. In only five of those instances does the word seem to have atonement related connotations (Romans 3:25; Hebrews 2:17; 9:15; 1 John 2:2; 4:10). Romans 3:25 uses *hilastērion*, which is often translated "propitiation" (ESV, NASB, HCSB) and "sacrifice of atonement" (NIV, NRSV). However, the same word is rendered "mercy seat" elsewhere (Hebrews 9:5).[9]

Where the noun *hilastērion* is used in the Old Testament, the corresponding Hebrew *kapporet* regularly refers to the "mercy seat."[10] Recalling the discussion in chapter two, the term refers to the symbolic throne for God. Consider also the insights from chapter four, where we saw that the verb *exilaskomai* translates *kpr*, and sometimes *ḥlh*, conveying the act of entreating God's favor (i.e., propitiation). Daniel Bailey further demonstrates the standard meaning of *hilastērion* in the first-century context. For ancient Greeks, *hilastērion* identifies a "votive gift," a thing that is able to gain favor of a god.[11] At the same time, "*hilastērion* never denotes an animal victim in any known source."[12]

Accordingly, it is less than clear how best to translate *hilastērion* in Romans 3:25 to make sense of the statement that Christ is *hilastērion*. What is obvious is that *hilastērion* appears to be emblematic of what Christ accomplishes. Therefore, one must be cautious not to claim too much from this single word without an extensive study of *hilastērion* and *kapporet* in their Old Testament context. In addition, in the few verses where the noun is used, we are limited in what we can infer about its meaning other than that it signifies a specific holy place in the temple.

Bailey's detailed study expounds on the Old Testament background that informs Paul's comments in Romans 3:21-26. Bailey agrees that Jesus is the "mercy seat" in Romans 3:25. Notably, Paul's imagery suggests a pattern or "sequence of the exodus leading to the sanctuary."[13] The mercy seat is the

---

[9]Per ESV, NASB, NRSV, HCSB. The NIV uses "atonement cover."

[10]In the LXX, *hilastērion* is found in Ex 25:17, 18, 19, 20, 21, 22; 31:7; 35:12; 38:5, 7, 8; Lev 16:2, 13, 14, 15; Num 7:89; Amos 9:1; Ezek 43:14, 17, 20.

[11]Daniel Bailey, "Jesus as the Mercy Seat: The Semantics and Theology of Paul's Use of *Hilasterion* in Romans 3:25" (Cambridge: Cambridge University, 1999), 15-75. Along this line of thinking, Jesus is designated as a votive gift entreating God's favor on our behalf.

[12]Daniel Bailey, "Jesus as the Mercy Seat: The Semantics and Theology of Paul's Use of *Hilasterion* in Romans 3:25," *TynBul* 51, no. 1 (2000): 156. Since his article and dissertation share the same title, other references refer to his dissertation.

[13]Bailey, "Jesus as the Mercy Seat," 197. The following paragraphs reflect Bailey (177-217).

quintessential synecdoche for the temple.[14] That is, it is the indispensable part that represents the whole.

Furthermore, the verb *protithēmi* (put forth, Romans 3:25) routinely refers to the "setting out" of bread in the sanctuary. Bailey says, "From this developed the technical biblical use of the related noun *prothesis*, which can qualify as the sacred table or its setting (Exod 40:4)."[15] Whereas the priests acknowledge God's presence in laying out the bread, God in Romans 3:25 "is the one who 'sets out' Jesus, leading to a *demonstration* of the divine presence and righteousness."[16] Bailey adds that scholars "have too often focused on *propitiation* and *expiation* to the exclusion of *revelation*, the primary purpose of the mercy seat."[17]

Priests used blood as a way of restoring or initiating worship in the sanctuary each year (Leviticus 16:16-20). Accordingly, Bailey summarizes his interpretation in this way: "Paul's statement about God's presenting Jesus in his blood indicates how Jesus was installed permanently as the centre and focal point of the new community's worship. The idea of atonement for sin is presupposed rather than emphasized. This will become clear as we consider the second half of Rom 3:25."[18] There is no room here to recount Bailey's full argument; however, his reading well suits the surrounding context of Romans in which Paul underscores the revelation and demonstration of God's righteousness (Romans 3:21, 25-26).

One additional comment may prove helpful. The argument and context of Romans 3:24 resembles that of 2 Corinthians 5:21 (discussed in chap. 9). In Romans, Paul refers to Christ's death, describing him as a mercy seat, put forth for the sake of demonstrating God's righteousness. Paul connects Christ's death, sacrificial language, and God's righteousness. Similar themes appear in 2 Corinthians 5–6, where Christ is a reconciliation offering. Also, an intertextual reading suggests that the phrase "God's righteousness" carries similar ideas in both passages. Many evangelicals argue that "the righteousness of God" in Romans 3:25-26 refers to God's wrathful judgment against sin. It is not likely that these interpreters would say that, in 2 Corinthians 5:21, we become the wrathful judgment

---

[14] A synecdoche is a figure of speech in which a part represents the whole, or vice versa. For example, saying I got a "new pair of wheels" means that I got a new car. Likewise, the "White House" represents the United States government.

[15] Bailey, "Jesus as the Mercy Seat," 201.

[16] Bailey, "Jesus as the Mercy Seat," 201.

[17] Bailey, "Jesus as the Mercy Seat," 202.

[18] Bailey, "Jesus as the Mercy Seat," 211.

of God. I've argued elsewhere that God's righteousness in Romans 3 refers to his saving righteousness, not his punitive condemnation against sin.[19]

Put simply, Romans 3:24-26 by itself sheds little direct light on the specific meaning and nuance of the atonement as a concept. Certain similarities between Romans 3 and 2 Corinthians might suggest that the latter can help us to interpret the former.

Why then does Isaiah 53:6 use "laid"? According to the NRSV, Isaiah 53:6 says, "The LORD has laid on him the iniquity of us all." If this verse does not support a traditional view of penal substitutionary atonement, why then does Isaiah 53:6 use "laid"?

The preposition *b* may be the cause of confusion. Its meaning depends on the verb's meaning. If we compare other instances where *b* follows this hiphil-stem verb, we find that *b* can also function as the means by which some result is achieved.[20] The following two verses use the same verb and preposition. In Jeremiah 15:11, "The LORD said, 'Have I not set you free for their good? Have I not *pleaded for you* before the enemy in the time of trouble and in the time of distress?'" (ESV). Then, in Jeremiah 36:25, "Even when Elnathan and Delaiah and Gemariah *urged the king* not to burn the scroll, he would not listen to them."

In other places, the *b* preposition's complement is a person (e.g., Isaiah 53:6). The person often is God's means. For example, in Exodus 9:35, "So the heart of Pharaoh was hardened, and he did not let the Israelites go, just as the LORD had spoken *through Moses*." More literally, it says, "through the hand of Moses."[21] First Kings 22:28 adds, "And Micaiah said, 'If you return in peace, the LORD has not spoken *by me*.' And he said, 'Hear, you peoples, all of you!'"[22] When deciding how to translate *b*, we must consider the context and its normal usage.

---

[19]See Jackson W., *Reading Romans with Eastern Eyes*, 72-75; Wu, *Saving God's Face*, 261-63; Wu, "Why Is God Justified in Romans? Vindicating Paul's Use of Psalm 51:4 in Romans 3:4," *Neot* 51, no. 2 (Dec 2017): 291-314.

[20]I refer only to instances where this verb in the hiphil (not all hiphil verbs) is followed by the preposition *b*, a preposition with great flexibility. Concerning its frequent *beth instrumenti* usage, see Christo van der Merwe, Jacobus A. Naude, and Jan H. Kroeze, *BHRG*, 340-41. With the verb *pg'* (to intercede, plead to, for), see Jer 15:11; 36:25; with other verbs, see Ex 17:5 ("with which you struck"); Ezek 12:5; 2 Chron 5:13 (using hiphil); cf. Job 39:12. Also, note a similar construction in Ex 4:17.

[21]Cf. Lev 8:36.

[22]Plowed with ox and donkey (Deut 22:10); trodden with foot (Is 28:3); prophesied by Baal (Jer 2:8); cursed David by his gods (1 Sam 17:43); swear to me here by God (Gen 21:23); the song was raised, with trumpets and cymbals and other musical instruments (2 Chron 5:13); cf. Gen 48:20.

At this point, I'll briefly reiterate two paragraphs from chapter seven. Isaiah 53:6 says, "All we like sheep have gone astray; we all turned to our own way, and the Lord *has laid* [*pg ʿ*] on him the iniquity of us all." The NRSV translates the same word (hiphil of *pg ʿ*) differently in Isaiah 53:6, 12 despite it sharing the same context. Isaiah 53:6 renders *pg ʿ* as "laid." Isaiah 53:12 translates *pg ʿ* as "makes intercession." The word typically means "to intercede for" or "look after someone."

A more natural rendering of Isaiah 53:6 is "the LORD made intercession *through him* for the iniquity of us all." Our observations about the preposition *b* are consistent with the translation "through him." Isaiah 53:12 reinforces this reading while also using *pg ʿ*. The one making intercession in Isaiah 53:12 is the servant through whom the Lord makes intercession in Isaiah 53:6. In what way is intercession made for "the iniquity of us all"? According to Isaiah 53:11, he shall take away our iniquity.

What if we dismissed this evidence and supposed the correct translation of Isaiah 53:6 is "the LORD has laid on *him* the iniquity of us all"? Even if that were true, the "laying on" language completely fits with the imagery of "carrying away" our sorrow and sin (Isaiah 53:4, 12).

Wasn't it God's will to crush Jesus in Isaiah 53? Finally, we look at Isaiah 53:10. This verse can lead to much confusion. The NRSV (author's adaptation) translates Isaiah 53:10 in this way: "Yet it was the will of the LORD to crush him with pain. / When you *make his life an offering for guilt,* / he shall see his offspring, / he shall prolong his days; / through him the will of the LORD shall prosper." Some readers will suppose that the opening phrase undermines or weakens the interpretation offered in this book.

Both Isaiah 53:5, 10 use the same Hebrew word (*dk ʾ*), translated as "crush." In context, this crushing is due to unjust affliction. It comes from his enemies, that is, those who reject him.[23] This scenario is essentially equivalent to Acts 2:23, 4:28, where we see that Christ's crucifixion was God's plan and will.

> This man, handed over to you according to the definite plan and foreknowledge of God, you crucified and killed by the hands of those outside the law. (Acts 2:23)

> For in this city, in fact, both Herod and Pontius Pilate, with the Gentiles and the peoples of Israel, gathered together against your holy servant Jesus, whom you

---

[23]Cf. Is 53:3, 4, 6.

anointed, to do whatever your hand and your plan had predestined to take place. (Acts 4:27-28)

Saying that God's will is that Pilate and the Jewish leaders will unjustly punish the Christ does not require that God himself unjustly killed Jesus. By comparison, in Isaiah 45:7, the Lord says, "I make well-being and *create calamity*, I am the LORD, who does all these things" (ESV). The word for "calamity" (*raˈ*) often refers to evil or wicked things. God in his sovereignty wills that evil occur. Saying that God "creates calamity" does not necessitate that evil is God's will in the sense that he delights in it. He only creates evil by his letting it occur (though the verb *create* is more likely to confuse or mislead readers). We should not confuse what God commands with what he allows.

In short, the people misunderstand God's servant in Isaiah 53:2-4. Therefore, they unjustly condemn him. Yet, these events were the Lord's will because the servant suffers for our sake (Isaiah 53:5-6, 10-12).

11

DOES CHRIST BEAR OUR SHAME?

THIS CONCLUDING CHAPTER will sketch a few implications and applications that stem from the interpretation presented in this book. To be sure, I do not claim that everything in this chapter comes only from this view. That is, other theories might lead to some suggestions mentioned below. Still, the previous discussion does reinforce the need for certain applications. In addition, the preceding chapters open our minds to discern theological connections that have been underappreciated for too long. Throughout the book, I peppered practical ideas for contextualized theology and practice. The following few pages leave just enough room to make suggestions and propose fresh paths of inquiry.

In keeping with the goal of contextualizing the atonement, this chapter underscores honor and shame more explicitly than previously (except for chap. 5). My goal is not to develop a robust theology of atonement in terms of honor and shame. I simply show some of the possibilities for anyone wanting to explore further the relationship between these themes and atonement.

While contextualization begins with interpretation, it matures in the work of communication and application. Contextualization shapes our theology and practice. Accordingly, the content of this chapter reflects that dual emphasis.

CHRIST BEARS OUR SHAME

Given our discussion about bearing sin, what can be said about bearing shame? Frankly, one could expound on this question for an entire book. For now, I simply outline a few ideas. It should first be noted that the Bible never explicitly speaks of Christ bearing our shame. We must consider what the phrase can legitimately mean in light of Scripture.

Given our observations in chapter seven, we understand the word *bear* as it is used in the Bible. The basic metaphor conveys the notion of carrying, removing, and so on. The precise connotation of bearing shame will depend on the context, specifically whose shame is borne and by whom. To say "Christ bore our shame" cannot mean that God puts Christ to shame (as he otherwise would put us to eternal shame because of our sin).

The idea that Christ bears our shame can refer to several things. Inasmuch as sin is a source of shame, it is possible that bearing shame functions similarly to "bearing sin." He takes away the shame associated with sin, such as exile, guilt, and impurity. Furthermore, Christ removes shame when he changes our identity. We are adopted as his children with glory. This is *ascribed* honor. Also, the new covenant effects in us a new heart. As a result, we can obey the Lord "from the heart" (Romans 6:17). In this way, the Spirit *achieves* honor in our lives. Christ's people belong to a new community, the church, which is not beholden to any particular set of social norms. Those who are disgraced or marginalized within their culture find new honor within the family of God. Their shame is transformed through their identification with Christ. Finally, Christ's resurrection defeats death, removing the threat of eternal shame. Instead, he gives us his own glory (John 17:22).

Imagine the power of this message to transform lives. I never knew my birth father until I was forty years old. As a child, someone said to me, "Your brother looks like your (step)dad. Your sister looks like your mom. But you don't look like anyone." They were correct. I wondered whether there was someone out in the world who did look like me. I felt a certain sense of not fully belonging. Many children and adults who were abandoned or adopted often feel shame, as though they are outsiders. After finding my father, I saw countless pictures of him and my siblings spanning several decades. The likeness between he and I was obvious. With joy and relief, I told my sister, "I've never looked like someone before."

In like manner, the Bible proclaims a message by which atonement makes reconciliation and adoption possible. Like us, Christ endured shame and understood the pain of rejection. Yet his shame bearing ultimately changes our identity. In Christ, the Father makes sons and daughters of the socially marginalized. By the Spirit, we are enabled finally to look like him.

OTHER ASPECTS OF SUBSTITUTION

Our study opens us to consider other ways in which Christ acts as a substitute. First, Christ pays our honor debt. In *Saving God's Face*, I explain.

> As the second Adam, the perfect "image of God," Christ pays the original debt owed by every human—honor to God. Honor substitution is an essential aspect of atonement theology, balancing a one sided emphasis on penal substitution. . . . Unless one sees *both* humanity's honor-debt and the Son's perfectly glorifying the Father, then one has not addressed the problem that justification presumes relative to God. His demand for honor is satisfied via Christ's obedience and his death, which pay both debts owed to God, that of honor and death. Hence, Christ's death is not so much a "bribe" as it is "restitution" (cf. Lev 5:16; Num 5:8).[1]

Those familiar with historical theology will hear echoes of Anselm's satisfaction theory of atonement. Reconciliation is only possible because Christ magnifies God's honor before a world that disparages his name.

From this perspective, Christ's sinless life not only gives significance to his death; his death gives his life its full value. His death completes the life that manifests God's name by doing the work given to him (John 17:4, 6). For this reason, Paul in Philippians 2:9-11 says Christ is exalted by the Father. "The cross perfects Jesus's God honoring life since not even death compels Jesus to forsake and thus shame his Father."[2]

One discerns another aspect of substitution from the discussion in chapter eight. We noted that *pasach*, traditionally translated "passover," means "protect" or "spare." Thus, Exodus 12:13 is better translated, "when I see the blood, I will *protect* [*pasach*] you." Tigay even calls the Passover lamb a "protective sacrifice."[3] How then might we describe the work of Christ, whom Paul explicitly calls "our Passover lamb" (1 Corinthians 5:7)? Rather than "penal substitutionary atonement," perhaps the acronym PSA might better mean "protective substitutionary atonement."[4]

---

[1] I develop this idea more fully in Jackson Wu, *Saving God's Face: A Chinese Contextualization of Salvation Through Honor and Shame*, EMS Dissertation Series (Pasadena, CA: WCIUP, 2012), 211.
[2] Wu, *Saving God's Face*, 199.
[3] J. H. Tigay, *Deuteronomy: The Traditional Hebrew Text with the New JPS Translation* (Philadelphia: Jewish Publication Society, 1996), 153.
[4] It's possible that when Paul says Christ died "for our sins" in 1 Cor 15:3, he continues to draw from the Passover imagery in 1 Cor 5.

REMOVING RELATIONAL BARRIERS

A fundamental goal of atonement in the Bible is to bring about reconciliation. Atonement removes relational barriers, even if the reason (i.e., uncleanness) is not an overt "moral" decision. Yet, getting rid of the problem is a moral issue. Until such obstacles are taken away, we bear the responsibility to do so. Consider the following situations.

American southerners have countless sayings that would make an outsider turn their head. More than a few are as offensive as they are old. Growing up, I picked up a common expression used to describe negotiating: "Jew down." To "Jew someone down" meant trying to get a good deal from a seller. However, I was completely oblivious to the obvious reference to ethnicity. Not until I was around thirty years old did it occur to me that the phrase alluded to Jewish people. I had never read or written the idiom. On realizing it was a racial slur, I was horrified. Once I became aware of its meaning, I immediately stopped using the phrase. Prior to that time, someone could easily have misinterpreted my intentions and racial sentiments. It became my responsibility to remove any obstacle that would get in the way of conveying love to people.

Contemporary conversations about racism underscore the point. During the Covid pandemic and quarantine of 2020, Mississippi State football coach Mike Leach sent out a tweet saying, "After 2 weeks of quarantine with her husband, Gertrude [Leach's wife] decided to knit him a scarf." The tweet included a picture of a woman knitting a noose. In the American South, nooses are historically associated with racist lynching. Because Leach spent much of his life in the American northwest, he did not immediately perceive the way the image would be interpreted in his new context. He quickly deleted the tweet and issued an apology. At least one of his players left the school. Leach was required to attend "listening sessions" and visit a Mississippi civil rights museum.[5]

The culture war over Confederate statues has raged for years in the United States. While some people defend them as tributes to history, many others argue that "monuments in prominent public places honoring the Confederacy are inconsistent with [racial] reconciliation."[6] Creating right relationships with

---

[5]Wilson Wong, "Mississippi State Football Player Transferring After New Coach Posts Tweet With a Noose," NBCNews.com, April 8, 2020, www.nbcnews.com/news/nbcblk/mississippi-state-football-player-transferring-after-new-coach-posts-tweet-n1177911.

[6]Richard Nelson, "Do Confederate Symbols Stand in the Way of Racial Reconciliation?," *The Leaf Chronicle*, April 17, 2017, www.theleafchronicle.com/story/opinion/contributors/2017/08/17/confederate-symbols-racial-reconciliation/570690001/.

others requires intentionality, especially when past wrongs hang in the air. To begin the work of atonement, so to speak, we must first examine the potential threats to reconciliation and social harmony.

BEARING OTHERS' BURDENS

In Galatians 6:2, Paul says, "Bear one another's burdens, and so fulfill the law of Christ." A few sentences earlier, he writes, "For the whole law is summed up in a single commandment: 'You shall love your neighbor as yourself'" (Galatians 5:14). Paul uses the bearing metaphor to explain what it means to love, to fulfill the law.[7] What does this look like in practice?

Jennifer McBride portrays Christ's crucifixion as an act where Christ takes responsibility for the world's sin even though he is guiltless. Her emphasis is on responsibility, not on blame.[8] Like Christ, his followers are called to accept responsibility for the sin and evil in the world, even if they think they should not be blamed. In a small way, Christians demonstrate one aspect of what it means for the priests, and ultimately Christ, to bear sin.

Navy SEAL Jocko Willink's books are not written with theology in mind, but his concept of "extreme ownership" helpfully reflects the mentality of burden-bearing.[9] He argues that leaders must take extreme ownership. By this, he says they are responsible for everything under their charge, even the mistakes of subordinates. After all, the leader could have trained them better or clarified the purpose of a task. What about when bad weather results in a failed mission during battle? While inclement weather is not the commander's fault, it is his responsibility to anticipate problematic contingencies that could arise. What might this look like in daily life?

I recently heard from a man who was constantly frustrated with the mess left by other people at his fitness gym. Free weights and equipment were always strewn around the place. His seething did not incline him to befriend some fellow gym members. Having read *Extreme Ownership*, he thought of an idea. "If I want an orderly workout area, why don't I bear responsibility for picking them up?" And he did. Not only did he improve his own experience exercising,

---

[7]In Rom 15:1-3, Christ's atoning work is the basis for urging readers to bear with the weak.

[8]Jennifer McBride, "Repentance as Political Witness," in *Christian Political Witness*, ed. George Kalantzis and Gregory W. Lee (Downers Grove, IL: IVP Academic, 2014), 179-95.

[9]Jocko Willink and Leif Babin, *Extreme Ownership: How U.S. Navy SEALs Lead and Win* (New York: St. Martin's Press, 2015).

but he also served those around him. As trivial as this example might seem, it well typifies the multitude of ways that the mentality of bearing another's burden can be transformative.

FORGIVENESS AS DIVINE RELEASE

A biblical vision of atonement will spur some people to reconceive of forgiveness. *Forgiveness* is a dead metaphor. We are so accustomed to the word that we forget that it previously concerned the letting go of debts. Nowadays, pastors exhort congregations to forgive and forget, even if the offender does not apologize. Is that possible from a biblical perspective?

Before you dismiss the question right away, consider the fact that worshipers in the Old Testament had to bring their offering to God and confess their sin. They had to take some public step of acknowledging their need for God. Only then do they receive forgiveness. When a wrong is done, a debt is created. How can forgiveness be given without the debt paid?

A few answers can be given. First, concerning brothers and sisters in Christ, God has forgiven them. Sin above all creates a debt to God. We find ourselves in the same spot as the unforgiving servant in Matthew 18:21-35. Having been forgiven much, will we forgive others whose debt toward us is smaller? Even this story, however, brings us back to our original dilemma. In the parable, the man still asked the unforgiving servant to forgive his debt. What if the offender does not ask for forgiveness?

Let us rethink what we mean by forgiveness. Even in Scripture, no one is forgiven without some sort of response, faith, or repentance. In other words, we find no one in the Bible who receives forgiveness without some sort of change. However, there is the constant *offer* of forgiveness. Perhaps, when people say we should forgive, what they mean, in biblical terms, is that we should be *willing to forgive*.

One scholar, drawing from Numbers 30, explains "Forgiveness is divine release from sin."[10] We want people to be freed from the burden of sin. We desire for others to receive payment for their debt. We want all people to have new hearts. In this way, we follow Christ's example and extend the genuine offer of forgiveness so that there can be reconciliation. We give up the absolute

---

[10]D. F. Kennedy, "The Concept of Forgiveness in the Pentateuch," *Old Testament Essays* 12, no. 1 (1999): 104.

demand for punishment because of what someone else has done. Unless they somehow desire or seek forgiveness (in some culturally appropriate expression), an obstacle to reconciliation remains.

Forgiveness also does not mean there are no consequences for sin. As Moses intercedes for his people at Sinai in Numbers 14, the Lord extends forgiveness; yet, they are still forced to wander in the wilderness for forty years (Numbers 14:20-23). In this case, God's forgiveness seems to suggest that he does not utterly destroy the nation as they deserve. Moreover, forgiveness "appears to be a more relational process in which the forgiver removes or bypasses the obstacle which obstructs the relationship with the one forgiven, thus restoring/maintaining the relationship."[11]

What if *we* seek forgiveness? How should we think about being forgiven? Sometimes, our simply asking someone, "Will you forgive me?" is enough. But not always. Reconciliation is costly. This is why God often demands that restitution be made when his people do harm to one another (Exodus 21:33-36). Likewise, the sacrifices testified to the worth that worshipers place on their relationship to God. Frequently, we think our goal is mere forgiveness, being released from the consequences of sin. But God's people seek genuine reconciliation. With a more robust view of atonement, we affirm the words of Brenda McNeil. She writes, "Reconciliation is about how to relate even after forgiveness and justice have occurred. It's about how to delve even deeper into relationship with one another. An absence of hostility is possible without a spiritual dimension, but reconciliation is not."[12] The atonement reminds us that God's grace is never truly free. We must sacrifice our pride just as he sacrifices his son.

We'll only move past forgiveness to reconciliation when we love people more than we fear punishment. When this happens, we will see the cost of reconciliation not as an unjust burden to bear but an opportunity to open new doors for hope. Consider the ongoing debate about race reparations in America. Admittedly, few people even agree on the practical meaning of *reparations*. Whatever the term might mean, many can agree that the "Zacchaeus Fund" is a step in the right direction.[13] Timothy Dalrymple, president and CEO of *Christianity Today*, explains,

---

[11]Gudmundur Olafsson, "The Use of nś' in the Pentateuch and Its Contribution to the Concept of Forgiveness" (PhD diss., Andrews University, 1992), 212.

[12]Brenda Salter McNeil, *Roadmap to Reconciliation: Moving Communities into Unity, Wholeness and Justice* (Downers Grove, IL: InterVarsity Press, 2015), 21.

[13]Examples of Zacchaeus Funds can be found at www.tapestrylachurch.com/zacchaeus-fund and www.theleadership400fund.com.

Christians who believe that African Americans have been subjected to four centuries of injustice and plunder are beginning to do their humble part to make it right. A majority-black committee assigns the funds to support rising black leaders in the church and in the marketplace. It will not be enough, but it will be something. What if there were Zacchaeus funds in every city and believers gave sacrificially, so our brothers and sisters could be restored and so our neighbors could see once again the Christlike love that overcame the world?[14]

In effect, efforts like these are attempts to restore to right what has been wrong for far too long.

BEARING CHRIST'S REPROACH (SUFFERING)

Paul wrote to a Roman church fractured along socioethnic lines. In Romans 14, he candidly addresses an area of conflict within the church. He then says, "We who are strong ought to put up with the failings of the weak, and not to please ourselves. Each of us must please our neighbor for the good purpose of building up the neighbor. For Christ did not please himself; but, as it is written, 'The insults of those who insult you have fallen on me'" (Romans 15:1-3). He quotes Psalm 69:9 as the basis for his exhortation. The church maintains harmony by following Christ's example in bearing with others in their weakness. In the context, the psalmist suffers unjustly. Why? Psalm 69:7 says, "For it is for your sake that I have *borne* reproach, that dishonor has covered my face" (ESV).

God is honored when the church lives in holy harmony. Yet, the glory of that end comes through much endurance, suffering, and humility. Like Christ, his followers bear the world's reproach in order to effect reconciliation among people. Being misunderstood and even rejected are the norm, not the exception. Yet, this is the burden that must be borne if we hope to see churches together with "one voice glorify the God and Father of our Lord Jesus Christ" (Romans 15:6).

The writer of Hebrews also draws on this language. He urges readers to persevere in their imitation of Christ. It is not the temple offerings that give lasting hope. Why? Like the temple sacrifices, "Jesus also suffered outside the gate in order to sanctify the people through his own blood. Therefore let us go to him outside the camp and bear the reproach he endured" (Hebrews 13:12-13).

[14]Timothy Dalrymple, "Justice Too Long Delayed," *Christianity Today*, June 10, 2020, accessed July 24, 2020, www.christianitytoday.com/ct/2020/june-web-only/justice-too-long-delayed.html.

To remain steadfast entails two things in context. First, followers must look "to Jesus the pioneer and perfecter of our faith, who for the sake of the joy that was set before him endured the cross, *disregarding its shame*, and has taken his seat at the right hand of the throne of God" (Hebrews 12:2). Second, they must consider what lies at the heart of true worship. Hebrews 13:15-16 says, "Through [Christ], then, let us continually offer up a sacrifice of praise to God, that is, the fruit of lips that confess his name. Do not neglect to do good and to share what you have, for such sacrifices are pleasing to God." For ancient Jewish followers of Christ, embracing a true heart of worship would quickly isolate them from their contemporaries who primarily located worship within the temple. To honor God in truth, we must be willing to sacrifice our own "face" (to use a Chinese expression).

Redeemed from Lingering Shame (Identity)

I still have dreams at night that focus on people and events that occurred when I was seventeen or eighteen years old. These are not pleasant dreams. Driving home one day, I wondered why. It is certainly wrapped up in the shame I experienced during that time in my life. "Why do I have such lingering shame?" I asked. Something that's not quite an audible voice replied, "Lingering shame is rooted in your sense of identity. Shame lingers when you hold onto certain identities that are not necessarily worthy of honor." If a person is defined by academic achievement, what happens when they fail out of college because they lost focus during their freshman year? What if a young Christian loses his virginity as a teenager after internalizing the teaching of purity culture and "True Love Waits" rallies? When he is thirty-five years old, he will still feel shame if he does not see his identity wrapped up in more than the sexual activities of his youth. Lingering personal shame thrives when we continue to have a misconstrued sense of identity.

In the Old Testament, people became unclean for numerous reasons. In some cases, one might experience isolation and shame. An individual needed to move from being unclean to being categorized as "clean." Offering sacrifices not only removed a barrier between God and worshiper; it also removed social shame and restored harmony within the community.

In Hebrews 9–10, Christ's atoning work brings about a new heart and thus a new identity. External measures of cleanness no longer define God's people.

Yet, we in the church are still prone to assign value to people based on common criteria and social identities. In the same way, we make judgments about ourselves. The Bible's teaching on atonement requires us to rethink the boundaries that define our measures of worth, those who are insiders and outsiders.

Something like Karen Fratti's story could have been written by a marginalized person in the first century. She is not a drug user nor a sex worker. She is a heterosexual, white woman who grew up in the suburbs. Yet, she says, "I have HIV, but it's stigma that makes me sick."[15] She explains further: "I'm not that scared about my health. I'm very scared about what you'll think of me. . . . When I was diagnosed, I told pretty much no one, not even my family, because I was ashamed. I felt dirty. I didn't want my parents to know that their honor roll, J. Crew-wearing, golden daughter had *H.I.V.*" After two years, she finally informed her parents. She told them, "I'm not telling you because I'm 'sick,' I'm telling you because I want to stop hating myself and hiding from it." She concludes with a testimony to the power of shame.

> Because stigma is a dirty little Gremlin—it's snarky and taunting and mean and if you listen to stigma, it will take over you and everyone you touch. The shame turns into a beast and possesses you. The shame lends itself to some sort of twisted pride. Stigma isolates you like an abusive partner. *Oh, of course you don't want me. I'm infected. You don't even know. You can't know. Because I won't even be able to tell you.*

Similar stories could be told of others who have allowed shame to define their identity. The cross and resurrection do not immediately eradicate sickness and common social markers. But they do create a new people with changed hearts. Biblical communities assess honor and shame by an uncommon standard. Christ followers pursue honor through shame. They dismiss caustic social labels because they embrace their identity in Christ.

Christ's sacrificial offering redefines purity. This point is especially potent in cultures around the world. In a fascinating and important documentary, *The Honor Diaries*, several women discuss the rationale behind the practice of female circumcision.[16] One midwife explains, "Purified girls grow taller and get marriage proposals, but unpurified girls grow short and stubby." Girls who

---

[15]Karen Fratti, "I Have HIV, But It's Stigma That Makes Me Sick," *Medium*, October 6, 2016, medium .com/@karenfratti/i-have-hiv-but-its-stigma-that-makes-me-sick-3ab4879ff324.

[16]Also called female genital mutilation. See *The Honor Diaries*, clarionproject.org/free-stream.

receive female genital mutilation are considered "purified." Why? Egyptian cleric Sheikh Yussuf al Badri, adds this: "Circumcision is the reason why Muslim women are virtuous, unlike Western women who run off to their sexual appetite in any place with any man." Women often are the primary maintainers of this practice because mothers fear their daughters won't get married if they don't receive the procedure.

What if these men and women heard a more robust message of the cross? Christ hung mutilated on a cross so that people would have circumcised hearts. This is true purity.

OFFERING SACRIFICES AS SPIRITUAL FORMATION

Paul sought to embody the "cruciform" life of Christ.[17] That is, he labored to ensure that the cross shaped every aspect of his life. Yet, Christ's life portrays the truth behind Israel's ancient sacrifices. He is the ultimate reconciliation offering. We are called to be "living sacrifices" (Romans 12:1). So, what can we learn about spiritual formation from the sacrificial system?

As James K. A. Smith argues, our rituals, habits, and practices amount to liturgies that move our hearts to love one kingdom and its values over another.[18] Ancient Israel was shaped by its many laws, including the daily practice of offering sacrifices in the temple. These rituals reinforced the assumptions and images discussed in this book. What might they and we learn?

Atonement requires that we give ourselves entirely to God. This happens symbolically in presenting offerings. Ultimately, it is Christ's self-sacrifice that completes then consummates God's covenants with his people. God called his people first to follow the sacrificial rituals and then to imitate Christ, the sacrifice itself. These two things form our ambitions and reflect our affections for God. They spur the holistic and habitual formation of character.

The Eucharist (i.e., the Lord's Supper) is a foundational practice, rooted in Israel's Passover. Israel's sacrificial offerings reinforced its sense of identity. So too does the Eucharist. For Paul, this sacred meal was not only symbolic but the substantiation of the church's unity. To partake in the blood and bread constituted a profession of allegiance (1 Corinthians 10:1-22). Whereas the old

---

[17]For more on this perspective, see Michael Gorman, *Inhabiting the Cruciform God: Kenosis, Justification, and Theosis in Paul's Narrative Soteriology* (Grand Rapids, MI: Eerdmans, 2009).

[18]See James K. A. Smith, *Desiring the Kingdom: Worship, Worldview and Cultural Formation* (Grand Rapids, MI: Baker Books, 2009).

covenant sacrifices sought reconciliation with God, the Eucharist—the meal of the new covenant—looks back to the reconciliation secured in Christ. Thus, we are empowered to seek reconciliation with one another (1 Corinthians 11:17-34). Not only that, but we show hospitality, inviting people into the holy family of God.[19] They are no longer kept at a distance, outside as if without a sacrifice to clear a way forward.

RETHINKING EVANGELISM

Our study challenges certain habits and thinking when it comes to evangelism. For most evangelical Christians, the gospel refers to the Bible's message about how to "get saved." Certainly, salvation and forgiveness from sin are intricately woven into a robust view of the gospel. Elsewhere, however, I have argued at length that the gospel is not first the message about *how* one gets saved; rather, it is the message one must believe *in order to* be saved.[20] Its central proclamation is that Jesus is king.

Common gospel tracts and presentations focus on doctrines of salvation (e.g., justification, atonement) at the expense of the message of Christ's kingship. For many, Jesus as king is just one of various other identities, such as shepherd, healer, savior, and teacher. Countless Christians rightly emphasize that Jesus gave his life as a sacrifice. What gets overlooked in the process of sharing the gospel and teaching the Bible? The royal dimension of atonement. As we saw in chapter two, the ark carries definite royal connotations. The inner sanctuary is where the high priest approaches the throne of God. Making a sacrifice to this king is an act of allegiance giving. If we proclaim the message of atonement as found in the Bible, we must take seriously its royal overtones. Atonement is more than a transaction that saves us from sin. It enables us to enter the presence of the King of kings.

Second, we should reflect on the tone and stress of our gospel presentations. Evangelical Christians have long defended the biblical idea that God hates sin. His wrath will ultimately destroy evil. We sometimes emphasize wrath for two reasons. First, it is effective in capturing people's attention. Second, we have a zeal to reach people with the gospel. But an overemphasis on this one

---

[19]See Joshua Jipp, *Saved by Faith and Hospitality* (Grand Rapids, MI: Eerdmans, 2017).
[20]See Jackson Wu, *One Gospel for All Nations: A Practical Approach to Biblical Contextualization* (Pasadena, CA: William Carey Library, 2015).

dimension of God's character quickly consumes our attention. It can then distort biblical interpretation and doctrine. More than we'd like to admit, this emphasis frequently does not reach hearts.

Our look at Psalm 22 in chapter nine serves as a needed corrective. The psalmist underscores the coming victory of God amid our suffering despite his apparent absence from our lives. The world might say that God forsakes us. But Psalm 22 reminds us that things are not always as they seem. What if we stressed in our teaching the same aspects that we find emphasized in the text? How often do we focus excessively on the feeling of forsakenness without moving to climactic hope?

I suspect other questions still linger in the minds of some readers with respect to evangelism. Does all this talk of atonement metaphors overcomplicate evangelism? In brief, no. We regain an appreciation for how the Bible itself testifies to the gospel of salvation. We should not feel pressure to say everything to everyone in every evangelistic conversation. Instead, we should rejoice at the diversity and creativity of God's revelation. We should feel grateful and free to discuss different parts of Scripture as best suits the person and occasion. With time and opportunity, we can share more of the biblical message in all its fullness.

What about my emphasis on honor and shame? Do I minimize the legal dimensions of atonement? I've heard this question reworded and asked in countless ways. First, some wonder whether this view of atonement downplays guilt. I suggest quite the contrary. In fact, the perspective offered in this book redeems the notion of guilt such that we can see in its biblical context. How so? When we looked at "bearing sin" or "bearing guilt," I explained such language underscored *responsibility*. Today, *guilt* is often reduced to the concept of blame. Asking, "Who is to blame?" is not the same as asking, "Who takes responsibility?" Our study helps us better grasp what it means to bear guilt as biblical writers speak of it.

How else might we respond to those who think this book minimizes law and legal language? Put simply, their objection often misunderstands the nature of the biblical law. On the one hand, it is the Mosaic law itself that presents us with a rich array of metaphors! On the other hand, we cannot speak of law in the Bible as an abstract concept. It formed a nation, underscoring collective identity. The Mosaic law was contextualized for an ancient context, using cultural concepts, values, and symbols. These include honor, shame, group identity, and the various metaphors discussed in this book.

How We Read the Bible

Our reading of Psalm 22 leads to another area of application. Perhaps another reason people press in on Jesus' words, quoted from Psalm 22:1, is because they sympathize with him in his suffering. They so grieve his agony that they have difficulty imagining that Christ might be making a larger, more significant appeal to the entire psalm. However, when reading Scripture, we must remind ourselves that feelings don't determine reality. They may influence how we perceive and respond to reality. But we do well to realize the importance of context for biblical interpretation. On the one hand, sentiment might push us to affirm or reject a set of ideas. On the other hand, the Bible's meaning is inextricably wrapped up in its original context, regardless of what we feel.

This point has practical significance. The same inclination that spurs us to overread the forsakenness of Christ can mislead us in other ways. For example, one might begin to see any suffering as God's forsaking us rather than as a tool for our good (Hebrews 12). Simply because God's enemies forsake the psalmist in Psalm 22:1 and the servant in Isaiah 53 does not mean that God does. Ultimately, others do not define our forsakenness.

Finally, we return to the place we began. The cross brings reconciliation to the world; yet debates about atonement divide the church. This book explores the diverse imagery that saturates the biblical picture of atonement. If we want a robust view of the atonement, we must embrace nuance, not merely tolerate it.

When I was about sixteen years old, I got into a big argument with my parents. Voices were raised to match our blood pressure. Weary of the back and forth, I wanted to end the fight, but not without a little mischief. I finally interjected, "Listen . . . you think you're right. I *know* I'm right. Let's just move on." Needless to say, the conversation prolonged from there.

I'm grieved that much of the church talks about the atonement in the same foolish manner that I used with my parents. We *know* what the Bible says, and so we feel little need to engage in genuine dialogue. It never occurs to us that two perspectives might not contrast as much as we think. I frequently tell people, "Even heretics aren't idiots." Even they often have a few good insights but then simply misapply them. It requires humility to temporarily set aside our atonement theories and embrace the messiness of the biblical text. Do we approach this doctrine in a way befitting its message?

HISTORICAL ATONEMENT THEORIES

THE FOLLOWING IS A BRIEF overview of major historical theories of atonement. This survey is intentionally broad. Our primary aim is to discern how each theory represents a fusion of biblical, cultural, and historical contexts.[1]

RECAPITULATION THEORY

Irenaeus (130–202 CE) and Athanasius (296–373 CE) were early advocates of the recapitulation theory of atonement. According to this view, Christ is the "last Adam" (1 Corinthians 15:45) who undoes the effects of the original Adam's fall. He is the embodied image of God, head of the human family. Through his life and death, Christ effectively restores the world to God's originally intended design.

This theory draws on several key passages. Not surprisingly, these include Romans 5:15-21 and 1 Corinthians 15:40-49. Both texts contrast two "Adams." Likewise, various passages that speak of new creation align with recapitulation theory. These include much of John's Gospel and Revelation 21:1, which foretells "a new heaven and a new earth."

Recapitulation theory emphasizes the atonement's result: the restoration of humanity and creation according to its original design. Aside from the incarnation, it focuses little on "how" questions. In other words, it does not detail the mechanism by which Christ achieves atonement.

RANSOM THEORY

Another ancient theory of atonement is called ransom theory. Distinct versions of this theory exist. Still, a few features broadly characterize this perspective. Origen (185–254 CE) espoused this view in the early church. It claims that

---

[1]This book primarily focuses on atonement theories popular within the Catholic and Protestant traditions. The Eastern Orthodox Church emphasizes human nature's transformation. They draw on texts like 2 Pet 1:3-4. Historically, this is a minority view. God, through Christ's death and the Spirit's coming, changes our disposition. Traditionally, Eastern Orthodox emphasize theosis. This process makes people more and more like God. People do not become a god, but they become increasingly holy like God.

Satan enslaved humanity as a consequence of sin. However, Christ gives his life as a ransom, liberating us from slavery. To whom is the ransom paid? Since God does not enslave humanity, Origen surmised, the ransom must have been paid to the devil.

Gregory of Nyssa (335–394 CE) adds his own twist. In his view, God uses Christ as "bait" to deceive Satan, who had legal rights over humanity. Satan believed that Christ was given in exchange for humanity. Gregory explains, "In order to secure that the ransom on our behalf might be easily accepted by him who required it, the Deity was hidden under the veil of our nature, that so, as with ravenous fish, the hook of the Deity might be gulped down along with the bait of flesh."[2] To the devil's shock, God raises Christ from the dead three days later. This perspective has received mixed responses. People are reluctant to accept a theory that seems to portray God as dishonest.

Mark 10:45 is one of the most famous texts that depict Christ as a ransom. Jesus says, "For even the Son of Man came not to be served but to serve, and to give his life as a ransom for many" (ESV). Paul also says Christ is a "ransom for all" in 1 Timothy 2:6.

Ransom certainly is a biblical metaphor. But how far does it extend? All metaphors have limits. Different versions of ransom theory arise from how one answers a series of questions. For example, does a ransom merely highlight the liberation of humanity? Or does it also imply some sort of payment? Who receives the ransom? Satan? God? If we are slaves, who is our master?

Christus Victor

A third atonement theory is Christus Victor (Latin for "Christ the Victorious"). This patristic model shares a certain affinity with the ransom theory. Both Ambrose (340–397 CE) and Augustine (354–430 CE) espoused this view. Gustaf Aulén (1879–1977) and N. T. Wright are its more recent popularizers.[3]

Christus Victor underscores the various ways that Christ defeats his enemies, including sin, Satan, disease, and death. Through his life and resurrection, he

---

[2]Gregory of Nyssa, "The Great Catechism 24," in *Nicene and Post-Nicene Fathers*, Series 2, vol. 5, ed. Philip Schaff, trans. William More and Henry Wilson (Grand Rapids, MI: Eerdmans, 1892), 494.

[3]See Gustaf Aulén, *Christus Victor: An Historical Study of the Three Main Types of the Idea of Atonement* (London: SPCK, 1931); N. T. Wright, *The Day the Revolution Began: Reconsidering the Meaning of Jesus's Crucifixion* (San Francisco: HarperOne, 2016). Some theologians see Christus Victor as a variation of ransom theory.

conquers worldly powers, that is, corrupt and unjust officials, social leaders, and so on. In this way, Christ is king.

Christus Victor paints sin (or death) as a master who enslaves humanity. Several texts in Romans exemplify this portrayal. For example, Paul says, "We know that our old self was crucified with him in order that the body of sin might be brought to nothing, so that we would no longer be enslaved to sin. For one who has died has been set free from sin" (Romans 6:6-7 ESV). Those who are "set free from sin, have become slaves of righteousness" (Romans 6:18).

Other passages add support to this view. The writer of Hebrews says, "Since therefore the children share in flesh and blood, he himself likewise partook of the same things, that through death he might destroy the one who has the power of death, that is, the devil, and deliver all those who through fear of death were subject to lifelong slavery" (Hebrews 2:14-15 ESV). John adds, "The reason the Son of God appeared was to destroy the works of the devil" (1 John 3:8 ESV).[4]

Some people seem to equate Christus Victor and ransom theory. The two theories appear wed in Colossians 2:13-15. Paul writes,

> And when you were dead in trespasses and the uncircumcision of your flesh, God made you alive together with him, when he forgave us all our trespasses, erasing the record that stood against us with its legal demands. He set this aside, nailing it to the cross. He disarmed the rulers and authorities and made a public example of them, triumphing over them in it.

Though similar, these theories have different focal points. Christus Victor highlights Christ's victory and kingship rather than simply his sacrifice and ransom. Also, Christus Victor highlights the results of atonement. Christ achieves a royal victory and wins our freedom. Ransom theory lays more emphasis on paying a ransom, the process or means of securing atonement. For this reason, scholars like Kathryn Tanner argue, "Christus Victor is not a model [of atonement] at all in that it fails per se, to address the question of the mechanism of the atonement."[5]

SATISFACTION THEORY

Anselm of Canterbury (1033–1109 CE) developed the satisfaction theory of atonement. In *Cur Deus Homo*, he tries to explain why the incarnation was

---

[4]Also, see Jn 16:11; Rom 8:3-4; 1 Cor 15:21-28.
[5]Kathryn Tanner, *Christ Is Key* (Cambridge: Cambridge University Press, 2010), 253.

necessary. He rejected ransom theory's claim that God is obligated to pay Satan. Rather, Anselm says atonement is necessary because God will not allow his creation to remain corrupt. The Creator must achieve his purposes. Otherwise, a corrupt creation dishonors the Creator.

According to satisfaction theory, God deserves perfect honor. Humanity's utmost duty is to live to the glory of God. However, when people dishonor God, they incur a debt. We cannot pay back this debt. Why? Anselm says that we cannot accrue merit. This is because all good behavior is simply one's duty to the divine Patron.

The satisfaction theory primarily underscores what I'll call a "positive" debt. Our positive debt refers to humanity's original, natural obligation. That is, we owe God honor. Adam and Eve, before the fall, had this positive debt of obedience. By contrast, contemporary readers are more likely to think of a negative debt. This is the debt incurred through sin. It is more like a moral deficit that necessitates some punitive consequence. Satisfaction theory lays stress on humanity's positive debt, that is, what we should do.

Anselm draws from biblical imagery. For Anselm, the atonement centrally concerns God's honor. Several texts point to the fact that Christ's incarnation upholds God's glory.[6] Also, Matthew depicts sin as a debt that God forgives (Matthew 6:12; 18:23-25). Anselm even appeals to Matthew's Gospel when making his argument.[7]

Since all humans are sinners, God must send a "God-man" to set the world right. Only a God-man can pay humanity's debt. According to medieval Catholic theology, people could attain merit before God. Christ's perfect life not only gave him merit for himself; his death provides a surplus of merit. He then shares that merit with humanity.

MORAL INFLUENCE THEORY

The moral influence theory is sometimes called the "moral exemplar theory." An early representative of this view is Peter Abelard (1079–1142 CE). The French theologian and philosopher proposed a subjective theory of atonement. By focusing on subjective aspects of Christ's atonement, he counters objective

---

[6]Cf. Jn 17:4, 22; Phil 2:8-11.
[7]*Cur Deus Homo* 1, 15 and 19; noted in David Neelands, "Substitution and the Biblical Background to Cur Deus Homo," *SAJ* 2, no. 2 (Spring 2005): 83.

theories, like those of Anselm and the Reformers. The latter emphasize what Christ objectively accomplishes before God, such as a transaction or change in legal status.

By contrast, Abelard asserts that Christ's holy life effects atonement. his moral example and self-sacrifice inspire us to live a good life. Abelard believed that nothing prevents God from indiscriminately forgiving people's sin. In other words, forgiveness does not require God receiving satisfaction or appeasement.

How might interpreters defend this perspective? Perhaps, one could cite 1 Peter 2:21-24.

> For to this you have been called, because Christ also suffered for you, leaving you an example, so that you should follow in his steps. "He committed no sin, / and no deceit was found in his mouth." When he was abused, he did not return abuse; when he suffered, he did not threaten; but he entrusted himself to the one who judges justly. He himself bore our sins in his body on the cross, so that, free from sins, we might live for righteousness; by his wounds you have been healed.

Contemporary supporters of the moral influence theory are largely found among liberal, mainline denominations. Many conservative evangelicals would argue that the problem with this atonement theory is not what it affirms as much as what is denies (i.e., objective aspects of Christ's atonement).

PENAL SUBSTITUTION

Contemporary evangelicals commonly affirm penal substitutionary atonement (PSA). Although elements of PSA exist throughout church history, it rose to prominence during the Protestant Reformation. The Reformers developed Anselm's theory. They argued that atonement is rooted in God's justice.

According to PSA, God regards sinners as enemies (Romans 5:10; Philippians 3:18). God demonstrates his justice by enforcing his law. Since people break God's law, they deserve the sentence of death. Yet, God loves humanity, so he sends Christ to die in our place. First Peter 2:24 says Christ "bore our sins in his body on the tree" (ESV). Instead of sinners bearing their sin, PSA states that Christ bears our sin. In other words, our sin is put on Jesus. Theologians cite 2 Corinthians 5:21, "For our sake he made him to be sin who knew no sin, so that in him we might become the righteousness of God."

Therefore, God pours out his wrath on Jesus. Jesus receives the punishment of death that sinners deserve. This is a common way of reading Romans 8:3, where Paul says, "By sending his own Son in the likeness of sinful flesh, and to deal with sin, he condemned sin in the flesh." What does it mean to say Christ died *for* us? Those who adopt PSA not only say Christ dies on our behalf; he also dies in our place.

AFFIRMING PENAL SUBSTITUTION BUT NOT ITS LOGIC

SEEING HOW BIBLICAL WRITERS use bearing and payment language, what are the implications for penal substitutionary atonement (PSA) theory? Advocates of PSA rely heavily on these metaphors. However, the logic of many writers does not seem consistent with the Bible's normal way of speaking. Below, I will affirm key ideas affirmed by PSA while demonstrating flaws in the logic used by many PSA theologians.[1] To avoid rehashing the various verses and arguments presented in the main chapters, I will assert conclusions that have been defended previously.

THE LOGIC FOR PSA

In the broad swath of literature affirming PSA, the implicit logic found often looks something like the following:

1. Ransom *implies* atonement.

2. Atonement *implies* punishment.

   therefore

3. Ransom *implies* punishment.

Many arguments for PSA depend on at least two premises. First, the presence of a ransom payment implies that atonement is achieved. Conversely, if there is not atonement, we can assume a ransom has not been paid. Second, atonement implies a punishment or retribution of some kind. From these assumptions, they surmise that the concept of a ransom suggests the existence of some punishment. A persistent concern for PSA theorists is defending God's wrath and the necessity that sin be punished.

---

[1]For example, the view in this book is consistent with criteria suggested by J. I. Packer, "What Did the Cross Achieve? The Logic of Penal Substitution," *TynBul* 25 (1973): 42-43, though one could quibble about whether his list is distinct or necessary for PSA.

This appendix explains why that argument is flawed. Previous chapters refute the claim that atonement (and ransom) implies retribution.[2] Rather, I argue that ransom brings atonement (and can appease wrath) yet apart from retribution. As a sacrifice, Christ pays our ransom to God. He does not receive our deserved retribution from God.

COUNTERING THE LOGIC OF TRADITIONAL PSA

This section challenges the second premise of the argument supporting PSA (atonement implies punishment). The Bible contains many examples of atonement without the presence of retribution. Thus, the ransom that brings atonement does not imply retribution. In the context of atonement, payment is not synonymous with punishment.

Interpreters often say that Jesus is the sacrifice that pays our debt, receiving the punishment of death that we deserve. They conflate debt and death. However, the biblical writers distinguish between paying a debt and the punishment that comes from one's inability to pay the debt. Thus, we too should be mindful not to confuse a person's debt with a person's death (i.e., the ultimate punishment, the consequence of sin).

Below I highlight two groups of passages. They together demonstrate that ransom cannot be identified as the punishment of sin. Our ransom is not our retribution. Various examples in the book show that an atoning payment (i.e., ransom) makes us avoid punishment. Some might object that the reason punishment is averted is because the ransom includes death. Therefore, in the second set of passages, we see that punishment (particularly in the form of death) is *not* a part of the ransom.

First, the following passage clearly distinguishes some sort of compensation payment and the punishment that would otherwise fall on an offender. We studied Exodus 30:11-16 in chapter eight. A ransom payment brings atonement, removing or appeasing God's wrath. Exodus 30:12 notes a *possible* sin (i.e., not paying ransom) and its consequence. Without a ransom, punishment would follow. People's lives are at stake. Sin could bring a plague. In Exodus 30:15-16, people gain atonement. Ransom brings atonement. Exodus 30:13, 15-16 make explicit that the ransom refers to money. The ransom payment atones for the life. In other words, God allows them to use a monetary offering to take away his wrath.

---

[2]We've also seen that atonement (and the presence of a ransom) does not *necessarily* imply appeasing wrath.

In the second set of texts, we find that atonement does not require people receiving the death penalty as retribution. These include Exodus 21:29-30; 32:30-32; Leviticus 5:11-13, 16; 10:17; Numbers 16:44-50; 31:48-51. Outside the Pentateuch, noteworthy passages include 2 Kings 12:16; Proverbs 6:34-35; 13:8. Much of this ground was covered in chapters eight and nine.

As we've seen, other passages further support this point: ransom (or payment) and punishment are distinct ideas. For example, Jesus tells the story of an unforgiving servant in Matthew 18. Concerning the servant, Matthew 18:25 says, "And, as he could not pay, his lord ordered him to be sold, together with his wife and children and all his possessions, and payment to be made." Yet, the master showed him mercy. Sadly, this servant was then ungracious to another man who owed him a smaller debt. So, in Matthew 18:34-35, Jesus says, "And in anger his lord handed him over to be tortured until he would pay his entire debt. So my heavenly Father will also do to every one of you, if you do not forgive your brother or sister from your heart." Note the link—if the man pays his debt, the master will remove the punishment.

People often confuse debt and punishment. Therefore, people say Jesus paid our debt, but their meaning is Jesus paid our death, that is, our punishment. However, they conflate metaphors. Jesus distinguishes three ideas: anger, debt, and punishment. In Jesus' parable, paying the debt removes or alleviates our punishment. Notice this metaphorical way of speaking applies even to our relationship with God. Debt *precedes* punishment. Therefore, paying the debt allays or removes wrath. As a result, we no longer receive punishment.

Implicitly, people assume that appeasing God's wrath means that he punishes the sinner. We contest that assumption, having seen in chapter four that even where "atone" connotes appeasement, it does not necessarily imply that someone is punished.

A HIDDEN AND FATAL ASSUMPTION

A fatal assumption underlies popular versions of PSA. Many people presume that God must punish every sin. For this reason, they say that atonement includes the appeasing of God's wrath. In other words, since scholars assume God must punish every sin, they infer that the sacrificial offerings secure atonement by enduring God's wrath instead of us. The flawed supposition is buried in the phrase "*every* sin."

Sin comes in two varieties. First, we have sin that God has forgiven. Second, there are sins that are not forgiven. *Penal substitutionary atonement proponents assume God even punishes every sin that is forgiven.* Unless God punishes sin, they say, he cannot forgive sin. God only forgives those sins that he punishes. They conclude that any sin that has been forgiven was already punished. Sin is forgiven because God punished people's sin in Jesus. Forgiveness necessitates punishment.[3]

Whereas PSA says that punishment is the means of God's forgiveness, punishment in fact is the consequence of God *not* forgiving sin. Chapter eight contains supporting arguments for this conclusion.

AFFIRMING PENAL SUBSTITUTIONARY ATONEMENT

In what sense can we affirm PSA? I put forth the following five affirmations. I affirm

- Christ's sacrifice effects atonement (chaps. 4, 6–8).
- Christ bears our sin (chap. 7).
- Christ's atonement involves a penalty (chap. 8).
- Christ's atonement involves substitution (chaps. 6–8).
- Christ's atonement appeases God's wrath (chaps. 2, 4, 8).

Each assertion is a biblical truth. I've argued for each idea throughout this book. Chapter ten also touches on several of these ideas explicitly. In conclusion, what I suggest is this: we can affirm each of these statements without claiming that God the Father kills or condemns Christ the Son on the cross (per popular views of PSA).

---

[3]In this book, I've not mentioned another latent assumption of traditional PSA. Advocates suppose that a perfect sacrifice is needed for atonement because it needs to absorb sin. The death of an imperfect being would not suffice. Yet, how do we explain Num 25:1-23? Phinehas kills the offender, yet this somehow makes atonement for the people of Israel. The problem seems to be this: according to PSA, the man's death should have no effect on whether the congregation's sin is atoned for. He is not a perfect sacrifice. If the people have sin, the man's death theoretically should not bring about atonement. They themselves deserve judgment.

"BEARING" IN THE OLD TESTAMENT

THE FOLLOWING GIVES EVIDENCE for the claim that *naśa* (to bear) has seemingly opposite connotations depending on the precise context and usage. For example, in texts where someone bears their own sin, iniquity, and so on, the word generally, though not always, conveys the idea of receiving punishment. In passages where a second party (e.g., God, people, animals) bears another person's sin, iniquity, and so on, the word has saving connotations. Specifically, it indicates the removal of a burden.

In any case, *naśa* is a metaphor that suggests "carrying, lifting." We can summarize its meaning most broadly as "taking responsibility for." How one does this can vary depending on the specific circumstance.

This list only mentions unambiguous verses. For certain debated texts, I do not beg the question, assuming a conclusion prematurely. In other words, we cannot presume straightaway the connotation of passages that speak about Christ or the servant in Isaiah as bearing our iniquity. That decision requires we see how terms are consistently used throughout the Bible.

CLEAR EXAMPLES WHERE SOMEONE "BEARS" (*NAŚA*) THEIR OWN SIN, INIQUITY, GUILT, OR TRANSGRESSION

Exodus 28:43; Leviticus 5:1, 17; 7:18; 17:16; 19:8, 17; 20:17, 19-20; 22:9, 24:15; Numbers 5:31; 9:13; 14:34; 18:22, 32; Job 34:31; Proverbs 19:19; Ezekiel 14:10; 16:58; 23:35, 49; 44:10, 12; Micah 7:9.

CLEAR EXAMPLES WHERE A SECOND PARTY "BEARS" (*NAŚA*) ANOTHER'S SIN, INIQUITY, GUILT, OR TRANSGRESSION

Genesis 50:17; Exodus 10:17; 23:21; 28:38; 32:32; 34:7; Leviticus 10:17; 16:22; Numbers 14:18, 19; 18:1, 23; Joshua 24:19; 1 Samuel 15:25; Job 7:21; Psalm 25:18; 32:1, 5; 85:2; Isaiah 33:24; Hosea 14:2; Micah 7:18. Also, cf. Psalm 99:8 (LXX 98:8); Hosea 1:6.

VERSES NEEDING ADDITIONAL COMMENT

Some verses require additional comment to clarify their interpretation. In the following, each text has a second party bearing another's sin. The word *naśa* seems to convey "endure, receive, or take" (with no definite punitive connotation).

Numbers 14:33. "And your children shall be shepherds in the wilderness for forty years, and *shall suffer* [*naśa*] for your faithlessness, until the last of your dead bodies lies in the wilderness." The key phrase literally translates "bear your faithlessness." Here, the children are not substitutes who take the place of parents. Their suffering does not remove the suffering of the elder generation. They do not "atone" for the parents' sin. Rather, they temporarily suffer the burden inherited from the parents. We observe that they share in the suffering only as long as the first generation of sinners lives. In community, the burden of sin is shared. Compare Numbers 14:34 where the parents "bear iniquity."

In the prior context, we see that the kids eventually get the blessing. Note Numbers 14:31-32, "But your little ones, who you said would become a prey, I will bring in, and they shall know the land that you have rejected. But as for you, your dead bodies shall fall in this wilderness" (ESV). In short, they endure the consequences of the parents' sin.

Numbers 30:15. "But if he makes them null and void after he has heard of them [the woman's vows], then *he shall bear her iniquity*" (ESV). The man shall take away her iniquity, just as the Lord will forgive her in Numbers 30:12. Although it says "her iniquity," the man is in fact the one guilty since he approves of breaking the pledge. Therefore, this verse does not count as a vicarious exchange of guilt or sin from the guilty to the innocent. This is not substitutionary in the sense of his absorbing punishment instead of his wife; instead, he takes responsibility.

We interpret Numbers 30:15 in light of Numbers 30:12-13, "But if her husband nullifies them at the time that he hears them, then whatever proceeds out of her lips concerning her vows, or concerning her pledge of herself, shall not stand. Her husband has nullified them, and the LORD will forgive her. Any vow or any binding oath to deny herself, her husband may allow to stand, or her husband may nullify."

Proverbs 6:35. "He will accept [*naśa*] no compensation, and refuses a bribe no matter how great." The verse simply indicates "take" or "receive" and does not have "sin" as the verb's object.

Isaiah 53:12. "Therefore I will allot him a portion with the great, / and he shall divide the spoil with the strong, / because he poured out himself to death, / and was numbered with the transgressors; / yet he *bore* the sin of many, / and made intercession for the transgressors." This book specifically addresses the ambiguity of this disputed text. So, we cannot beg the question. Based on the context and the previous discussion in this book, it appears this usage is positive, that is, taking away our transgressions.

Ezekiel 4:4-6. "Then lie on your left side, and place the punishment of the house of Israel upon it; you shall *bear* their punishment for the number of the days that you lie there. For I assign to you a number of days, three hundred ninety days, equal to the number of the years of their punishment; and so you shall *bear* the punishment of the house of Israel. When you have completed these, you shall lie down a second time, but on your right side, and *bear* the punishment of the house of Judah; forty days I assign you, one day for each year." Although these verses are unique, they reinforce the pattern argued in this book. Ezekiel symbolizes the fate of Israel. His actions illustrate how they will bear the punishment for their own sin. This action is symbolic for the community bearing their own sin. The passage clearly does not show Ezekiel being punished in their place, nor does he take away their sin.

Ezekiel 18:19-20. "Yet you say, 'Why should not the son *suffer* [*naśa*] for the iniquity of the father?' When the son has done what is lawful and right, and has been careful to observe all my statutes, he shall surely live. The person who sins shall die. A child shall not *suffer* [*naśa*] for the iniquity of a parent, nor a parent *suffer* [*naśa*] for the iniquity of a child; the righteousness of the righteous shall be his own, and the wickedness of the wicked shall be his own." This key text argues the exact point in question. If *bear* means "to be punished" for someone else's sin, then Ezekiel 18 flatly rejects the idea as unjust. The meaning of *bear* here is meant to be understood as suffering punishment.

Ezekiel 39:26. "They shall *forget* [*naśa*] their shame, and all the treachery they have practiced against me, when they live securely in their land with none to make them afraid." This bearing of their own shame indicates a positive, saving state. In essence, they have a proper, moral sense of shame.

Hosea 4:8. "They feed on the *sin* of my people; *they are greedy* [*naśa*] for their iniquity." Whatever the meaning, it is not penal substitution.

Noteworthy Texts with Related Verbs

Isaiah 6:7. "And he touched my mouth and said: 'Behold, this has touched your lips; your guilt is *taken away* [swr], and your sin atoned for'" (ESV).

Isaiah 27:9. "Therefore by this the guilt of Jacob will be atoned for, and this will be the full fruit of the *removal* [swr] of his sin" (ESV). Neither text carries punitive connotations. They instead underscore salvation.

THE METAPHORS OF HEBREWS 9–10

HOW DOES CHRIST'S BLOOD secure the blessings of the new covenant? We turn to Hebrews 9:22, a famously difficult text that alludes to Leviticus 17:11. How does Leviticus 17:11 influence Hebrews 9:22? The writer does not directly quote Leviticus; he merely draws from it. Instead of speaking of freedom or release, Leviticus 17 refers to atonement. Still, the prominent thread in both texts is the use of blood.

Interpreting Hebrews 9:22 in its context can feel daunting for anyone. The writer leaves much unsaid, allowing an array of images to speak for themselves. Even where the logic in Hebrews 9–10 is explicit, it is dense. My purpose in the following pages is modest. I do not offer a verse-by-verse commentary on these chapters. Instead, I simply show the intricate way the writer interweaves several atonement metaphors. Such metaphors reinforce one another and derive meaning from the biblical narrative.

How does Hebrews 9:22 fit within the broader argument of Hebrews 8–10? Hebrews 9:22 says, "Indeed, under the law almost everything is purified with blood, and without the shedding of blood there is no freedom [or release]."[1] We face two pressing issues when understanding Hebrews 9:22. First, what is the meaning of *haimatekchysia* (the shedding of blood, pouring of blood)? Second, how should we translate *aphesis* (forgiveness, freedom, release)?

Concerning the shedding or pouring of blood, does the writer refer to the animal's slaughter, the application of blood (upon the altar, etc.), or both? Choosing one over the other is difficult. The slaughter alone seems insufficient.[2] In a sacrificial context, atonement and forgiveness never result from bloodshed alone. Something else is needed, whether sprinkling, rubbing, pouring, and so on. We saw this in previous chapters. Of course,

---

[1]Many translations use "forgiveness," not "freedom" or "release." I discuss this below.
[2]Another option suggests that the writer doesn't refer to the mechanics of making a sacrificial offering. Perhaps, the blood symbolically points back to the death of the covenant maker in Heb 9:15-17. Norman H. Young, "*Haimatekchysia*: A Comment," *The Expository Times* 90, no. 6 (1979): 180. This view is attractive, but the following observations and logical flow of the immediate context make it unlikely.

applying blood presumes a slaughter. In this respect, the answer might be both.

HEBREWS 9:21-26

And in the same way *he sprinkled with the blood* both the tent and all the vessels used in worship. Indeed, under the law almost everything is purified with blood, and without the shedding of blood there is no *freedom/release* [*aphesis*].

Thus it was necessary for the sketches of the heavenly things to *be purified with these rites*, but the heavenly things needs with better sacrifices than these. [Why "better"?]

For Christ did not enter a sanctuary made by human hands, a mere copy of the true one, but he entered into heaven itself, now to appear in the presence of God on our behalf.

Nor was it to offer himself again and again, as the high priest enters the Holy Place year after year with blood that is not his own,

> **for** then he would have had to suffer again and again since the foundation of the world. But as it is, he has appeared once for all at the end of the age to *remove* ["bear," *naśa*] sin by the sacrifice of himself. (NRSV, author's adaptation)

The context helps us to minimize guesswork. Let's begin with a few observations. First, Hebrews 9:22b is the third in a series of verses repeating the same phrase.[3]

Hebrews 9:7	*ou chōris haimatos*
	"not without blood"
Hebrews 9:18	*oude . . . chōris haimatos*
	"not even the first covenant was inaugurated without blood"
Hebrews 9:22b	*chōris haimatekchysias . . . ou*
	"without the shedding/pouring of blood there is no release"

Second, Hebrews 9:21-22 contains a gradual intensification of thought. The text does this by using *kai* to begin three consecutive thoughts. *Kai* is a connecting word with various shades of use and meaning.[4]

Hebrews 9:21 And [*kai*] in the same way he sprinkled with the blood both the tent and all the vessels used in worship.

---

[3]William L. Lane, *Hebrews 9–13*, Word Biblical Commentary, vol. 47B (Grand Rapids, MI: Zondervan, 2015), 246.
[4]These include "and," "indeed," "likewise," "also," "both . . . and," "not only . . . but also," among others. See "*kai*," BDAG.

Hebrews 9:22a Indeed [*kai*], under the law almost everything is purified with blood.

Hebrews 9:22b and [*kai*] without the shedding of blood there is no release. (NRSV, author's adaptation)

Each consecutive *kai* creates an intensification. Third, what follows beginning in Hebrews 9:23 stems directly from Hebrews 9:22.[5] Likewise, the message shifts sharply from that in the passage preceding Hebrews 9:22. I emphasize these observations to say this: *the primary import of Hebrews 9:22 is discerned by looking at Hebrews 9–10, not Leviticus 17:11* (quoted in Hebrews 9:22).

The point is underscored by the fact that Hebrews makes significant adjustments to Leviticus 17:11. For example, whereas Leviticus speaks of "atonement," Hebrews refers to "release" (*aphesis*). Likewise, the writer dramatically alters the actual message.[6] Leviticus states, "For the life of the flesh is in the blood; and I have given it to you for making atonement for your lives on the altar; for, as life, *it is the blood that makes atonement.*" By contrast, Hebrews makes a more absolute claim using the negative: "Without the shedding of blood there is no release."

The Day of Atonement in Hebrews 9–10

Consider how the Day of Atonement in Leviticus sheds lights on the structure and substance on Hebrews 9–10. A study of Leviticus 16 provides clues for interpreting Hebrews 9:22, especially the meaning of *haimatekchysia* (shedding of blood) and *aphesis* (release).[7]

First note the contrast, via intensification, within Hebrews 9:22. In Hebrews 9:22a, the writer says, "Under the law almost everything is purified with blood." He reemphasizes that he speaks of purification "under the law." He then adds the qualification "nearly everything" (*schedon . . . panta*).[8] Hebrews 9:22b, however, makes a sweeping claim, "without . . . there is no" (*chōris . . . ou*).

Hebrews 10:18 confirms the shift in 9:22b. Hebrews 10:18 says, "Where there is *release* [*aphesis*] from these, there is no longer an offering of the reconciliation offering."[9] The verbal link to Hebrews 9:22 is unmistakable. In fact, Hebrews 10:18

---

[5]Note "thus" (*oun . . . men*) in Heb 9:23.

[6]As previously noted, ancient Jewish sources routinely mention Lev 17:11 for various purposes, especially when discussing the efficacy of blood manipulation (e.g., sprinkling of blood at the altar).

[7]Keep in mind that, for the writer of Hebrews, Lev 17 immediately follows Lev 16 in its canonical form.

[8]See William Johnsson, "Defilement and Purgation in the Book of Hebrews" (PhD diss., Vanderbilt University, 1973), 319.

[9]The NRSV says "any offering for sin," yet we've shown above why rendering *peri hamartias* as "reconciliation offering" is preferable.

is the climax to the entire unit of thought in Hebrews 9:23–10:18 that follows from Hebrews 9:22b. Hebrews 9:18 is an implication from Hebrews 9:22b.[10] Whereas Hebrews 9:22b asserts "If there is no shedding of blood, there is no release," Hebrews 10:19 affirms the contrapositive. In other words, if there is release, then bloodshed has occurred; thus, there is no need for a reconciliation offering. The comments in Hebrews 9:23–10:18 clearly highlight the supremacy of Christ's atoning work over the system under the law.

Finally, we mustn't overlook another critical observation. Following Hebrews 9:22, the writer unloads a litany of words evoking similar imagery. Look at the following verses.

Hebrews 9:26   But as it is, he has appeared once for all at the end of the ages *to put away* [*athetēsis*] sin by the sacrifice of himself (NRSV, author's adaptation)

Hebrews 9:28   so Christ, having been offered once *to bear* [*anapherō*] the sins of many

Hebrews 10:4   For it is impossible for the blood of bulls and goats *to take away* [*aphaireō*] sins.

Hebrews 10:9   then he added, "Behold, I have come to do your will." He *does away with* [*anaireō*] the first in order to establish the second. (ESV)

Hebrews 10:11   And every priest stands daily at his service, offering repeatedly the same sacrifices, which can never *take away* [*periaireō*] sins. (ESV)

Each of these words is related to the metaphor of loadbearing. Why does this sort of language suddenly appear here with such density?

The key is found in the shared vocabulary from Hebrews 9:22b; 10:18. Both texts refer to *aphesis* (release). When this word pairs with the genitive of *hamartia* (of sins), it is typically translated as "forgiveness of sins."[11] Otherwise, *aphesis* takes on different connotations. Throughout Scripture, *aphesis* routinely denotes freedom or release. For example, Jesus (quoting Isaiah 61:1) says,

---

[10]Likewise, Benjamin Ribbens, "Levitical Sacrifice and Heavenly Cult in Hebrews" (PhD diss., Wheaton College, IL, 2013), 214; Gareth Lee Crockerill, *The Epistle to the Hebrews*, NICNT (Grand Rapids, MI: Eerdmans, 2012), 414.

[11]Eph 1:7 uses *paraptōma* and so says "forgiveness of our trespasses."

"The Spirit of the Lord is upon me, because he has anointed me to proclaim good news to the poor. He has sent me to proclaim *release* to the captives and recovering of sight to the blind, to let the oppressed *go free*" (Luke 4:18 ESV).

Nearly "half of the occurrences of *aphesis* in the LXX occur in Leviticus."[12] In speaking of the year of Jubilee, LXX Leviticus 25:10 says, "And sanctify the year, the fiftieth year, and proclaim loudly a time of *release* concerning the land to all those inhabiting it; a year of *remission* this signal will be to you, and a person will go out, each one to his possession, and each one shall go to his family property" (LES).[13]

Most importantly, we find *aphesis* at a critical point in Leviticus 16. The Greek version of Leviticus 16:26, "And the person who sends out the he-goat that was set apart for *release* [*aphesis*] must wash his garments and must bathe his body with water. And after these things he will return to the encampment" (LES).[14] One goat is sacrificed as a reconciliation offering in the sanctuary; the living goat bears the sins of the people. LXX Leviticus 16:21-22 says, "[Aaron] will *place* [Israel's transgressions and injustices] *upon* the head of the living he-goat, and he will send it forth, by the hand of a person prepared for this, into the desert wilderness. And the he-goat will *take their injustices upon itself into a desolate wasteland*, and he will send forth the he-goat into the desert wilderness" (LES). The text depicts the goat as taking away the sins of God's people. The word's occurrence is hardly coincidental. Hebrews 9–10 is packed with allusions to the Day of Atonement.[15]

The writer uses Leviticus 16 to structure the argument of Hebrews 9–10. On the Day of Atonement, the priest sheds the blood of the reconciliation offerings. Only then is the living goat released outside the camp.[16] The first part of Hebrews 9 focuses on purification in the sanctuary. After Hebrews 9:22, Christ is the one who bears or removes sin. In short, Christ is presented as both the reconciliation offering and the living goat that takes away sin. Every year required a new Day of Atonement. This is because the high priest and the animals could not ultimately accomplish what Christ achieved for all time. Since Christ finally purifies and removes our sin, there is no longer need for a reconciliation offering.

---

[12]Johnsson, "Defilement and Purgation," 326.

[13]Although *aphesis* shares a root with *aphiēmi* (forgiveness), interpreters must not ignore the potential ways they differ. Certainly, *aphesis* and *aphiēmi* draw from overlapping thought worlds. One gains freedom through forgiveness; cf. LXX Deut 15:2; LXX Ps 104:20.

[14]The NRSV uses the Hebrew MT: "And he who lets the goat go to Azazel shall wash his clothes and bathe his body in water, and afterward he may come into the camp."

[15]Cf. Heb 9:1-14, 23-28; 10:11-14.

[16]Conversely, once the living goat is released, there is no more need for a reconciliation offering. This statement resembles the logic of Heb 10:18.

What then might we say about the meaning of *haimatekchysia*, which the NRSV renders "shedding of blood"? This compound combines *haima* (blood) and *ekcheō* (shedding, pouring). The pairing of words can refer to a person's murder (Genesis 9:6; 36:22; Numbers 35:33). However, in the context of sanctuary sacrifices, *haima* and *ekcheō* overwhelming denote the pouring of blood. For example, the reconciliation offering is killed in Leviticus 8:15. The text says, "Moses took the blood, and with his finger put it on the horns of the altar around it, *purifying* [*katharizō*] the altar; and *poured out the blood* [*haima ex-echeen*] at the base of the altar. Thus he consecrated it, to make atonement for it."[17] This reconciliation offering included a death. But, in context, the writer seems primarily to stress the fact that Christ is a sacrificial offering.

Finally, the transition at Hebrews 9:22 also reflects the writer's focus on the new covenant promises. Before Hebrews 9:22, the passage builds on Hebrews 8, particularly emphasizing the promise that God will change the hearts of his people. Hebrews 9 expresses this idea when he says Christ's blood will "purify our conscience from dead works to serve the living God" (Hebrews 9:14). Following Hebrews 9:22, the writer underscores the promise that God will take away sin.[18] Hebrews 10:15-17 confirms this outline.

> And the Holy Spirit also bears witness to us; for *after* [*meta*] saying,
>> "This is the covenant that I will make with them after those days, says the Lord:
>>> I will put my laws on their hearts, and write them on their minds,"
> he *also* [*kai*] adds,
>> "I will remember their sins and their lawless deeds no more."

It is only after reiterating these two promises from Jeremiah 31 that the writer makes his climactic conclusion in Hebrews 10:18.

The brevity of this appendix reflects its purpose. It demonstrates how deliberate the author of Hebrews is when using metaphors. Hebrews 9–10 reflect the ways that other biblical authors use these metaphors to explain the atonement. In addition, the account here illustrates how the discussion in this book bolsters our ability to explain challenging passages, such as those in Hebrews.

---

[17]Other examples include Ex 29:12; Lev 4:18, 25, 34; 9:9. Also, see T. C. G. Thornton, "The Meaning of *Haimatekchysia* in Hebrews 9:22," *JTS* 15, no. 1 (April 1964): 63-65.

[18]Notably, the frequency that *hamartia* (sin) appears increases drastically (13 times) in Heb 9:26–10:26. This is over half of the references to *hamartia* in Hebrews. Past "transgressions" are mentioned in Heb 9:15.

DISCUSSION GUIDE

INTRODUCTION

1. What are a few concerns that motivate the writing of this book?

2. How might popular theories of atonement make interpreting the biblical authors more difficult?

3. How can studying the atonement help us to contextualize the biblical message?

1. RECONCILING ATONEMENT THEORIES

1. How might debates about atonement "lose at the starting line"?

2. How does the analogy of cooking ingredients suggest a better way to discuss the doctrine of atonement?

3. How have theologians contextualized the atonement in history?

4. How might our culture, background, and assumptions influence our view of doctrines like the atonement?

5. In what ways might you be personally challenged and encouraged in this study as you think afresh about this critical teaching?

2. PREPARING A SANCTUARY FOR THE KING

1. What is the significance of sacred space?

2. What are four basic categories used by the Israelites to categorize things in the world? How do these categories relate to one another?

3. What makes something unclean?

4. What is the basic problem with uncleanness or impurity?

5. What are three primary metaphors used to talk about the problem that atonement solves?

6. What is the relationship between impurity and debt language?

3. Offering a Way to God

1. What is the basic meaning of the Hebrew word for "offering"?

2. What are the primary sacrifices found in Leviticus and discussed in this chapter?

3. In light of the discussion about the reconciliation offering, how might we define *sin*?

4. Depending on the context, blood from the reconciliation offering binds, though in different ways. What are these two ways?

5. What is common to all sacrificial offerings?

6. What is a devoted thing?

4. Atonement and the Significance of Blood

1. Before reading this chapter, how would you have explained the atonement? How have you heard the idea taught?

2. How does this chapter summarize the fundamental objective achieved by the atonement?

3. We observe a constant pattern. What routinely precedes the announcement that atonement has been made?

4. In Scripture, what are the primary objects of atonement?

5. What seem to be two specific but distinct functions of atonement? (They are illustrated most clearly in our study of the Levites.)

6. What do we find is the relationship between atonement and death?

7. Why does God forbid the Israelites from eating blood?

5. Seeking God's Face Through Sacrifice

1. From an honor and shame perspective, how can we explain holiness?

2. What is the relationship between purity, uncleanness, honor, and shame?

3. What is the fundamental purpose of a sacrifice from the perspective of honor?

4. How do sacrifices affect the honor or shame of worshipers?

5. How might observations from this chapter challenge our understanding of Christ's atonement and correct how we explain the message of salvation?

6. What Does Christ Purify?

1. What are the functions of the two reconciliation offerings and the burnt offerings presented on the Day of Atonement?

2. According to this chapter, why is uncleanness called "iniquity" in Leviticus 16?

3. In light of our reading of Leviticus 17:11 in Hebrews 9, Christ's blood appears to effect what type of transition?

4. Does Hebrews 9 discuss the covenant or a will? How do we know?

5. How does Christ's inauguration of the new, better covenant bring purification?

7. Who Bears the Burden of Sin?

1. How is the phrase "bear sin" usually interpreted by evangelicals?

2. What are the two seemingly contrary meanings of "bear sin" as seen in the Bible?

3. Why do readers of the Bible often overlook or miss these two meanings?

4. How do we discern between these two meanings when biblical writers speak of bearing sin?

5. What is the function of the living goat on the Day of Atonement?

6. From the context of Isaiah 52–53, what does it likely mean when the writer says the servant bears iniquity and sin?

8. Does God Want Recompense or Retribution?

1. What biblical texts best help you to grasp the link between restitution-compensation with either atonement or wrath?

2. What is the interrelationship between the payment, purity, and burden metaphors?

3. Conceptually, how might we distinguish payment, penalty, and punishment?

4. What function does the Passover lamb serve?

5. Why is the Passover lamb not a penal substitute that is punished in the Israelites' place?

6. In the context of Scripture, what does it mean to say Jesus is the Lamb of God?

9. Does the Father Punish the Son?

1. How have evangelicals traditionally interpreted Jesus' meaning when he quotes Psalm 22:1?

2. What does "forsaken" imply within the context of Psalm 22?

3. According to this chapter, why does Jesus quote from Psalm 22?

4. Does Galatians 3:13 contribute to our theology of atonement? If not, why not? If so, explain how.

5. What biblical texts explicitly state that God punishes or pours out this wrath on his son or on a reconciliation offering?

10. Answers to Lingering Questions

1. What are two or three questions posed in this chapter that you also have? What answers were most helpful for you? Why?

2. What other questions (not asked above) do you have?

3. How do the insights provided in this book begin to contribute to answering your questions?

11. Does Christ Bear Our Shame?

1. Before reading this book, what explicit applications of the atonement have you heard taught?

2. What are two areas of application mentioned in this chapter that you found helpful? Why? How might these suggestions be applied in your life, church, and ministry?

3. What other applications stem from the insights and discussion presented in this book?

GLOSSARY

AS WE REORIENT OUR MENTAL paradigms about the atonement, one can easily get lost amid an ocean of terms. So, to help readers navigate their way through this book, I provide a glossary. I do not intend for these definitions to be exhaustive. Rather, readers would do well to think of the following as *descriptions* more than definitions. These brief comments seek to capture key ideas about these words *as expressed in this book*.

atone—to entreat one's favor, appease, propitiate

bear—to lift, raise, carry, take away, remove, endure

burden—a weight associated with difficulty or hardship

common—ordinary, everyday, profane, not holy

compensation—recompense, reparation, restitution, payment, restore or pay back what is owed

consecrate—to set apart as holy

debt—an obligation, what one owes to another

devoted—a gift given completely to God thus no longer available for common use

forgive—to release or free from a debt or obligation; not hold against

forsake—to not intervene on one's behalf (contrary to expectation), to be far from

guilt—objective guilt, the responsibility one has for doing wrong; subjective guilt, the feeling that one has done something wrong

holy—sacred, set apart for God, belonging to God, pertaining to the divine, worthy of unique honor, not ordinary

honor—glory, having public status or esteem, recognized as having worth, right of respect

impure—unclean, whether for ritual or moral reasons

mercy seat—symbolic throne atop the ark within the Most Holy Place, the symbolic throne room of God within the temple or tabernacles' inner sanctuary, the Holy of Holies

offering—a means of drawing near to God

penalty—required due to wrongdoing (in order to avoid punishment or retribution)

retribution—punishment in response to wrongdoing

purity—clean; can describe something common or holy, but is inherent to holiness

ransom—payment leading to freedom or release, compensation for debt

reconciliation—restoration of right relationship

redemption—"A concept found in the OT to express the action of a relative in setting free a member of his family or buying back his property (Lv. 25:25ff.) or in general that of purchasing something for a price."[1]

sanctify—to regard or set apart something as holy

shame—the state of being judged unworthy or lacking value, sensitivity to the views of others, especially regarding moral issues

---

[1]Sinclair B. Ferguson and J. I. Packer, "Redemption," *NDT*.

SELECTED BIBLIOGRAPHY

Allender, Dan B., and Tremper Longman. *In the Cry of the Soul: How Our Emotions Reveal Our Deepest Questions About God*. 2nd ed. Colorado Springs, CO: NavPress, 2015.

Anatolios, Khaled. *Deification Through the Cross: An Eastern Christian Theology of Salvation*. Grand Rapids, MI: Eerdmans, 2020.

Anderson, Gary. *Sin: A History*. New Haven, CT: Yale University Press, 2009.

Arnold, Jack. "Propitiation: A Study of Romans 3:24-26." *IIIM Magazine Online* 1, no. 22 (July 16, 1999). reformedperspectives.org/newfiles/jac_arnold/NT.Arnold.Rom.19.html.

Aulén, Gustaf. *Christus Victor: An Historical Study of the Three Main Types of the Idea of Atonement*. London: S.P.C.K., 1931.

Bailey, Daniel. "Jesus as the Mercy Seat: The Semantics and Theology of Paul's Use of *Hilasterion* in Romans 3:25." PhD diss., Cambridge University, 1999.

———. "Jesus as the Mercy Seat: The Semantics and Theology of Paul's Use of *Hilasterion* in Romans 3:25." *Tyndale Bulletin* 51, no. 1 (2000): 155-58.

Barclay, John. *Paul and the Gift*. Grand Rapids, MI: Eerdmans, 2015.

Barrick, William. "Penal Substitution in the Old Testament." *The Master's Seminary Journal* 20, no. 2 (Fall 2009): 149-69.

Bauckham, Richard. Interview with London Christian Thinkers, January 29, 2015. www.youtube.com/watch?v=oHSoovmy4cw.

———. *Jesus and the God of Israel*. Grand Rapids, MI: Eerdmans, 2008.

Bavinck, Hermon. *Reformed Dogmatics*. Vol. 3. Edited by John Bolt. Translated by John Vriend. Grand Rapids, MI: Baker Academic, 2006.

Beale, Greg. "Eden, the Temple and the Church's Mission in the New Creation." *Journal of the Evangelical Theological Society* 48, no. 1 (2005): 5-32.

———. *The Temple and the Church's Mission*. Downers Grove, IL: IVP Academic, 2004.

Beck, Richard. *Unclean: Meditations on Purity, Hospitality, and Mortality*. Eugene, OR: Cascade, 2011.

Beckwith, R. T. "Sacrifice." In *New Dictionary of Biblical Theology*, edited by T. Desmond Alexander and Brian S. Rosner, 754-61. Downers Grove, IL: InterVarsity Press, 2000.

Belousek, Darrin Snyder. *Atonement, Justice, and Peace: The Message of the Cross and the Mission of the Church*. Grand Rapids, MI: Eerdmans, 2012.

Bennett, Matthew A. *Narratives in Conflict: Atonement in Hebrews and the Qur'an*. Eugene, OR: Pickwick, 2019.

Boteach, Shmuley. "Should Jews Owe Gratitude to Trump?," *Jerusalem Post*, September 18, 2018. www.jpost.com/opinion/should-jews-owe-gratitude-to-trump-567466.

Brown, Francis, S. R. Driver, and Charles Briggs. *The Enhanced Brown-Driver-Briggs Hebrew and English Lexicon*. Oak Harbor, WA: Logos, 2000.

Burnhope, Stephen. *Atonement and the New Perspective: The God of Israel, Covenant, and the Cross.* Eugene, OR: Pickwick, 2018.

Burton, Ernest D. "Redemption from the Curse of the Law: An Exposition of Gal. 3:13, 14." *The American Journal of Theology* 11, no. 4 (1907): 641-45.

Campbell, Constantine. *Paul and Union with Christ: An Exegetical and Theological Study.* Grand Rapids, MI: Zondervan, 2012.

Caneday, Ardel. "'Redeemed from the Curse of the Law': The Use of Deut 21:22-23 in Gal 3:13." *Trinity Journal* 10 (1989): 185-209.

Capehart, Jonathon. "How Segregationist George Wallace Became a Model for Racial Reconciliation: 'Voices of the Movement,' Episode 6." *Washington Post*, May 16, 2019. washingtonpost.com/opinions/2019/05/16/changed-minds-reconciliation-voices-movement-episode/.

Carey, George. "The Lamb of God and Atonement Theories." *Tyndale Bulletin* 32 (1981): 97-122.

Carey, Holly J. *Jesus' Cry from the Cross: Towards a First-Century Understanding of the Intertextual Relationship Between Psalm 22 and the Narrative of Mark's Gospel.* New York: T&T Clark, 2009.

Carmichael, Calum. "The Origin of the Scapegoat Ritual." *Vetus Testamentum* 50, no 2 (2000): 167-82.

Chou, Abner (blog). "'The Big Picture of God's Mission': A Concise Overview of the Entire Bible." July 25, 2015. https://adam-setser-hlrz.squarespace.com/blog/2015/7/25/the-big-picture-of-gods-mission-a-concise-overview-of-the-entire-bible-by-dr-abner-chou.

Constantineanu, Corneliu. *The Social Significance of Reconciliation in Paul's Theology: Narrative Readings in Romans.* Library of New Testament Studies 421. New York: T&T Clark, 2010.

Cooke, Gerald. "The Israelite King as Son of God." *Zeitschrift für die Alttestamentliche Wissenschaft* 73 (1961): 202-25.

Cowan, J. Andrew. "The Curse of the Law, the Covenant, and Anthropology in Galatians 3:10-14: An Examination of Paul's Use of Deuteronomy 27:26." *Journal of Biblical Literature* 139, no. 1 (2020): 211-29.

Craig, William Lane. *Atonement and the Death of Christ: An Exegetical, Historical, and Philosophical Exploration.* Waco, TX: Baylor University Press, 2020.

Crezo, Adrienne. "We Used to Put Radium in Coffee." *The Atlantic*, October 10, 2012. www.theatlantic.com/health/archive/2012/10/we-used-to-put-radium-in-coffee/263408/.

Crisp, Oliver. *Approaching the Atonement: The Reconciling Work of Christ.* Downers Grove, IL: IVP Academic, 2020.

Crisp, Oliver and Fred Sanders, eds. *Locating Atonement: Explorations in Constructive Dogmatics.* Grand Rapids, MI: Zondervan, 2015.

Crockerill, Gareth Lee. *The Epistle to the Hebrews.* NICNT. Grand Rapids, MI: Eerdmans, 2012.

Dalrymple, Timothy. "Justice Too Long Delayed." *Christianity Today*, June 10, 2020. www.christianitytoday.com/ct/2020/igo-web-only/justice-too-long-delayed.html.

Demarest, Bruce. *The Cross and Salvation: The Doctrine of God*. Wheaton, IL: Crossway, 2006.

DeSilva, David. "Despising Shame: A Cultural-Anthropological Investigation of the Epistle to the Hebrews." *Journal of Biblical Literature* 113 (1994): 459-81.

———. *Honor, Patronage, Kinship and Purity*. Downers Grove, IL: IVP Academic, 2000.

Dever, Mark, and Michael Lawrence. *It Is Well*. Wheaton, IL: Crossway, 2010.

DeYoung, Kevin, and Jerry Bridges. *The Good News We Almost Forgot Rediscovering the Gospel in a 16th Century Catechism*. Chicago: Moody, 2010.

Dillman, Augst. *Die Bücher Exodus und Leviticus*. Leizig: Hirzel, 1897.

DOCSology. "I Survived I Kissed Dating Goodbye." Documentary, August 30, 2019. youtu .be/ybYTkkQJw_M.

Douglas, Mary. "Pollution." In *International Encyclopedia of Social Sciences*, edited by David L. Sills, 335-41. Vol. 12. New York: Crowell Collier and Macmillan, 1968.

———. *Purity and Danger: An Analysis of Concepts of Pollution and Taboo*. London: Routledge, 1966.

———. "Symbolic Classification." In *International Encyclopedia of Social and Behavioral Sciences*, edited by James Wright, 557-62. Oxford: Elsevier, 2015.

Dunn, J. D. G. "Paul's Understanding of the Death of Jesus as Sacrifice." In *Sacrifice and Redemption: Durham Essays in Theology*, edited by S. W. Sykes, 35-56. Cambridge: Cambridge University Press, 2007.

Eberhart, Christian. "A Neglected Feature of Sacrifice in the Hebrew Bible: Remarks on the Burning Rite on the Altar." *Harvard Theological Review* 97, no. 4 (2004): 485-93.

Eder, Jacob. "Germany Is Often Praised for Facing Up to Its Nazi Past. But Even There, the Memory of the Holocaust Is Still Up for Debate." *Time Magazine*, January 27, 2020. time .com/5772360/german-holocaust-memory/.

Feder, Yitzhaq. *Blood Expiation in Hittite and Biblical Rituals: Origins, Context, and Meaning*. Atlanta: Society of Biblical Literature, 2011.

———. "On *kuppuru, kipper*, and Etymological Sins That Cannot Be Wiped Away." *Vetus Testamentum* 60 (2010): 535-45.

Fiensy, David A. "Crucifixion." In *The Lexham Bible Dictionary*, edited by John D. Barry and Lazarus Wentz. Bellingham, WA: Logos Bible Software, 2012.

Fratti, Karen. "I Have HIV, But It's Stigma That Makes Me Sick." *Medium*, October 16, 2016. medium.com/@karenfratti/i-have-hiv-but-its-stigma-that-makes-me-sick-3ab4879ff324.

Gaffin, Richard. "Atonement in the Pauline Corpus." In *The Glory of the Atonement: Biblical, Theological & Practical Perspectives*, edited by Charles E. Hill and Frank A. James III, 140-62. Downers Grove, IL: IVP Academic, 2004.

Gallusz, Laszlo. *The Throne Motif in the Book of Revelation*. New York: Bloomsbury, 2013.

George, Timothy. "The Atonement in Martin Luther's Theology." In *The Glory of the Atonement: Biblical, Theological & Practical Perspectives*, edited by Charles E. Hill and Frank A. James III, 263-78. Downers Grove, IL: IVP Academic, 2004.

Gilders, William K. "Sacrifice in Ancient Israel." *SBL Newsletter*. n.p. Accessed August 21, 2020. www.bibleodyssey.org/en/passages/related-articles/sacrifice-in-ancient-israel.

Glasson, T. Francis. "The 'Passover,' a Misnomer: The Meaning of the Verb 'Pasach.'" *The Journal of Theological Studies* 10, no 1 (April 1959): 79-84.

Gorman, Michael. *Inhabiting the Cruciform God: Kenosis, Justification, and Theosis in Paul's Narrative Soteriology*. Grand Rapids, MI: Eerdmans, 2009.

Greenberg, James. *A New Look at the Atonement in Leviticus: The Meaning and Purpose of Kipper Revisited*. University Park: Penn State University Press, 2020.

Gregory of Nyssa. "The Great Catechism 24." In *Nicene and Post-Nicene Fathers*, Series 2, vol. 5, edited by Philip Schaff, 492-95. Translated by William More and Henry Wilson. Grand Rapids, MI: Eerdmans, 1892.

Gruenler, Royce Gordon. "Atonement in the Synoptic Gospels and Acts." In *The Glory of the Atonement*, edited by Charles E. Hill, Roger R. Nicole, and Charles Evan Hill, 90-105. Downers Grove, IL: IVP Academic, 2004.

Haas, Volkert. *Materia et Medica Hethitica*. Berlin: De Gruyter, 2013.

Hahn, Scott. "Broken Covenant Curse and the Curse of Death: A Study of Hebrews 9:15-22." *Catholic Biblical Quarterly* 66, no. 3 (July 2004): 416-36.

Hamilton, Victor. *Exodus: An Exegetical Commentary*. Grand Rapids, MI: Baker Academic, 2011.

Hartley, John E. *Leviticus*. Word Biblical Commentary 4. Grand Rapids, MI: Zondervan, 1992.

Hendel, Ronald. "Table and Altar: The Anthropology of Food in the Priestly Torah." In *To Break Every Yoke: Essays in Honor of Marvin L. Chaney*, edited by R. B. Coote and N. K. Gottwald, 131-48. Sheffield: Sheffield Phoenix Press, 2007.

Hill, Daniel J., and Joseph Jedwab. "Atonement and the Concept of Punishment." In *Locating the Atonement: Explorations in Constructive Dogmatics*, edited by Oliver Crisp and Fred Sanders, 139-53. Los Angeles Theology Conference Series. Grand Rapids, MI: Zondervan, 2015.

Hoskins, Paul. "Deliverance from Death by the True Passover Lamb: A Significant Aspect of the Fulfillment of the Passover in the Gospel of John." *Journal of the Evangelical Theological Society* 52 (2009): 285-99.

Hughes, John. "Hebrews IX 15ff. and Galatians III 15ff: A Study in Covenant Practice and Procedure." *Novum Testamentum* 21 (1979): 27-96.

Hundley, Michael. "Objects, Offerings, and People in the Priestly Texts: A Reappraisal." *Journal of Biblical Literature* 132, no. 4 (2013): 749-67.

Imes, Carmen. *Bearing God's Name: Why Sinai Still Matters*. Downers Grove, IL; IVP Academic, 2019.

"Imran Khan Says 3 Actresses Told Him About Vikas Bahl, Feels Dirty About Not Speaking Up Earlier." *Hindustan Times*, October 10, 2018. www.hindustantimes.com/bollywood /imran-khan-says-3-actresses-told-him-about-vikas-bahl-feels-dirty-about-not-speaking -up-earlier/story-0yrKBBeJ9IjDClmWKeJIUJ.html.

Jackson, Charles Gregory. "The Retributive Justice of God." PhD diss., The Southern Baptist Theological Seminary, 2012.

Jamieson, R. B. "Not Without Blood: Jesus' Death and Heavenly Offering in Hebrews." PhD diss., Selwyn College, 2017.

Jeffery, Steve, Michael Ovey, and Andrew Sach. *Pierced for Our Transgressions: Rediscovering the Glory of Penal Substitution.* Wheaton, IL: Crossway, 2007.

Jenson, Philip Peter. *Graded Holiness: A Key to the Priestly Conception of the World.* Journal for the Study of the Old Testament Supplement 106. Sheffield: JSOT Press, 1992.

Jipp, Joshua. *Saved by Faith and Hospitality.* Grand Rapids, MI: Eerdmans, 2017.

Johnsson, William. "Defilement and Purgation in the Book of Hebrews." PhD. diss., Vanderbilt University, 1973.

Keil, C. F., and F. Delitzch. *Commentary on the Old Testament.* Logos Edition. Peabody, MA: Hendrickson, 1996.

Kellermann, D. "עטר ʿātar." In *Theological Dictionary of the Old Testament.* Vol. 11, edited by Helmer Ringgren, Heinz-Josef Fabry, and G. Johannes Botterweck, 18-27. Translated by David E. Green. Grand Rapids, MI: Eerdmans, 2015.

Kennard, Doug. "Hebrew Metaphysic: Life, Holy, Clean, Righteousness, and Sacrifice." *Answers Research Journal* 1 (2008): 169-95.

Kennedy, D. F. "The Concept of Forgiveness in the Pentateuch." *Old Testament Essays* 12, no. 1 (1999): 94-113.

Kennedy, Lindsay. "Parallels Between Creation and the Temple." mydigitalseminary.com /parallels-between-creation-and-the-temple.

———. "Was the Garden of Eden the First Temple?," October 3, 2012. mydigitalseminary.com /was-the-garden-of-eden-the-first-temple/.

Kesari, Godfrey. *The Atonement Creating Unions: An Exploration in Inter-Religious Theory.* Eugene, OR: Pickwick, 2019.

Kim, Kyu Seop. "The Meaning of χειρόγραφον in Colossians 2:14 Revisited." *Tyndale Bulletin* 68, no. 2 (2017): 223-39.

Kitchen, K. A. "Crown." In *The New Bible Dictionary,* edited by I. Howard Marshall, 247. 3rd ed. Downers Grove, IL: IVP Academic, 1996.

Klawans, Jonathan. *Impurity and Sin in Ancient Judaism.* Oxford: Oxford University Press, 2000.

Köhler, Ludwig, Walter Baumgartner, and Johann Jakob Stamm. *The Hebrew and Aramaic Lexicon of the Old Testament.* Vol. 4. Leiden: Brill, 1994.

Kwon, Duke L., and Gregory Thompson. *Reparations: A Christian Call for Repentance and Repair.* Grand Rapids, MI: Brazos, 2021.

Lamont, Michele, Sabrina Pendergrass, and Mark Pachucki. "Symbolic Boundaries." In *International Encyclopedia of Social and Behavioral Sciences,* edited by James Wright, 15341-47. Vol. 23. Oxford: Elsevier, 2015.

Lane, William L. *Hebrews 9–13.* Word Biblical Commentary 47B. Grand Rapids, MI: Zondervan, 2015.

Levine, Baruch. *Presence of the Lord: A Study of Cult and Some Cultic Terms in Ancient Israel.* Leiden: Brill, 1974.

Lewis, John. "Forgiving George Wallace." *New York Times.* September 16, 1998. www.nytimes .com/1998/09/16/opinion/forgiving-george-wallace.html.

London Christian Thinkers. "Richard Bauckham Interview." January 29, 2015. www.youtube .com/watch?v=oHSoovmy4cw.

Lust, Johan, Erik Eynikel, and Katrin Hauspie. *A Greek-English Lexicon of the Septuagint*. Rev. ed. Stuttgart: Deutsche Bibelgesellschaft, 2003.

Luther, Martin. *The Complete Works of Martin Luther*. Vol. 6. Harrington, DE: Delmarva Publications, 2015.

———. "Ipse Deus percussit et punivet Christum." *Werke: Kritische Gesamtausgabe*: vol. 40, part 3, edited by J. F. K. Knaake. Weimar: Bohlaus, 1930.

———. *Luther's Works: Lectures on Galatians*. Vol. 26. Saint Louis: Concordia, 1963.

MacArthur, John and Richard Mayhue. *Biblical Doctrine: A Systematic Summary of Bible Truth*. Wheaton, IL: Crossway, 2017.

Macaskill, Grant. *Living in Union with Christ: Paul's Gospel and Christian Moral Identity*. Grand Rapids, MI: Baker Academic, 2019.

Marshall, Christopher. *Beyond Retribution: A New Testament Vision for Justice, Crime, and Punishment*. Grand Rapids, MI: Eerdmans, 2002.

Marshall, I. Howard. "The Theology of Atonement." In *The Atonement Debate: Papers from the London Symposium on the Theology of Atonement*, edited by Derek Tidball, 49-68. Grand Rapids, MI: Zondervan, 2008.

Matera, F. J. "The Kingship of Jesus: Composition and Theology in Mark 15." SBL Dissertation Series 66. Atlanta: SBL Press, 1982.

McBride, Jennifer. "Repentance as Political Witness." In *Christian Political Witness*, edited by George Kalantzis and Gregory W. Lee, 179-95. Downers Grove, IL: IVP Academic, 2014.

McKnight, Scot. *A Community Called Atonement*. Nashville: Abingdon, 2007.

McNall, Joshua. *The Mosaic of Atonement: An Integrated Approach to Christ's Work*. Grand Rapids, MI: Zondervan, 2019.

McNeil, Brenda Salter. *Roadmap to Reconciliation: Moving Communities into Unity, Wholeness and Justice*. Downers Grove, IL: IVP, 2015.

Milgrom, Jacob. "Israel's Sanctuary: The Priestly 'Picture of Dorian Gray.'" *Revue Biblique* 83 (1976): 390-99.

———. *Leviticus 17–22*. New York: Doubleday, 2000.

———. "Prolegomenon to Leviticus 17:11." *Journal of Biblical Literature* 90, no. 2 (1971): 149-56.

Miller, Lisa, Paul Rozin, and Allan Page Fiske. "Food Sharing and Feeding Another Person Suggest Intimacy: Two Studies of American College Students." *European Journal of Social Psychology* 28 (1998): 423-36.

Mischke, Werner. *The Global Gospel*. Scottsdale, AZ: Mission One, 2014.

Moffitt, David M. "Atonement at the Right Hand: The Sacrificial Significance of Jesus' Exaltation in Acts." *New Testament Studies* 62 (2016): 549-68.

Moon, Jay. "Chicken Theology: Local Learning Approaches from West Africa." In *Challenging Tradition: Innovation in Advanced Theological Education*, edited by Perry Shaw and Havilah Dharamraj, 382-405. Carlisle, UK: Langham Global Library, 2018.

Morris, Leon. *Apostolic Preaching*. Grand Rapids, MI: Eerdmans, 1965.

Nam, Daegeuk. "The 'Throne of God' Motif." ThD diss., Andrews University, 1989.

Neelands, David. "Substitution and the Biblical Background to Cur Deus Homo." *The Saint Anselm Journal* 2, no. 2 (Spring 2005): 80-87.

Nelson, Richard. "Do Confederate Symbols Stand in the Way of Racial Reconciliation?" *The Leaf Chronicle*, April 17, 2017. www.theleafchronicle.com/story/opinion/contributors /2017/08/17/confederate-symbols-racial-reconciliation/570690001/.

Nichols, Stephen (blog). "The Doctrine of Imputation: The Ligonier Statement on Christology," Ligonier.org, April 16, 2016. www.ligonier.org/blog/doctrine-imputation-ligonier -statement-christology/.

Njibwakale, Wabomba S. "Atonement in African Pluralistic Context: Examples from the Luhya of Western Kenya." *Perichoresis* 14, no. 1 (2016): 21-39.

Nolland, John. "Sin, Purity, and the חטאת Offering." *Vetus Testamentum* 65 (2015): 606-20.

Olafsson, Gudmundur. "The Use of nś' in the Pentateuch and its Contribution to the Concept of Forgiveness." PhD diss., Andrews University, 1992.

Packer, J. I. "The Necessity of Atonement." In *Atonement*, edited by Gabriel N. E. Fluhrer, 1-17. Phillipsburg, PA: P&R Publishing, 2010.

——. "What Did the Cross Achieve: The Logic of Penal Substitution." *Tyndale Bulletin* 25 (1974): 3-45.

Peterson, Robert A. *Salvation Accomplished by the Son: The Work of Christ*. Wheaton, IL: Crossway, 2012.

Piper, John. "The Demonstration of the Righteousness of God." *Journal for the Study of the New Testament* 2, no. 7 (Jan 1980): 2-32.

——. *The Future of Justification: A Response to N. T. Wright*. Wheaton, IL: Crossway, 2007.

——. "Why Is God Just to Punish Jesus for Our Sins When Doing a Similar Thing Would Be So Unjust for a Human Judge to Do?" September 4, 2020. www.desiringgod.org /interviews/why-is-god-just-to-punish-jesus-for-our-sins-when-doing-a-similar-thing -would-be-so-unjust-for-a-human-judge-to-do.

Porter, Steven. "Rethinking the Logic of Penal Substitution." In *Philosophy of Religion: A Reader and Guide*, edited by William L. Craig, 596-608. Edinburgh: University of Edinburgh Press, 2002.

Pugh, Ben. *Atonement Theories: A Way Through the Maze*. Eugene, OR: Cascade, 2014.

Rahn, Kim. "Moon Vows Fact-Finding for Jeju Massacres." *Korea Times*, April 3, 2018. korea times.co.kr/www/nation/2018/04/356_246662.html.

Reid, D. G. "Sacrifice and Temple Service." In *Dictionary of New Testament Background: A Compendium of Contemporary Biblical Scholarship*, edited by Craig A. Evans and Stanley E. Porter, 1037-50. Downers Grove, IL: InterVarsity Press, 2000.

Reid, Kenneth James. "Penal Substitutionary Atonement as the Basis for New Covenant and New Creation." PhD diss., Southern Baptist Theological Seminary, 2015.

Ribbens, Benjamin. "Levitical Sacrifice and Heavenly Cult in Hebrews." PhD diss., Wheaton College, 2013.

Rienzi, Greg. "Other Nations Could Learn from German Effort to Reconcile After WWII." *Johns Hopkins Magazine*. Summer 2015. hub.jhu.edu/magazine/2015/summer/germany -japan-reconciliation/.

Rillera, Andrew. "Paul Does Not Have a Kippēr Theology: Understanding Paul's Sacrificial Imagery Applied to Jesus." Paper presented at the Society of Biblical Literature Annual Conference, San Antonio, TX, November 21, 2021.

Ross, Allen P. *A Commentary on the Psalms*. Grand Rapids, MI: Kregel Academic, 2011.

Rutledge, Fleming. *The Crucifixion: Understanding the Death of Jesus Christ*. Grand Rapids, MI: Eerdmans, 2015.

Ryken, Leland, James Wilhoit, and Tremper Longman III, eds. *Dictionary of Biblical Imagery*. Downers Grove, IL: IVP Academic, 2000.

Sandel, Michael. *Justice: What's the Right Thing to Do?* New York: Farrar, Straus and Giroux, 2010.

Saysell, Csilla. "The Blood Manipulation of the Sin Offering and the Logic of Defilement." In *Holding Forth the Word of Life: Essays in Honor of Dr. Timothy Meadowcroft*, edited by Csilla Saysell and John de Jong, 44-67. Eugene, OR: Wipf & Stock, 2020.

Schwartz, Baruch. "The Bearing of Sin in Priestly Literature." In *Pomegranates and Golden Bells*, edited by D. Wright, D. N. Freedman, and A. Hurwitz, 3-21. Winona Lake, IN: Eisenbrauns, 1995.

Scott, James. *Exile: A Conversation with N. T. Wright*. Downers Grove, IL: IVP Academic, 2017.

———. "'For as Many as Are of Works of the Law Are Under a Curse' (Galatians 3.10)." In *Paul and the Scriptures of Israel*, edited by Craig A. Evans and James A. Sanders, 187-221. Journal for the Study of the New Testament Supplement 83. Sheffield: JSOT Press, 1993.

Scurlock, JoAnn. "The Technique of the Sacrifice of Animals in Ancient Israel and Ancient Mesopotamia: New Insights Through Comparison, Part 1." *Andrews University Seminary Studies* 44, no. 1 (2006): 13-49.

Shaker, Christiane. "The 'Lamb of God' Title in John's Gospel: Background, Exegesis, and Major Themes." PhD diss., Setan Hall, 2016.

Sipula, Sithembele. "The Sacrifice of the Mass and the Concept of Sacrifice Among the Xhosa: Towards an Inculturated Understanding of the Eucharist." ThD diss., University of South Africa, 2000.

Siyo, Athandile. "Abuse Is Already in My Blood, Says Teen Repeatedly Raped by Father." *Cape Times*, March 18, 2020. www.iol.co.za/capetimes/news/abuse-is-already-in-my-blood -says-teen-repeatedly-raped-by-father-45186856.

Skinner, Christopher. "Another Look at 'the Lamb of God.'" *Bibliotheca Sacra* 161 (2004): 89-104.

Sklar, Jay. *Sin, Impurity, Sacrifice and Atonement: The Priestly Conceptions*. Sheffield: Sheffield Phoenix, 2005.

Smith, James K. A. *Desiring the Kingdom: Worship, Worldview and Cultural Formation*. Grand Rapids, MI: Baker Books, 2009.

Storms, Sam. "10 Things You Should Know About Penal Substitution." Accessed April 13, 2020. www.samstorms.org/all-articles/post/article-10-things-you-should-know-about -penal-substitution.

Stott, John. *The Cross of Christ*. Downers Grove, IL: IVP Academic, 2012.

Streett, Daniel. "Cursed by God? Galatians 3:13, Social Status, and Atonement Theory in the Context of Early Jewish Readings of Deuteronomy 21:23." *Journal for the Study of Paul and His Letters* 5, no. 2 (2015): 189-209.

Tanner, Kathryn. *Christ Is Key*. Cambridge: Cambridge University Press, 2010.

Ten Elshof, Gregg. *For Shame: Rediscovering the Virtues of a Maligned Emotion*. Grand Rapids, MI: Zondervan, 2021.

Thielmann, Frank. "The Atonement." In *Central Themes in Biblical Theology*, edited by Scott Hafemann and Paul House, 102-27. Nottingham: Apollos, 2007.

Thiessen, Matthew. *Jesus and the Forces of Death: The Gospels' Portrayal of Ritual Impurity Within First-Century Judaism*. Grand Rapids, MI: Baker Academic, 2021.

Thomas, Bruce. "The Gospel for Shame Cultures." *Evangelical Missions Quarterly* 30, no. 3 (July 1994): 284-90.

Thornton, T. C. G. "The Meaning of αἱματεκχυσία in Hebrews 9:22." *The Journal of Theological Studies* 15, no. 1 (April 1964): 63-65.

Tibbs, Eve. "Eastern Orthodox Theology." In *Global Dictionary of Theology: A Resource for the Worldwide Church,* edited by William Dyrness and Veli-Matti Kärkkäinen, 244-50. Downers Grove, IL: IVP Academic, 2008.

Tigay, J. H. *Deuteronomy: The Traditional Hebrew Text with the New JPS Translation*. Philadelphia: Jewish Publication Society, 1996.

Tova Ganzel. "The Defilement and Desecration of the Temple in Ezekiel." *Biblica* 89, no. 3 (2008): 369-79.

Treat, Jeremy. *The Crucified King: Atonement and Kingdom in Biblical and Systematic Theology*. Grand Rapids, MI: Zondervan, 2014.

Trudinger, L. Paul. "Eli, Eli, Lama Sabachthani? A Cry of Dereliction or Victory?" *Journal of the Evangelical Theological Society* 17, no. 4 (Fall 1974): 235-38.

Turner, David L. "Paul and the Ministry of Reconciliation in 2 Cor 5:11–6:2." *Criswell Theological Review* 4, no. 1 (1989): 77-95.

Van der Merwe, Christo, Jacobus A. Naude, and Jan H. Kroeze. *A Biblical Hebrew Reference Grammar*. 2nd ed. New York: Bloomsbury, 1998.

Van Imschoot, Paul. *Theology of the Old Testament*. Vol. 1, *God*. Translated by K. Sullivan and F. Buck. New York: Desclee, 1954.

Vidu, Adonis. *Atonement, Law, and Justice: The Cross in Historical and Cultural Contexts*. Grand Rapids, MI: Baker Academic, 2014.

Vriezen, Th. C. *An Outline of Old Testament Theology*. Newton Centre, MA: Branford, 1966.

W., Jackson. *Reading Romans with Eastern Eyes*. Downers Grove, IL: IVP Academic, 2019.

Walton, John. *The Lost World of Genesis One*. Downers Grove, IL: IVP Academic, 2009.

Walton, John and J. Harvey Walton. *The Lost World of the Torah: Law as Covenant and Wisdom in Ancient Context*. Downers Grove, IL: IVP Academic, 2019.

Warnock, Adrian (blog). "2 Corinthians 5 and Romans 5—Two Critical Passages on Justification." November 14, 2007, www.patheos.com/blogs/adrianwarnock/2007/11/2-corinthians-5 -and-romans-5-two.

Watts, Rikk. "Mark." In *Commentary on the New Testament Use of the Old Testament*, edited by G. K. Beale and D. A. Carson, 111-249. Grand Rapids, MI: Baker Academic, 2007.

Wenham, Gordon. *Leviticus*. Grand Rapids, MI: Eerdmans, 1979.

Wesley, Charles. "'All Ye That Pass By,' Hymn 707." In *A Collection of Hymns*, edited by John Wesley London: Wesleyan-Methodist-Book-Room, 1889. Accessed April 13, 2020. www .hymntime.com/tch/htm/a/y/e/ayetpaby.htm.

Wilcox, Max. "'Upon the Tree': Deut 21:22-23 in the New Testament." *Journal of Biblical Literature* 96, no. 1 (1977): 85-99.

Willink, Jocko, and Leif Babin. *Extreme Ownership: How U.S. Navy SEALs Lead and Win*. New York: St. Martin's Press, 2015.

Wisdom, Jeffrey. "Blessing for the Nations and the Curse of the Law: Paul's Citation of Genesis and Deuteronomy in Gal 3.8-10." PhD diss., Durham University, 1998.

Wong, Wilson. "Mississippi State Football Player Transferring After New Coach Posts Tweet with a Noose." *NBC News*, April 8, 2020. www.nbcnews.com/news/nbcblk/mississippi -state-football-player-transferring-after-new-coach-posts-tweet-n1177911.

Wright, Christopher J. H. "Atonement in the Old Testament." In *The Atonement Debate: Papers from the London Symposium on the Theology of Atonement*, edited by Derek Tidball, David Hilborn, and Justin Thaker, 69-82. Grand Rapids, MI: Zondervan, 2008.

Wright, N. T. *The Climax of the Covenant*. Minneapolis: Fortress, 1993.

———. *The Day the Revolution Began: Reconsidering the Meaning of Jesus's Crucifixion*. San Francisco: HarperOne, 2016.

———. "The Letter to the Romans." In *The New Interpreter's Bible,* 12 vols., edited by Leander E. Keck, 396-770. Vol. 10. Nashville: Abingdon, 1994-2004.

———. "On Becoming the Righteousness of God." In *Pauline Theology*, edited by D. M. Hay, 200-208. Vol. 2. Minneapolis: Augsburg Fortress, 1993.

———. *Paul and the Faithfulness of God*. Vol. 2. Minneapolis: Fortress, 2013.

Wu, Jackson. *One Gospel for All Nations: A Practical Approach to Biblical Contextualization*. Pasadena, CA: William Carey Library, 2015.

———. *Saving God's Face: A Chinese Contextualization of Salvation Through Honor and Shame*. EMS Dissertation Series. Pasadena, CA: WCIUP, 2012.

———. "Why Is God Justified in Romans? Vindicating Paul's Use of Psalm 51:4 in Romans 3:4." *Neotestamentica* 51, no. 2 (Dec 2017): 291-314.

Yates, Roy. "Colossians 2:14: Metaphor of Forgiveness." *Biblica* 71, no. 2 (1990): 248-59.

Yonge, Charles Duke, with Philo of Alexandria. *The Works of Philo: Complete and Un-abridged*. Peabody, MA: Hendrickson, 1995.

Young, Norman H. "*Haimatekchusia*: A Comment." *The Expository Times* 90, no. 6 (1979): 180.

Zohar, Noam. "Repentance and Purification: The Significance and Semantics of חטאת in the Pentateuch." *Journal of Biblical Literature* 107, no. 4 (Dec 1988): 609-18.

GENERAL INDEX

SCRIPTURE INDEX